St. Louis Community College

Forest Park
Florissant Valley
Meramec

Instructional Resources
St. Louis, Missouri

GAYLORD

Media-tions

Media-tions
Forays into the
Culture and Gender Wars

By Elayne Rapping

South End Press   Boston, MA

Cover design by Bri McAlevey.
Text design and production by the South End Press collective.

Library of Congress Cataloging-in-Publication Data
Rapping, Elayne.
Media-tions: forays into the culture and gender wars/
by Elayne Rapping.
p. cm.
ISBN 0-89608-479-5: $30.00. --ISBN 0-89608-478-7: $15.00 (pbk)
1. Sex role in motion pictures. 2. Sex role in television. 3. Popular cul-
ture--United States--History--20th century.
    I. Title. II. Title: Mediations.
    PN1995.9.S47R36 1994
    305.3--dc20   93-29356
                                    CIP

South End Press, 116 Saint Botolph Street, Boston, MA 02115
99 98 97 96 95 94   1 2 3 4 5 6

Contents

We're not where we *want* to be. And we're not where we're *going* to be. But we sure are a long way from where we *were*.

-Martin Luther King, Jr.

For Al

Acknowledgements

I am grateful to many people who have helped and supported me over the years. The staff members of the many publications I have written for have often been active supporters of both my work and my perspective, even when they have been highly controversial. Dan Cohen, John Trinkl, Jill Benderly, and Ann Wagoner of *The Guardian* have been particularly supportive friends and colleagues, in more ways than I can know. I am also grateful to Erwin Knoll, Linda Rocawich, Ruth Conniff—and most especially Matthew Rothschild—of *The Progressive* for giving me the space to develop my ideas with almost no restrictions on content and very little (although always excellent) editing. I have never worked with an editorial group so respectful of an author's ideas and so committed to freedom of expression. Matthew's support has been vigorous and constant.

Laurie Oullette and Merle Hoffman of *On The Issues*, and Ellen Cantarow and Linda Gardiner of *The Women's Review of Books* have also been a pleasure to work with. Ellen and Linda, especially, offer a rare kind of editorial guidance that combines political seriousness with a refreshing sensitivity to literary style.

Loie Hayes and Sonia Shah of South End Press deserve thanks for their excellent editorial help and advice. Loie was instrumental in the development of this project and I am grateful to her for encouraging me to undertake it. Her intelligent support was invaluable.

Beatrice Woulfe and Christine Gilewski have given me unusually valuable clerical help, since their commentary on my work has often helped me clarify my ideas.

I am particularly grateful to my students, who always teach me as much as I teach them, and to my children, Alison and Jonathan, who have shared the greater part of my viewing experience with me. All too often no one else was willing to watch the endless stream of movies and TV shows I did over the years. When they were children, they were my most delightful and astute "sources." Now that they are adults, they are even more fun. Indeed, Jon and Alison are my favorite movie and TV companions and my most accurate barometers of cultural change and inflection as it occurs. They have the great gift—in my view—of appreciating what is truly wonderful in American culture, while recognizing and reviling, even at its subtlest, what is ugly and inane.

Introduction

As I write this Introduction, in the summer of 1993, we are at the end of the Reagan/Bush era, a long dry period of rightwing ascendancy and political reaction that, understandably, has left liberals and Leftists alike feeling depressed and pessimistic. For women, especially, the 1980s and early 1990s have been experienced—and almost universally labeled—as an age of "backlash," in which the cultural and material advances made by feminists in the 1960s and 1970s were vigorously and hostilely driven back by the forces of white, male supremacy.

In women's meetings, conferences, and casual political conversations, in the last few years, I have often felt weighed down by the despair and powerlessness engendered by the so-called "backlash." One might think—to listen to growing numbers of women—that we are no better off today than when the Second Wave of feminism began in the 1960s: that feminism has had no real or lasting effect on American life.

I am puzzled by the backlash rhetoric. I came of age in the

1950s, participated, and was transformed by, Second Wave feminism. I raised a son and a daughter whose own lives, identities, choices, and attitudes, where gender and sexuality are concerned, are radically different from mine and their father's, when we were their ages. I often feel as though I am living in a parallel universe in which all sorts of things are happening that no one I know is noticing.

Yes, of course, there is a backlash. The white, straight, rich men who own and run most things still are more than a bit apoplectic over feminism's challenge, spanning virtually every area of social and personal life, to their power. Wouldn't you be? And, yes, they are waging campaigns against feminism so that their "Father Knows Best" world will not erode further.

But why are *their* efforts all we can see these days? And why, I wonder, are *their* successes seen to negate ours? We feminists have had an enormous impact upon gender relations and attitudes since the 1960s, and our influence—despite rightwing resistance— grows every day, in the realm of representation and discourse as well as in the material world of society and politics.

It seemed, when Clarence Thomas was confirmed, for example, that *they* had won. But narrative closure—the frozen last frame of a single, short-term, narrative line—in life and in art, is not the proper gauge of a process of struggle. Thomas was confirmed, but he, and his allies, did not "win" the sexual harassment battle. Sexual harassment—as an issue constructed by feminists in the 1970s and fought for and circulated in various arenas, media and others, ever since— has proven far more powerful politically than Thomas's impact as a Supreme Court Justice will be likely to match.

The feminist perspective on sexual harassment—most interestingly, from the perspective of this collection—has been exercised most visibly and effectively through the endless media events—docudramas, soaps, talk shows, and news reports—since the hearings, which have generally presented the feminist perspective more positively. Indeed, one year after the hearings, popular opinion on the matter has changed dramatically, in part because of all this media play. Whereas most people then "believed" Thomas, the reverse is true today. The rush to conclusion, as the final depressing gavel fell on that grim October day, was clearly premature, as are many similar judgments based on "common sense" assumptions about the power of the backlash against the forces of feminist agitation.

In this case, as in many others, my evidence for feminism's impact comes, interestingly enough, from the very sources that offer so many others grounds for despair—mass media and popular culture. As a media theorist and critic, I have spent much of the last 20 years studying popular culture—movies, soap operas, pulp fiction, self-help books, rock music, docudramas—in an effort to understand the relationship between women audiences and media representation from the stance of the female consumer. In that time, I have seen the influence of women grow and expand exponentially, as a result of feminist activities of many kinds.

A quick scan of the years since "I Love Lucy" and "Leave It To Beaver" dominated our imaginative lives reveals a media industry in a state of radical—if uneven, contradictory, and always reluctant—transformation as a result of feminism.

The essays that follow, written over the last 20 years, present evidence of feminism's successful struggle to change gender representation, as a significant part of the broader struggle—also more successful than it may sometimes seem these days—to change gender relations in the material world. They represent an effort to place the sometimes depressing historic moment in a broader, more dynamic context. They show feminism not as a defensive posture, but rather as a militant force which, since the late 1960s, has forced its way into the major channels of discourse and representation in both subtle and dramatic ways.

The earliest piece was written in 1973, as one of a series of regular columns on "Culture" I wrote for a New Left newspaper. It was an effort, from the stance of feminist activism, to understand why daytime soap operas appealed to American women. I knew that women who watched soap operas and other "low" forms were not stupid or duped, because I myself was one of them. And so I tried to figure out, from my own mixed, often contradictory reactions to American pop culture, and from young mothers in the park where I sat with my children, working-class students in my classes, and women on buses, in restaurants, and in malls, why soaps so pleased and compelled us, in spite of our clear knowledge that they were unrealistic, sentimental, corny, and manipulative.

(Women and others who openly admit to a love of schlock do indeed know its faults.)

Analyzing pop forms from this very self-conscious, woman-identified stance, I came to see how media and their audiences differ and change, and how media respond to progressive forces and ideas in subtle ways. While the top priorities of those who control media are profits and ideological control, they have often been dragged, kicking and screaming, away from those ends by progressive pressures. Nor would I analyze our influence on media in terms of "co-optation," which implies defeat. I prefer the term "incorporation." We have made inroads into mainstream discourse through political struggle.

That first soap opera piece was titled "Daytime Soap Opera: Where Time Stands Still," an indication of how stuck in time the soaps then appeared—stuck and unlikely to move.

At that time, feminists had only recently begun to exert pressure on media and were focusing on more visible, less "ghettoized" forms than television, such as billboard advertisements. Soap operas were a bastion of near-medieval conventions about marriage, monogamy, and woman's role in the home and family. Nonetheless, they appealed to women, I argued, by offering a fantasy-like, female-centered world in which emotional realities of male-dominated, sexist life for women gave way to a kinder, gentler set, in which, indeed, men themselves organized every enterprise around a highly preposterous, but delicious, concern for the needs and values of the women in their lives.

As long as the male world refuses to change its economic and political ways, women will enjoy an occasional private foray into the kinder, gentler world of soap opera life, where those things don't matter so much, while relationships and feelings and humanistic values, as women are raised to understand them, prevail. This was and is enough, in my view, to explain and justify their popularity with women, from the days of radio to the present. But there is today—because of political changes we have engineered—much more to justify female loyalty.

Over the last 20 years, as the three pieces on soap operas included here document, soaps beefed up and considerably expanded their representations of women's concerns and desires, as feminism raised and stretched the consciousness of a nation. While many retrograde aspects of the form remain and always will—until Proctor and Gamble is put out of business—the feminist overhaul of the Pine Valley/Bay City/Springfield imaginative map has clearly disproven the idea that "Time Stands Still" on soaps. The men, the corporations, the government agencies and hospitals, still revolve, preposterously, around the needs and concerns of women and personal life. But the portrayal of women's needs and concerns now goes beyond love and romance to include date rape, sexual harassment, professional equity, and the demand that men share in child care and domestic responsibility—issues identified and politicized by feminism. Not to mention a significant number of other politicized issues, such as interracial relationships, homelessness, AIDS, gay- and race-bashing, and corporate pollution, which originated from a more broad "humanist" progressive agenda.

Most media did not easily or happily accommodate themselves to the demands of feminists. But feminism did compel all media, across the differences *among* media, and in public discourse in general, to address and respond to its political agenda. This is an informing principle of this collection. While I don't deny the existence of a backlash against feminists' gains (which would be absurd), the overly reductive and pessimistic understanding of what that backlash actually means and how it should be talked about and responded to troubles me.

The backlash model of media dynamics assumes an ahistoric, one-dimensional, either/or, them/us, then/now (in current academic jargon, "binary") playing field. According to backlash theorists, feminists made certain strides in the late 1960s and then, in the early 1980s, were pushed back to point zero by the monolithic, misogynist forces of the backlash. The foundational premises of this argument owe much to the kind of media theory that has dominated Left analyses since the days of the Frankfurt School.

In those days (and still, to a great extent today), progressive media analysts wrote about "The Media" as though they were a monolithic, unchanging bastion of ruling-class power with a unified, uninflected agenda of social control and manipulation. From this angle—and it is still the most common, if unspoken one in most mainstream media critiques, even among liberals—all movies, pulp fiction, television, and pop music could be easily "read" as one-dimensional ideological messages from the centers of power, meant to confuse us all into buying their wares and doing their bidding.

Even my most naive and conservative students, as a matter of fact, understand how power and commerce manipulate them through media. To that extent, I would say, the Left, and by extension, mainstream feminism—the very visible and important segment that battles against "negative" and "degrading" gender images—has won a significant ideological battle. "Everybody knows" (to quote a wonderful Leonard Cohen song) that the media are the bad guys, responsible for everything, some would have it, from street crime to bad haircuts. And "everybody" is mostly correct, at least as far as this overly simplistic analysis takes them.

But in adopting, wholesale, this uninflected view of media as unified and unchanging in purpose and action, we accept a seriously distorted picture of how media function and interact with other social forces. We miss the many nuances and contradictions within which the gains of feminism are most clearly seen. Even as *Fatal Attraction*, *Pretty Woman*, and the infamous Harvard/Yale study (which warned that educated single women were more likely to be shot by terrorists than to marry) offered their misogynist threats and taunts, counterforces—in perhaps less publicized places—offered respect and kindness. Aretha Franklin was demanding "R-E-S-P-E-C-T" at that very time, as were the many soap opera heroines, unnoticed by most critics, who were even then coming out as lesbians (on "All My Children") and forcing sexually abusive fathers to court and jail (on "Guiding Light").

Those 1980s "backlash" years were also the ones in which made-for-TV movies about issues feminists had placed on the national agenda—rape, domestic violence, incest, economic discrimination, and more—were reaching audiences of 75 to 100 million viewers. The bestseller lists were filled with the works of black feminists Toni Morrison, Alice Walker, Maya Angelou, Gloria Naylor, and others. Nancy Drew mysteries began to outsell Silhouette Young Love novels. Pulp fiction racks generally held fewer romance novels and more mysteries written by women, featuring feisty feminist street fighters such as Kinsey Milhone and V.I. Warshawski chasing after powerful, rich men in the interest of female dignity and justice.

Even *Fatal Attraction*, scary and vicious as its representation of independent, sexually aggressive women surely was, should not be interpreted as an ahistorical morality play. *Fatal Attraction* was indeed a watershed film, a call to arms against uppity women everywhere. But it was also a tacit acknowledgement that uppity women had already created the cultural changes cited above and were even then creating more.

Hollywood's representation of feminism in Glenn Close's cartoon-like character in *Fatal Attraction* was in a sense flattering. Think how scared these producers must have been. Way too scared to give us even the partially sympathetic villainesses we got in the 1930s—the Crawfords, Stanwycks, Davises, and Bacalls—who, untainted by the dread Women's Movement, were portrayed so much more believably and movingly.

No boiled rabbits for *Mildred Pierce*, the heroine of the 1940s film noir tragedy of female ambition and sexual license. She didn't need a fullblown psychosis to make her rage and downfall understandable. She lived in a world in which women's rights were not an issue, so she was simply portrayed as "unnatural" and seen to destroy herself through her inevitably useless efforts to escape the sexist restraints of her day.

There is, in fact, a masculinist bias built into the very criteria we accept in evaluating the representation wars. To privilege film over television, for example, and prime time over daytime, is to accept the idea, upon which all little boys and girls are raised, that what men watch and prefer is more important than what women watch. Movies, since the rise of television, have been increasingly brainless and macho because they are geared to the 18- to 24-year-old dating crowd, in which young males buy most of the tickets and choose most of the movies. Television, on the other hand, especially daytime, targets women, and is therefore, for the purposes of charting feminist influence on women audiences, more important. For it is this medium that can, at times, actually raise consciousness about various forms of sexism and encourage women to resist and refuse them.

Women dominate soap opera, daytime talk show, and TV movie audiences, but not the pool of box office ticket buyers. And so the producers and sponsors of soap operas, daytime talk, and

TV movie programs pay a lot of attention to the female sensibility. Nor is it trivial to point out that TV, pulp fiction, and other "trash" industries are far more willing to hire women as production and creative staff than are the Hollywood studios. On some soap operas, I was told by a 30-year veteran actress who is now a director, there are many days when every person on the set, except the actors, is a woman.

Male tastes have dictated which TV shows and films are most discussed and honored. Meanwhile, the last two decades have given birth to a real growth in woman-centered and -oriented TV fare, geared to the increasingly influential female audience and creative staff. "Hill Street Blues" may have been the hottest show on prime time during the 1980s, but if you want to know what women were watching, check out the video rental stores—where made-for-TV movies about women, like *The Burning Bed* are still hot items. Or eavesdrop on the small talk that women of all ages, races, and classes engage in, wherever they gather, in which the histories—dating back 10 years and more—of favorite women soap characters and their increasingly politicized goings on are still recalled vividly.

Nor is it only consciousness that was changing, as women watched and discussed these programs. The issues raised in films such as *The Burning Bed* entered the realm of public discourse and policy making in dramatic ways. That film, based on a case brought to public attention by socialist-feminist activists, helped make an entire nation aware of the injustice of traditional attitudes about domestic violence, even as it helped activists successfully demand shelters, education, and changes in police procedures in dealing with domestic "squabbles," as they were then called. The very concept of "domestic violence," as a politicized way of understanding what was, until recently, considered normal family relations, has taken hold in large part because of feminist victories in this and other media arenas.

There are dozens of examples I could cite—*Something about Amelia*, about incest, and *When He's Not a Stranger*, about date rape, are only two—in which popular TV movies intervened in public debate and policy decisions in ways which furthered feminist political agendas. And these movies were produced by creative staffs increasingly influenced by feminist ideas.

The media are neither monolithic nor static. Nor are they produced according to the desires and needs of a constant, undifferentiated group of powerful men. This collection shows that in the last 20 years, in the period since Second Wave feminists began their organized battle to change the construction of gender relations and identities, feminism has become a major force in the representation wars. We have more chips than we started with; we are active on more fronts than ever; we are players to be taken seriously. Indeed, the powers that be understand this all too well. That is why they have been upping the ante. As the *Fatal Attraction* example shows, they are taking no prisoners in their most serious battles with feminist ideas and demands. But that is because they are suffering too many casualties to afford to.

From the Streets to the Academy:
What a Long, Strange Trip

The analysis of gender and media just put forth was a long time in formulation. It marks a course of movement—personal and historical; political and theoretical—that many in my generation will relate to. My earliest cultural criticism was written in a period of radical activism and cultural revolt. It grew out of a time when my paid work—teaching English literature—was not connected to my cultural criticism, which was political, not academic. In those days, there were no media-studies programs or degrees. And I certainly did not put my movie reviews on my official *curriculum vitae* when I applied for jobs.

But in the ensuing decades things changed in complex ways. The euphoric radicalism of the 1960s and early 1970s gave way to the sobering 1980s, forcing Leftists to reevaluate our analyses, our strategies, and, not least, our cocky attitudes. In some ways the New Left and the counterculture changed the world for the better, just as feminism did. But, as in the case of feminism, the world has ways of changing the rules and the turf on us.

On the positive side, media studies became a hot theoretical field. On the negative side, the days of organized, visible Left and feminist activism ended, marginalizing the activist Left and shifting much of the action to the academic, theoretical arena. I was not the only one to parlay what I learned as a political activist into an academic career. But as I continued to write political journalism, from an activist perspective, I sometimes found myself uncomfortably straddling a fence—worried about using too much jargon for one audience, not enough for another, and so on. And I was increasingly frustrated by the sharp turn among now-academic Leftists toward textual rather than activist politics.

In media studies, the emphasis on texts over institutions has manifested itself most noticeably in the emphasis on "audience" and "reader response" theories, in which "liberatory" potential is found in the private viewer's or reader's ability to "read against the grain" of "dominant" ideological texts.

The great insights into how audiences do indeed "read" and use texts, offered by this school of thought, have been invaluable to me, since my own interest in women as active, oppositional viewers has been central to my work from the start. Nonetheless, the tendency to call such oppositional reading "emancipatory" and to assume that texts themselves constitute the only arena of ideological struggle is troubling. By limiting our work as feminists and Leftists to private reading, viewing, listening, and perhaps dancing, and ignoring the economic and social functions of the production process itself, we move far away from the realm of political struggle within and against institutions, as Leftists and feminists have always understood it.

Also, by limiting ourselves and our theories to an elite group of scholars, we in the academy, whether we call ourselves Leftists or not, have opted out of the great public debates that construct and amend national consciousness and policy. The most sophisticated theories of culture and media today are too often being produced in an ever more narrow arena and addressed to an ever more narrow range of political issues and problems.

In any event, amidst all of these developments, I have continued upon a fairly consistent path, for all its detours and pitfalls, trying to keep a balance between theoretical and activist impulses, between sophisticated discourse and engaged public voice. It is this blending of the theoretical, the political, the personal, and the emotional into a recognizable human "voice" that is distinctly mine that I have striven for as a writer.

Cinema, Schlock, and Political Turmoil:
As the World Turns

The pieces assembled here are taken from a variety of publications to which I have contributed, more or less regularly, for many years. Among the publications most often represented are *The Guardian*, the now-defunct radical newsweekly for which I served as culture critic throughout the 1980s; *Cineaste*, a journal of cinema and politics; *The Women's Review of Books*; and *The Progressive*, a political monthly to which I now contribute a bi-monthly column on culture. There are also pieces culled from other publications, most prominent among them *Radical America*, *Socialist Review*, *The Nation*, and *On the Issues: The Progressive Women's Quarterly*, to which I now contribute a column.

Before commenting on the contents, let me briefly mention certain obvious omissions, since they may seem rather glaring to some readers. Since the subject here is the representation of gender—women, men, children, and the family in society—and since the texts examined are mostly mainstream, commercial films and TV shows, there is a strong bias toward white, middle-class subject matter. That bias is the media's, not mine. The decision not to challenge it more often by taking up issues of racial representation is conscious, however. I have always written, as a feminist, from my own perspective as a straight, white, middle-class woman. The Women's Movement, long ago, set the guidelines for this kind of self-identified writing, and for good reason. One of the great truths (which the Right is understandably distressed about) to come out of New Left politics was that knowledge and truth are socially constructed and reflect the subjectivities of different constituencies and individuals. And one of the great values of that lesson has been the flowering of, and attention to, film, literature, and video by and about those the dominant culture deems Other—women, gay men, lesbians, blacks, Latinos, Asians, and on and on.

This is as it should be. It is right that black characters figure in more and more novels and films, and it is right that those who share these cultures and experiences are given the chance to comment upon and explain them to others. In the 1960s, I remember bristling when men—as they really did in those days—got up at meetings to say things like "My wife is a feminist and she agrees with me" about some totally offensive thing or other, (obviously an updated version of "Some of my best friends..."). I am very careful on this score. Nor is my voice in these matters greatly needed, since we have so many brilliant women of color writing theory and criticism these days.

On the other hand, I have often addressed issues of sexuality and written quite a bit about lesbians and gay men in media. In the section on the representation of men, half of the pieces deal with gay men. There is no way to talk about changing images of sex and gender without discussing the tricky ways in which sexuality—for men and women—is constructed and reconstructed, socially and representationally.

Moving on to matters of selection and organization, I am struck, in going through the Contents, by how the categories I have set up—film, television, lifestyle trends, etc.—dramatize the differences among media, and their different reactions to feminism. The first three sections are about film. And yet, the pieces that most clearly illustrate my thesis about feminist influence on media are not in these sections so much as in the later sections, on television and other "lower" culture forms and trends.

The film sections, called—"Hollywood's Women," "Hollywood's Families," and "Hollywood's Men"—chart what was happening in Hollywood, as other media overtook it in relevance and cultural dominance. The gradual dwindling of movies with serious themes, figuring serious women, and the corresponding tendency to cater to the more boorish and boyish elements of society is a trend which these pieces, taken together, clearly map. These pieces also pay tribute to the many ways, even in the most misogynist of cases, in which Hollywood has been forced to deal with feminism and sexuality in spite of itself.

These three sections overlap to an extent because Hollywood tends to evaluate all change and difference in terms of their effects upon the traditional nuclear family. Not surprisingly, the independent films about gay men and lesbians—*My Own Private Idaho, Desert Hearts*—provide the most gratifying critiques of family life. The dominant movie industry, by contrast, ignores the more radical implications of gender politics, as we have defined it, and trivializes what it can't completely ignore. Nonetheless, even this negative response testifies to the influence and power of feminism.

Moving on to "Gender on Television" and "Lifestyles, Trends, and Trash," the news gets a bit better. The pieces in the first of these sections focus on places where women and other progressive forces have had most influence. In the early 1980s, for example, as "Made-for-TV Movies: The Domestication of Social Issues" makes clear, feminism had a great and positive influence on the docudrama, producing such exemplary dramas as *The Burning Bed* and *Lois Gibbs and the Love Canal*, which, for all their limits and sins, were admirably progressive. By the 1990s, the force of feminist agitation and influence could be felt in unexpected places. "The Three Faces of Amy Fisher," for example (like the MTV piece, "Sex, Commercials and Rock 'n' Roll"), documents how audiences themselves have increasingly revolted against media insult and injury and demanded to be taken more seriously and treated more respectfully. The winds of change and struggle continue, and the power of women and others to wage war against media attacks keeps growing and shifting arenas.

In the "Lifestyles" section, we see the very real struggles among various forces at work in creating our common culture. Way back in the 1970s, I wrote a piece about Tupperware in which I noted the many ways in which this astoundingly successful business and social formation managed to incorporate working-class women in ways which we in the women's movement had often theorized about but rarely successfully managed. The later essays continue to analyze social trends that attract and inspire large numbers of women to become active, or change their lives—the most recent trend being the Recovery Movement. This movement—based on 12-Step self-help groups, books, and ideologies that interpret personal suffering in terms of "addiction"—appeals to women (as a book-length study I am now working on explains more fully) by addressing them as "diseased" victims and offering spiritual and personal cures for what are primarily social problems. Reactionary as it generally is, it is deeply indebted to feminist ideas and processes in its analyses of family, sexual relationships, and "dysfunction." Since it addresses interpersonal and emotional suffering seriously, as pre-feminist dominant ideologies did not, it is at least a partially positive development.

Finally, the last section, "Contested Feminisms," consists mostly of book reviews on gender, sexuality, and representation. Some of these, "The Future of Motherhood" and "Pleasure and Danger," present my growing participation in some of the most heated controversies about what a feminist position on sexuality—and by extension motherhood, the family, reproductive technologies, and many other issues—should be. They are engaged, deeply felt, addresses to the feminist and Leftist communities about public policy affecting women in every arena of our private and public lives.

These pieces are in line with what is sometimes (unfortunately) called the "sex radical" position. They stress the importance of the liberatory approach to female sexuality, which insists that feminism grew out of a radical impulse to set ourselves free from the economic, sexual, and cultural constraints of patriarchy, and that sexual freedom, pleasure, choice, personal growth, and creativity must be among our most cherished values, no matter what the political climate. They were written—as were all the books and articles that make up the "sex war" debates of the 1970s and 1980s—in the context of political debate and struggle.

The "other" position, the "anti-porn" position as it is usually referred to, credits texts with more coercive power than they have by themselves, and—as the title of the book *Pleasure and Danger* makes clear—allows the very real danger of sexual violence and repression to scare us into losing sight of the more liberatory values we started with. Too often, in fact, this position has flirted dangerously with misogynist rightwing tendencies toward social and representational repression.

While this particular debate continues, it has less public prominence today than when these pieces were written. Nonetheless, the theoretical and political values that inform these reviews also inform the other book reviews—and many other pieces as well—that address representational and social interaction. "Girls Just Wanna Have Fun," "Feminism and Media in an Age of Reaction," and most notably my review of Susan Faludi's *Backlash: The Undeclared War Against American Women* and Naomi Wolf's *The Beauty Myth*, followed by the exchange of letters it produced in *The Women's Review of Books*—all take sides in a parallel debate in which a key issue is media representation of gender.

When I reviewed the Faludi book, I had no idea it would become the phenomenon it did; if I had I would certainly have approached it differently. At the time, I treated it not as the major "media event" it certainly was in its own right, but as one of many books on gender I have reviewed over the years. I received it before publication, and read it in large part as an example of a type of media analysis that I find limiting and distorted.

Certainly, had I foreseen its impact, I would have altered my emphases and contextual apparatus in various ways, calling attention—most obviously—to the fact that the book was a major phenomenon that had, to its credit, dramatically influenced public debate and opinion. Rereading the review, I am struck by how seriously I misjudged its potential impact. From my stance as a media theorist and critic, I was only aware of how very one-sided, simplistic, and distorted its depiction of popular culture in the 1980s was. I failed to gauge the appeal of the book, especially to self-identified feminists, as a political rallying cry.

As an attack on the most visible and misogynist elements of the male power structure, Faludi's book struck an emotional chord among angry feminists everywhere. But, I would still argue, it was seriously myopic in its reading of feminist and media history, because it assumed a "common sense," "everybody knows" approach to the horrors of mainstream culture that is both inaccurate and unfair to women, as viewers, producers, and activists.

To notice only the places where *their* values win out, without crediting the many other places in which the very terms of struggle have been radically altered to include our ideas and viewpoints, and to ignore our many large and small victories in winning hearts, minds, and air time for feminist views and concepts, is to simplify and misrepresent the complexity and nuance of media representation and the struggles that produce it.

As we emerge from the Reagan/Bush years and try to assess our positions in the 1990s, we need to take a broad and deep look at where we've been and what we've accomplished so far and to reassess our own achievements and our current positions in the culture and gender wars. "Roseanne" and "Murphy Brown" are a long way down the road from June Cleaver. Madonna and k.d. lang are equally far from Marilyn Monroe and Patsy Cline. Such cultural progress does not make a revolution. As Gil Scott-Heron reminded us in the days when we were beginning our struggle, the revolution will not be televised. But, as Dr. King reminded us, we may not be "where we want to be," or "where we're going to be, but we sure are a long way from where we were." We need to remember that, and make sure our daughters and granddaughters understand and take pride in it. Because they will need that confidence and pride to carry on.

–August 1993, New York City

Hollywood's Women

Fatal Attraction and the Backlash

Judging from the 1987 Best Actress nominee list, one would think 1987 was a banner year for women in film. I can't remember a year that boasted such an impressive number of dynamite performances by strong women leads. Every one of them—Meryl Streep in *Ironweed*, Glenn Close in *Fatal Attraction*, Holly Hunter in *Broadcast News*, Cher in *Moonstruck*, and Sally Kirkland in *Anna*—was larger-than-life terrific in a role that placed a female lead smack in the center of the psychic and dramatic action and let her really strut her stuff.

So why was I so depressed? Why was I feeling more and more irritated about the way in which women—especially strong, independent women—were being portrayed on the big screen? No, it wasn't the old sexist cliché that women are never satisfied, never know what they really want. It was something a lot more serious and disturbing. The fact was that women in those films—and the Academy list was no exception—were portrayed in ways that subtly and not so subtly undermined a lot of important feminist values. And, what's worse, the films were so sneaky and clever about it that it was often hard to notice.

Remember the late 1960s and 1970s when "women's lib" seemed to be all the rage in Hollywood? Films like *An Unmarried Woman* (1978) and *Alice Doesn't Live Here Anymore* (1975) certainly weren't feminist tracts. They always produced an obligatory "good man" in the final frames for our newly liberated heroine and they skirted issues of money and class, what we now call "the feminization of poverty," in ways that obviously distorted the real situation of most women. Still, they were fun to watch because they showed women leaving bad marriages to go off on their own in search of their own destinies, their true selves.

And then there was *Norma Rae* (1979), a film that actually treated the problems of working-class women with political sophistication. Not only did Norma lead a strike and go to jail for her union activities, she also transformed her way of relating to men as she gained self-respect in her work. Not bad for Hollywood.

Of course this same period also produced some very antifeminist Hollywood films, which portrayed independent women in ways that—in retrospect—were ominous signs of what the 1980s would bring. Alan (With Friends Like This Who Needs Enemies) Alda's *The Seduction of Joe Tynan* (1979) may have started it. Alda plays a political candidate who has an affair with an attractive attorney (played by Meryl Streep) who shares in his work life as his sweet little wife cannot. He returns to hearth and home, though (for reasons all of us Gary Hart experts will recognize as mostly opportunistic), leaving Streep to take her legal briefs to her cold bed.

If the earlier films were unrealistic in letting their heroines have it all—career, money, and a perfect man—this one was downright cruel in its message that women had to choose love or work. Men, of course, have never had to make that choice. The theme was repeated in at least two more recent films—*Violets are Blue* (1986) and *Just Between Friends* (1986). In both, the drama centers on the classic triangle—attractive male, sweet little homebody wife, dangerous but sexy colleague—and ends with the wife getting all the goodies while the successful career woman, attractive and exciting as she is, is left alone with her work, her empty apartment, and her frustrated libido. Who wants a partner/lover to share your life, these films say, when you can have the June Cleaver/Stepford Wife classic model?

As for working-class women, the descendants of *Norma Rae* have fared even worse. *An Officer and a Gentleman* (1982) virtually lifted the triumphant scene in *Norma Rae* in which Norma defies her bosses and stands on a table with a sign reading "Union" until the entire shop floor has stopped work to join her. This time, though, the factory worker heroine falls in love with a military man and, in true Cinderella fashion, is carried out of the shop floor to live happily ever after as a wife and mother. The now wholly reactionary work-stoppage scene, based so flagrantly on *Norma Rae*, is now in celebration and support of traditional marriage. Can you believe the nerve of these guys?

Looking now at the films of the 1987 season, it's easy to see the continuity. Marriage, men, and babies—to the exclusion of meaningful work—were being pushed down our throats in movie after movie. In one way or another, films like *Moonstruck, Someone to Watch Over Me, Overboard, Baby Boom, Hannah and Her Sisters,* and most interestingly, the two blockbusters, *Fatal Attraction* and *Broadcast News,* all pushed a similar theme. In each film, the nuclear family and old fashioned romantic love of the kind that leads to "happily ever after" were presented as more or less unproblematic ideals. Independent women, for their part, were portrayed as seriously in trouble, in one way or another, for reasons that ranged from garden-variety Freudian female neurosis to downright psychopathic evil.

In *Overboard,* Goldie Hawn plays a crabby, wealthy, frigid woman who is transformed, through amnesia, into a gushy, happily married wife and mother to a down-home carpenter and his messy brood. The more she mops, cooks, and serves her man, the happier she becomes. In *Someone to Watch Over Me,* a glamorous, jet-set journalist almost lures her policeman/body guard away from his far-from-glamorous, childhood-sweetheart wife. In the end, of course, the independent woman is left in her posh but lonely apartment and her lover goes home to his tried-and-true wife, to eat meatloaf at a formica kitchen table.

Moonstruck and *Hannah* are more clever. Almost unnotice-ably—because these films are so intelligent and amusing—they all end up with the most hokey endorsement of the kind of true love that hits you in the head, or heart, and instantaneously turns your life from dull and troubled to pure bliss. The spirit of Shakespeare's "A Midsummer Night's Dream" pervades these adult fairy tales. And their women, most incongruously the feisty Cher, end up or-ganizing their entire lives around the myth that every day is Valen-tine's Day and who could want anything more?

Baby Boom, about a financial whiz who gives up the fast lane for a baby, a strong supportive hunk, and a kitchen-based baby-food business in Vermont, is more explicit about where work fits into the life of the postmodern woman: between the cracks of romantic bliss.

So much has already been written about *Fatal Attraction* that it hardly seems necessary to point out that the film escalates the pro-family/traditional woman, anti-independent, sexy woman propaganda to outrageous heights. Glenn Close is just too smart, sexy, and aggres-sive to be anything but nuts, at least by 1980s standards. And Anne Archer, as the woman who devotes her entire life to hubby and kids and still looks great, is just June Cleaver in Vittadini clothing.

Broadcast News, on the other hand, about a female news producer and her two male colleagues—a gorgeous but shallow anchor and a klutzy but brilliant writer—is more contradictory and subtle in its message about strong, active women than any of the others. The characters are believable. Everyone I know knows at least three women like Holly Hunter's Jane. She's driven, serious about her work and her principles, making it in a man's world by forgoing a lot of social and leisure time, and showing the strains of her choices in her periodic crying spells.

The interplay of work and personal life, the ambiguities of a world in which women and men work intimately together amid confusing sexual tensions are all presented as accurately and wit-tily as the media hype about the film claims. Nonetheless, Jane's life and ultimate destiny aren't all that attractive. In fact, she comes off as very much like the career women characters discussed above. Not only is she forced (why?) to forego sex with the man she really digs, the hunky anchor, but she isn't allowed to have any fun at all. She eats on the run; she dresses dowdily; she does nothing but work and worry. And there is more than a subtle hint in this film that her obsessiveness, her ambition, are linked to a rather extreme case of sexual repression.

Even the ending, tagged on to please preview audiences, has the two males happily married while Jane—and this is the best she's allowed to dream of—has a maybe, sometimes boyfriend in another city. Not exactly "having it all," is it?

So how come Goldie Hawn, the drudge, and Cher, the moonstruck romantic, get to end up so ecstatically happy, while poor little Holly Hunter, the most believable cinematic incarnation of the New Woman, is doomed to a lifetime of nail biting, crying jags, and sensual repression? Is that justice? Is that feminism? A lot of people seem to think so, but I'm not buying it. As an old feminist song of the 1960s put it, "They've got women on TV but I still ain't satisfied."

Hollywood's Mid-1980s Feminist Heroines

Powerful, autonomous women have never been strangers to the Hollywood movie screen. The weak, simpering stereotypes that feminists, since the 1960s, have brought so vividly to our attention—the sex kittens and servants, the Marilyn Monroes and June Allysons—have always had their tougher counterparts.

In fact, as Molly Haskell demonstrated in *From Reverence to Rape: The Treatment of Women in the Movies*, the heroines of the 1930s and 1940s were generally far more active, assertive, and independent than their 1950s and 1960s sisters. Stars like Katharine Hepburn and Rosalind Russell often played women with serious careers who went toe to toe with their male counterparts and in some cases—Irene Dunne as the mayor of the town in *Together Again* or Russell as an advertising executive in *Take a Letter, Darling*—were socially and professionally above their male suitors.

Not that their positions were presented as unproblematic, of course. The conflict between work and love, "femininity" and "ambition," were central themes in all these films. As often as not these women were portrayed as deeply flawed and neurotic, or even, with the coming of *film noir*, downright evil. Joan Crawford, in *Mildred Pierce*, paid dearly for her business success, losing her husband and her children. Those women whose power—realistically enough—was portrayed as sexual rather than social or economic, were, in spite of their attractiveness, often shown as cold-blooded monsters. Joan Bennet in *Scarlet Street*, Barbara Stanwyck in *Double Indemnity*, and Bette Davis in any number of films were typical of Hollywood's underlying fear and hatred of the strong sexual woman.

The reemergence of the strong heroine in the 1970s was not, as is sometimes assumed, a great leap forward, although the "new woman" was presented differently, reflecting the influence of the newly visible women's movement, the changes in family life brought about by feminism, and changes in the economy and women's place in it. The most typical films of the 1950s and 1960s presented women in sexually and socially conservative, "Stand by Your Man" stereotypes. From *The Tender Trap* and *Pillow Talk*, to *Easy Rider* and *Alice's Restaurant*, women were seen as coy, game-playing man-traps or Earth Mothers.

No wonder, then, that the 1970s' preoccupation with "the problems of the modern woman," the breakdown of the traditional family, and the social upheaval caused by changing sex roles seemed progressive. Films such as *Alice Doesn't Live Here Anymore* and *An Unmarried Woman* seemed to—and in certain ways did—point out the very real oppression and diminishment of human capacity suffered by traditionally married women in families. In these films, the end of marriage—foisted upon the heroines by circumstance—was portrayed as liberating, offering the chance for growth, fulfillment, and independence at last. In fact, the futures of these heroines were not as realistic as they were portrayed to be. In both cases, a new, "better" man was a major part of the happy ending. In *An Unmarried Woman*—and this is typical of Hollywood's "women's lib" scenarios—class privilege allows the heroine to escape the most serious consequences of divorce, and the feminization of poverty.

In the later 1970s and early 1980s this genre switched its focus on women to the problems of men. In most "family breakdown" movies of that time, the father and husband suddenly becomes the "hero," the good guy who changes and grows into a responsible, nurturing provider/parent, while the estranged wife is the heavy. In *Kramer vs. Kramer* and *Ordinary People*, for example, it is Dad who "communicates," nurtures, and holds the family together while Mom is selfish, weak, and irresponsible in her emotional or actual abandonment of the family. Even in *Tootsie*, it is a man, impersonating a woman, who is the feminist heroine.

This brief and necessarily sketchy survey of major Hollywood trends in portraying women serves as background against which to understand the crop of mid-1980s films featuring strong independent women. For Hollywood, while responding to real changes in women's status, always has its own agenda, its own axe to grind, in its treatment of these themes. While its messages and images change, and are interestingly contradictory, it is not—with rare exceptions—wholeheartedly or sincerely on women's side. Without feminist interventions, it is Hollywood's style to "keep up with the times" while framing and limiting whatever apparently progressive messages it sends out in order to undercut the real demands and rights of women and to preserve the class- and sex-based power relations upon which our social and economic system is based.

The mid-1980s crop of movies featuring strong, independent women in responsible, successful positions provides an excellent opportunity to look closely at how this is done. The fall of 1985 gave us a remarkable number of releases featuring major stars in just such roles. Unlike any of the trends just described, these films actually took as a given that women were here to stay, in every important area of American public life, and that men, romance, and marriage were not indispensable components of a meaningful female existence. Five of these films—*Sweet Dreams, Jagged Edge, Marie, Agnes of God,* and *Plenty*—provide a nicely varied sample of the structural, stylistic, and dramatic ploys with which Hollywood manages to pay lip service to feminist themes and issues while at the same time seriously, if subtly, undermining those themes and demeaning, in many ways, the image of the "new woman" it seems to present.

That there are five—actually more—major actresses suitable to play strong female roles is itself a tribute to feminism and the women's movement. Jane Fonda, Meryl Streep, Jessica Lange, Glenn Close, and Sissy Spacek make up an impressive group, the likes of which have not been seen since the 1930s and 1940s, with the Crawfords, Davises, Stanwycks, and Bacalls. While the taint of "evil" associated with these women was gone in the 1980s, this new crop of women characters suffered from equally negative, if more subtle flaws, at least from a feminist perspective.

The five films fall into two categories. Three are standard Hollywood formula pieces, while two are more highbrow adaptations from stage dramas. *Marie* is actually closer to the conventions of made-for-TV movies about women than to any theatrical film genre. *Jagged Edge* is a courtroom/mystery thriller and *Sweet Dreams* is a typical Hollywood star biography of country singer Patsy Cline, which traces her path from rags to riches to tragic death. *Agnes of God* and *Plenty,* in contrast, were originally plays.

It is interesting that the women characters themselves, and their respective fates, are in certain ways more positively presented in the less serious offerings. Jessica Lange's Patsy Cline, for example, is a tough, talented, ambitious woman who knows she's as good as any man in the field, and isn't afraid to push the point. Since the real Cline lived decades ago, some of the characterization in the film is anachronistic in its feminist spirit. "Hell, no," she hoots at the promoter who asks her if she wants to be Kitty Wells, "I wanna be Hank Williams!"

Cline is also, unlike the other heroines considered here, blatantly and aggressively sexual. Unlike the 1940s heroines whose sexuality damned them, she is not a temptress of adventures. She wants a home and kids and loves her husband, played by Ed Harris, to distraction. The film does a good job of dramatizing the tensions that arise within the marriage because of Cline's fame and wealth. In recognizably 1980s fashion, in their relationship the man is ambivalent about the woman's success and power. He falls

for her because of her power and talent, but he wavers dangerously between adulation and resentment at what soon becomes his
secondary role in the household.

Because *Sweet Dreams* uses the Hollywood star tragedy formula, it avoids dealing with the sexual issues it raises. In fact,
while the fine performances of the principals tend to obscure this,
it is the slightest and most meaningless of the films. It has no point,
really, because it can't decide what the point of Cline's dilemma
should be. So it lets life provide an easy out: early death for the
heroine. Jessica Lange's performance is masterful and her character
intriguing, but we never get below the surface of the character or
the issues, and the film remains a clichéd piece of Hollywood fluff
about celebrity and its tragic costs.

Marie, on the other hand, does have a point. It too uses a hackneyed formula to get around the real issues of women in society today. It tells the "true story" of Marie Ragghianti, a formerly abused
wife and single mother, who gets a meant-to-be token job in the Tennessee governor's office and proceeds to single-handedly and doggedly expose the corruption she discovers in the penal system.

Sissy Spacek plays Marie as a modern-day Dickens heroine.
She is sweet, demure, immune to sensual urges, fanatical in her
mothering and so honest and determined to "do the right thing"
that she quickly becomes a tremendous bore to watch. In one
scene illustrating her competence and drive, she ingeniously saves
her son's life in a roadstop bathroom. In fact, her single-minded-
ness in questioning, facing down, and proving herself right against
a doctor's erroneous diagnosis of her son's condition is exactly
analogous to her behavior at work. There too she refuses to be intimidated or stopped by evil, incompetent, male authority figures.
A court finds her innocent of trumped-up charges made up to fire
her, and in the process exposes the state's financial hanky-panky.

Formally, this morality tale is dull as dust. In TV-movie manner it plods along from scenes of domestic violence, to the hard
work of going to college while raising kids and caring for an inva-
lid mother, to her professional triumphs and troubles. Nothing is
unpredictable here. Nothing is emotionally, politically, or psychologically subtle.

The character of Marie was meant, clearly, to be inspiration-ally feminist. It is, in fact, reactionary, both politically and sexually. Since these movies rarely provide a social or political context for their messages, the audience is left with some implicit but dangerous ideas. For one thing, Marie is a law-and-order girl, after the heart of Ronald Reagan. She acts out all the patriotic, mindless rules about "doing right" and "obeying the law" that the Right so loves. In fact, her efforts, though this is never spelled out, strengthen the penal code and ensure longer sentences and less likelihood of parole for all prisoners.

That "feminism" was used to sell this message is significant, and it fits perfectly with Marie's sexual persona. She is a true Madonna—of the Immaculate Conception, not the Material Girl, variety—of virtue and maternal instinct. Women are working these days, the film tells us, but they aren't slighting their motherly duties or becoming sexually loose because of it. And their work is an extension of their domestic mothering role: to uphold morality and keep things organized and running according to God's will.

Jagged Edge, in which Glenn Close plays an attorney who defends an accused wife-murderer, falls in love with him, wins his case, and finds out he's guilty, is as slick and formulaic as *Marie,* but far more interesting as a film as well as a social statement. It provides a nice example of how Hollywood formulas subvert and co-opt whatever serious, socially threatening issues a film may raise. If Patsy Cline has no real character, and Marie Ragghianti is a modern Little Nell, Glenn Close, as Teddy Barnes, is a real, contradictory woman. She is tough, competent, aggressive, and independent in her work, but she is also emotionally vulnerable and needy, idealistic, and, at times, manipulable. She is a devoted single mother, but her kids are not her whole emotional focus.

She is, then, what early feminist film critics used to cry out for—a "positive role model," but with enough flaws to be credible. In subtle ways, nevertheless, her character—because of her femininity—is portrayed as less capable of succeeding in a man's world than soppy little Sissy Spacek. Most obviously, she is taken in by a cold-blooded sociopathic murderer who happens to be a hunk, with charm to spare. She believes absolutely that he is innocent while her DA opponent, a political cynic and sleaze whose methods are unethical and illegal, sees through the guy immediately.

This film presents a world in which men, and the institutions they rule, are hopelessly corrupt, immoral, and unfeeling. A good woman, no matter how principled and competent, is no match for the devious male minds she must confront. The suggestion that Teddy lets her heart rule her head is obvious. In *Marie*, the Norman Rockwell world buckled easily in the face of Marie's moral authority, while in *Jagged Edge*, a much more believable.version of public life, Teddy buckles and can't really play with the big boys.

There are two aspects of the style and setting of this film that further subvert whatever progressive message it might have had. For one thing, all evil is seen to lie solely in political rather than corporate institutions, and in the hearts of individual "bad" men. Teddy, in fact, had worked for the sleazy DA, become disillusioned with criminal law, and moved over to what is presented as "cleaner" corporate work. From a Left perspective, this is definitely a frying-pan/fire decision.

The film's most clever subversion of social implications is the ending. Teddy actually faces down the killer and shoots him in cold blood, before he can kill her. This "solution" is a kind of feminist *Death Wish* ploy. The women in the audience are relieved—Teddy is dramatically returned to stature—but the problem of social evil, and of ruthlessness and violence in powerful men and their institutions, is ignored. Teddy represents many feminist virtues (if we ignore questions of class), but is socially and politically ineffectual precisely because of those virtues. She is left with no emotionally suitable male partners who are on her level intellectually or morally. The solution for Teddy is a retreat from public life, since her integrity and emotional priorities signal weakness, and, implicitly, social eccentricity, at least in the world she inhabits.

In all three films, we see the way Hollywood, at its commercial best, deals with social change and the demands of the relatively powerless. It is easier than one might think to present women as feminist role models and allow them to "be the best you can be," as a popular cosmetic commercial put it, as long as you can contain their strengths and virtues in a form which implicitly subverts their radical thrust. Popular genre forms, by definition, limit the scope and seriousness of subversive challenges to the status quo. The audience expects certain things and not others: it has been trained from childhood to understand these forms. Whether it's a star biography, an uplifting morality tale, or a courtroom thriller, most of the complexities and contradictions of American social and political life are left out.

The legal and governmental worlds of *Jagged Edge* and *Marie* are contained within the limits of the plot, the problem to be solved in a neat 90 minutes or so. No larger questions can arise about, say, the "left" or "right" of Marie's positions, or the political and economic context that produces the kind of corruption and immorality that Teddy Barnes confronts. We are primed to look for clues and happy endings, to find and expunge the bad guys. *Sweet Dreams* similarly flattens and frames the issue of success and celebrity.

Hollywood addresses some of the issues left out of classic pop genres in the stage adaptations. Not surprisingly, the images and fates of the heroines are a lot more depressing, for theses films were not necessarily made to be box office blockbusters. They were aimed, primarily, at a different audience—the relatively select group of thinkers and doers who read *The New York Times* rather than *USA Today* and watch the "MacNeil Lehrer News Hour" rather than CNN's "Headline News." Because they were meant to reach the educated "opinion makers," these films took feminism's challenge to established power far more seriously.

Their analyses of the "modern woman" were therefore more mean-spirited and philosophically devastating than the films mentioned above. In fact, both *Agnes of God* and *Plenty* represented a retreat to the Freudian, implicitly woman-hating and -fearing images of the 1940s. But the flaws upon which they focused, and the punishments meted out, were different. Because of the impact of feminism, it was no longer fashionable to portray sexually or socially powerful women as Jezebels or unfeminine victims of penis envy. Instead, they had more demeaning, even pathetic flaws.

In both films, the heroines present real challenges to the legitimacy of powerful institutions and the assumptions and values that sustain them. In both cases, the filmmakers presented a broad, intricate picture of the workings of those institutions, and then proceeded to discredit the heroines' challenges through character assassination.

In *Agnes*, Jane Fonda plays an ultra-rational psychiatrist determined to prove that a delusionary young nun, Sister Agnes (Meg Tilly), who has borne and apparently murdered a child, was raped rather than "visited by the Holy Ghost," which is the feisty Mother Superior's position.

The ideological issues dominate the film. Anne Bancroft's Mother Superior is a woman of the world—she married, had children, and finally turned to the convent as a solace (and escape) from the failures and disappointments of her earlier "normal" life. Fonda's Dr. Livingston, on the other hand, is single, childless, and has left the church because of her emotionally traumatic experiences with religion. The cards are clearly stacked from the start. Bancroft's reasons for turning to religion are seen as valid, since she is now content as she never was in the "world of sorrow" that society had been for her and for the young, emotionally disturbed nun. Agnes, we learn, was abused both mentally and physically as a child.

Dr. Livingston's life is less fulfilling. She is estranged from her mother, has no permanent man, no visible friends or family, and is all business, from her tailored beiges and grays, to her orderly, modern apartment. The church, on the other hand, offers a true community, tradition, culture, and the joy and passion that come with faith.

To see Bancroft and Fonda square off for the young nun's soul is to see Hollywood's dirtiest of dirty pools, where women are concerned. Bancroft, after all, is as tough and hip as Fonda, and more experienced to boot (she even smokes). But the institution she represents is anathema to feminist ideals, for reasons that surely don't need to be explained. Patriarchy, celibacy, retreat from social and political life—these are values that nuns themselves are fighting to change today.

In the end, the church wins and Fonda falters in her convictions. The film ends with a statement from the doctor to the effect that she has been moved and changed by the young nun's (deranged) faith and hopes that there just may be some truth to her religious beliefs, fantastic as they seem. Needless to say, the church in question bears no relation to the progressive church of liberation theology. The conclusion, therefore, must be interpreted as extremely reactionary, both sexually and politically. The "liberated woman" ends up looking very unattractive indeed, while mysticism and blind obedience to institutional authority win the day.

Plenty, which, like *Sweet Dreams,* was set in earlier times but informed by a 1980s sensibility, goes even further than *Agnes* in subverting feminist ideals, and making them, and those who try to live by them, seem seriously flawed and emotionally unstable. This time the setting and themes are political, not religious. Susan Traherne (Meryl Streep) had been a fighter in the French Resistance during World War II. She had loved the adventure and the sense of doing important work for deeply held political principles. Her return to civilian life is a letdown. She goes from job to job—diplomatic service, TV advertising, even office work—and finds them all deadening.

Plenty includes some truly remarkable lines and situations, given its early-1950s setting. Traherne's best friend, for example, is quite eloquent on the matter of male resentment of female friendships. At one point, Traherne enlists a young working-class man to father a child for her, which she will raise alone. At another point, we see her, the lone woman at a meeting, making a suggestion that is ignored, only to be enthusiastically endorsed when a male re-phrases it. Her response is a cynical shrug of the shoulders; she is used to such treatment. Finally, in one of the film's great lines, she tells her friend that she rarely says what she really thinks publicly, in front of the men she knows, "for fear of blowing them out of the room."

This is clearly a woman modern audiences will find familiar. The film, however, sets her up from the start as neurotic. Even in her war scenes she is seen giving in to fear and clinging to a male comrade. While men—heroes at least—never behave this way in war movies, fear is not, certainly, an unusual or abnormal reaction to war.

As the movie progresses, she goes from shaky to thoroughly incompetent. She marries her diplomat husband in a moment of weakness and gratitude after having a "breakdown" when her attempts to become pregnant fail. From there, the film drags us through a series of embarrassing and increasingly hysterical scenes in which she breaks protocol, shocks guests, and at times viciously tirades against British imperialist policies.

When her husband finally castigates her for her "selfishness" and unrealistic fantasies of a better, more meaningful life and world, the audience is meant to feel, "It's about time." He is, after all, a long-suffering, loving, if dull sort, who "deserves" a wife who will help, not hurt his career. The final scenes, which find her in a cheap room, stoned, and reliving the idealism and excitement of her political days, are a damning indictment of what her husband sees as her wasted life.

The film never explains why she does not pursue what at one point seems to be an interest in painting, or why she stays in such an unsuitable marriage. But the unmentioned answer is obvious— this was the 1950s. Because the film and the heroine are so very up-to-date, however, it's hard to remember that. And that is exactly the point of the film's entirely sexist strategy. It takes a woman easily identifiable as a modern-day feminist, a woman of power, drive, and social concerns, and puts her in a setting in which these traits are only interpretable as "crazy."

The 1980s in many ways were a return to 1950s values. The people who have always hated and feared feminism were more influential than ever. It makes sense, then, that this movie, like *Agnes of God,* put forth an image of the "liberated woman" in a contradictory way. On one level, all these films support and accept everything the Women's Movement pushed for in the 1960s and 1970s. On another, more subtle level, however, they are stabs in the back: reactionary attacks on those very ideals. "You've come a long way, Baby," they all seem to say, "Now let's see how you like the bed you've made for yourself."

Hollywood's bed, plush as it looked, was not the one women ordered. Feminism assumes that society itself needs to change in important, democratizing ways. By omitting or distorting every aspect of the larger social world, and its effects on women, Hollywood gives women a message so depressing that it is almost a threat. There is very little in any of these films that would make a young woman envy these heroines. In fact, the Katharine Hepburns and Lauren Bacalls look a lot more enviable in every way. "You've come a long way," indeed.

Do 1950s Values Tempt 1990s Women?

Wake me when it's over, I had been muttering, ever since the 1990s bit us. George Bush, recession, poverty, civil rights attacks, war. But at least, I kept telling myself, most of the cultural changes wrought by feminism are still standing. My daughter, after all, was in much better shape than I was at her age, in most ways.

And then I went to the movies and was harshly reminded of an obvious, sad truth: Feminist-raised daughters aren't the cultural markers of our time. Movies are, and have always been, a lot more revealing of broad social feeling and fantasy. The movie that brought me to my senses was not all that significant on its own. In fact, it could be described as easily forgettable, unless you're wild

for Holly Hunter or Richard Dreyfuss. It tells the improbable sentimental tale of a young, unemployable, unmarriageable woman—
part of a huge, symbiotically joined-at-the-hip Italian family. She
falls for a zillionaire eccentric who loves her to death but causes
friction in her family.

As a movie it was sweet but dumb; as a synthesis of dominant representation of women and families, however, it was very
interesting indeed. In the late 1980s and early 1990s, the relatively
few movies in which women figured at all prominently all were
obsessively concerned with the preservation of hearth, home, and
biological offspring. Once in a while, someone in a skirt left home
with a briefcase, but often as not she turned out to be temporarily
mateless, a situation that was usually rectified by film's end.

Remember Dianne Wiest in *Hannah and Her Sisters* or Dianne Wiest, again, in *Parenthood? Moonstruck* was the quintessential case. These films were and are part of an insidious trend. They
feature very large, extended families and plots that pivot on the
successful if improbable matings and child-rearing practices of the
principals to the exclusion of all else.

As I dragged myself to one after another of these depressing
movies about the burdens of baking birthday cakes and the non-
chemical highs of going daffy for whoever happens to be standing
nearby, I began to feel very un-American. I just didn't get it.

A Reactionary Fantasy

And then came *Pretty Woman,* a reactionary fantasy I could
understand. Here was a woman character with no marketable
skills, forced to stand on street corners selling herself to survive,
who is deep down inside really a virginal saint with the moxy of an
oil magnate. And lo and behold, someone recognizes her qualities.
Not just someone, really, but Richard Gere, gorgeous as ever,
metamorphosed incongruously into a character who has all the
money anyone could ever imagine but whose life is empty because
he lacks a streetwalker fitting our heroine's description.

From there, it was sheer party time. Gorgeous hotel suites,
champagne and escargot, endless shopping sprees in which she buys
everything she fancies and tells off snooty saleswomen who confuse

class with cold cash, a fatal error in post-industrial commerce.

This movie, I confess, tickled me. I saw it on a day when a particularly large dental bill arrived, among other bad news, and immediately I understood its appeal. Women, especially, were hurting, and *Pretty Woman* was a beautifully made piece of fluff in which our problems were resolved effortlessly. No need even to deprive ourselves of good sex, like all those boring housewives seemed to. The good girl/bad girl thing didn't seem to apply.

Pretty Woman surprised everyone by becoming a record-breaking smash, and was clearly a sign of the times. It was a purer, more preposterous version of the story told by *Working Girl* and *White Palace*, two other films about sexy, uneducated working-class women who snag wealthy hunks with no more equipment than Melanie Griffith's famous "mind for business and bod for sin." It acknowledged women's economic realities in post-feminist years and pretended that working-class women (a metaphor, it seems to me, for most women in these days of feminized poverty) could get all the economic goodies of Leona Helmsley by being innocently sweet, street smart, and good in bed.

This was a direct throwback to the 1950s of Marilyn Monroe and Debbie Reynolds. Julia Roberts's character in *Pretty Woman* combined the overt sexual manipulations of Monroe with the always phony sexual purity of nice girls like Reynolds and Audrey Hepburn. Innocence and helplessness on the surface, promises of hot nights as subtext. Isn't that what pre-feminist women were all about? We've come a long way around in a circle.

Which brings us to *Once Around*, a movie that begins and ends with people driving around in circles—singing "Fly me to the moon and let me play among the stars." Lest you doubt the cleverness of the Hollywood moguls, try this. Someone recognized that both these fantasies were hot right now and found a way—incongruously—to make them fit together: First you get the warm rock-solid extended family; then you get a fantastic romantic fairy tale filled with all the sex and luxury you want; and then it's back to the family with a new baby and an endless bankroll.

Holly Hunter plays Renata Bella, a truly pathetic young woman so desperate to marry that she grovels before her boyfriend on the day of her younger sister's wedding. When he responds by telling her, "I don't ever intend to marry you," she literally crawls home to her parents' bed for comfort. (Her sister and the new hubby are right next door in the same house; that's the kind of family this is.)

Hunter quits her waitress job to try selling condos in the tropics (it had to be a lush, romantic setting) where she meets multibillionaire Sam Sharpe (Dreyfuss), an insensitive, overbearing slob who somehow manages to tell stupid jokes in a way that makes people fork over their money and buy his condos. Renata immediately sets her cap for him and they return to Boston, where he promptly moves his business headquarters so she can stay with her family. "I wasn't real good at selling condos," she tells the folks.

After which she does nothing at all but play and giggle with her boorish bozo—"This is my adventure," she tells her amazed sister—and negotiate between her two fantasy lives of safety and security.

At this point, the film begins a discourse on ethnic conflict. Dreyfuss is Lithuanian and insists on inserting his culture into the family rituals, and sparks fly. What's really at stake, of course, is the patriarchal ownership of Renata, an aging girl who either has to be owned by someone or perish. So which strong older man will it be? Will she stay with Dad, who offers the warmth and predictability of tradition and order? Or will she choose wild and crazy Sam and a life of permanent fireworks and surprises, not to mention penthouses, chauffeured limos, and charge accounts?

The movie, correctly hedging its bets on the amount of time the audience can stand Sam—or believe that even an airhead like Renata can—kills him off. Now the original family is reunited and intact. Renata has lost nothing and has memories and money to burn. Oh, and a baby, the one essential commodity of the age.

Call me ditzy, but I could see the charm of this movie too. Things really are not easy for women these days. The promise of feminism, after all, depends on a little cooperation from government and the economy. But the 1980s gave us one kick in the shins after another. No wonder fantasies of security, of luxury, of someone to take us away from the worry of bills and child care and dreariness of the dayshift are so much fun, every once in a while.

Hollywood-made fantasies—like gin—bring major hangovers. They are just as dangerous now as they were in the 1950s. Marriage and motherhood didn't keep us happy or safe then either.

And exchanging sex for luxury—whatever the problems involved in these arrangements anyway—is not an option for anyone but Julia Roberts and a few others, for a few years.

I won't even comment on the projected returns of letting yourself be swept off your feet by the nearest man and merging your life with his. It's not a good idea; avoid full moons. Don't give up your day job. And above all, don't believe everything you see in the movies.

Privileging Patriarchy at the Movies

One of the things that has puzzled me more and more lately is how people—movie critics, film scholars, and casual viewers alike—continue to talk about the contemporary *cinema* (if you will) as if it still deserved to be taken seriously. Anyone searching for a Saturday night movie knows full well that mindless macho blockbusters have virtually dominated the cineplex screens and box offices for lo these many years, reducing us all to choosing between Arnold Schwarzenegger and Leonardo the Ninja Turtle or staying home with HBO or a good mystery.

The implicit hierarchies we accept when talking about film, fiction, and television need to be revised—especially where gender is concerned. The mall's paperback book sections are filled with science fiction, hard-boiled detective stories, and even family sagas in which tough, bright women solve crimes, fight galactic wars, and march triumphantly through history. The much-maligned TV screen offers "Roseanne," "Murphy Brown," the Lifetime channel's constant run of woman-oriented movies, and more. While the big screen offers ever more gruesome and mindless mayhem, most daytime soap operas showcase story lines about date rape, gay-bashing, hate crimes, sexual harassment, and other hot issues, with—almost invariably—women characters championing the progressive causes. The decision to read a trash novel or watch TV instead of dragging oneself to a movie makes sense.

By taking movies so seriously and discounting other forms in which women and feminism have had greater impact, we are buying into one of the more subtly insidious—because so rarely noted—ways in which sexism becomes internalized in our culture. My female students cringe in embarrassment when their young male classmates—avid fans of mindless sexist comedies and shoot-em-ups—guffaw and sneer at their milder, far more easily defended pop pleasures. They are mimicking the gendered biases of cultural power brokers in more sophisticated, intellectually respectable places. The privileged place of movies in our toniest journals of opinion is a source of continuing prejudice against things female—female taste, female sensibility, female experience, and, too often, female survival.

Let me take you on a brief tour of what's been playing at your local cineplexes for the last year or so and what it says about Hollywood's position in the gender wars. Women in movies today—when they appear at all—are not only far more demeaned and abused than in other media, proportionately; they are far more demeaned and abused, even, than they were in the pre-feminist 1930s, 1940s, and even 1950s. All the women in movies I've seen lately fall into two categories for single women and two for those attached to men. For single, independent women, the dominant trend is the bitch-from-hell horror film in which the frustrated, bitter, "independent" woman puts some version of the perfect American home or workplace in mortal danger.

Fatal Attraction was the grandmama of them all, the one in which "Leave It to Beaver" family bliss, so trendy in the Bush/Reagan era, was threatened by a mad, sexy, career woman out to get the Nice Girl's husband and baby through the worst possible means—hot sex and intelligent conversation. When that failed, of course, she resorted to mayhem, but what can you expect from a career woman with only her downtown loft and uptown deals to keep her warm?

In the wake of this blockbuster—among the "best" roles for a woman that year—came the inevitable spinoffs. *The Hand That Rocks the Cradle* showed a similarly perfect family threatened by a dispossessed, reproductively barren nanny from hell. *The Temp* portrayed a nice businessman stalked by an ambitious office worker. And *Single, White, Female* had a nice, properly boyfriended young woman terrorized by her less pretty, unbalanced roommate, crazed with envy. Finally, the classiest of all was *Basic Instinct*, in which the smart, gorgeous psychopath was also bisexual. In all these films the message was clear: women who choose, or are forced, to make it on their own inevitably become so deranged with unhappiness as to represent a threat to all of western civilization. Stop this woman before she ruins the whole world!

Single, White, Female, also fits into the second category. In "woman on the loose" films the heroine is not dangerous but pathetic because she can't really cut it in a man's world. She inevitably makes a mess of her life and career and nearly dies because of her stupidity and weakness: usually, there's a macho hero waiting in the wings to save her from herself. This version of the old 1970s "woman in danger" flick has been classed up a bit these days and now finds itself in A—rather than B—movies. Glenn Close of *Fatal Attraction* fame started this one, too, in the 1980s with *Jagged Edge*. Since then we've had many of these movies, most recently *Jennifer 8*, about a blind woman stalked by a psychopath and saved by a cop, and *Guilty as Sin*, about a hotshot lawyer whose woman-murdering client has his eyes on her for his next victim. She—and this is the best of the scenarios—manages, implausibly, to save herself and kill him. The point, however, is not her ultimate victory but her incompetence—as a vulnerable woman and not-so-great lawyer—in choosing her male associates. Like Close in *Jagged Edge*, she is no match for a man either personally or professionally. You get the message. And finally there's *Sliver,* another gory, voyeuristic mess in which a passive, vulnerable, dopey career woman is almost killed by a hunky psychopath.

These are the two trends, started in the 1980s, which warn single, ambitious women that they are no match for the male world they dare to enter on their own. In 1992, we saw a new set of demeaning movies in which women are neither ambitious nor in danger. They were simply—in the most medieval terms imaginable—the property and playthings of generally attractive and sympathetic men. In *Indecent Proposal, Mad Dog and Glory,* and *Honeymoon in Vegas*—three mainstream, lucrative movies with big stars—men negotiate to actually barter women. Both negotiating men want the women for one thing or another, but only one is rich and powerful enough to take full possession on his own terms. Demi Moore is bought for a million dollars, for one night, by superslick high roller Robert Redford in the first film. And, to confuse things utterly, Redford is a true hunk who really loves her, so what's the problem? (In real life, of course, such deals are made by men who look like Aristotle Onassis and smell like death.) The other two woman-bartering films, more lighthearted comedies than moral-dilemma vehicles, pay even less attention to the implications of their story lines for women. The heroines simply behave as though they were, indeed, living in the days of fairy tales and King Arthur's Round Table, and act as though it all made perfect, jolly sense, as they pack their things and move from one man's household to the next, all the time smiling and cooking and cleaning.

A darker, more troubling version of this theme was seen in *Point of No Return,* in which a smooth, fatherly government agent trains a tough young drug addict to be a very feminine, sexy, hired killer and then romantically "sets her free" when he falls in love with her. Love is portrayed in terms of the most barbaric ideas about women as human putty or property, and romanticized and eroticized to the point where such retro notions seem to almost make sense. He "gives her a life," twice, really, and she is grateful, as only the powerless and brainless can be grateful for what is already theirs.

Given this onslaught of humiliation and horror, one is almost grateful for the last category, in which fantasy men miraculously save women stuck with brutish mates, offering true love and companionship (of a kind generally not seen in movies or real life) with a man worthy of it. *Sommersby* and *Dave* both present this scenario in a way which, if one suspends all judgment, makes for a nice little fantasy. If indeed—as these movies seem to assume—divorce has become impossible and one must choose to live with some man or other who happens to turn up in one's front yard (since one does not ever leave home), then the conjuring up of a perfect fantasy mate is indeed the best of all happy endings. In *Dave*, for example, the choices are a George Bush-type president and a Clintonesque clone of the president, who replaces him. This, you will note, is very much the choice women actually had at the polls in 1992. The heroine does well under the circumstances. In a world in which women—in our personal lives at least—do in fact have the right to choose mates or matelessness, to divorce, to move to another town, to change careers, etc., the premises of these movies are absurd and insulting. To read the reviews, however, they represented the height of "romantic" comedy and drama.

And so we sit at home privately reading and viewing books and videos that don't insult us. And then, in public, we chat politely about the latest would-be Oscar nominee as though we agreed with our male friends and colleagues that popular culture still is the movies, while pulp fiction and TV are beneath contempt. We nod knowingly when it's implied that an actress making a docudrama or starring in a sitcom has somehow "come down" in the world artistically. And we warn our daughters away from lowbrow women's genres in the interest of their intellectual and cultural development.

Lesbian Interventions

Nineteen-eighty-five saw a remarkable flowering of fine films in which gay relationships are central, but not the thematic point. The British *My Beautiful Launderette* deftly allowed the relationship between a white working-class kid and a Pakistani immigrant go completely without comment as the larger racial and political themes emerged as dominant. *Parting Glances* similarly presented the sexual aspect of gay life in an offhand way, as larger issues of friendship, love, and the effects of the AIDS crisis on a community developed.

Desert Hearts, the desert-set late-1950s period piece about a love affair between a staid Columbia professor waiting for a Nevada divorce and a sexy, predatory casino "change girl," seemed to be more specifically "about" lesbian sex. It was surely among the most erotic gay films produced at the time. But its emphasis on eroticism at a time when gay male films were downplaying "sex for sex's sake" is itself politically telling. Gay male culture has been marked by a sexual openness, an almost militant flamboyance. Lesbian culture, on the other hand, has been far less visible or stereotypically "sexy." This is hardly surprising given the power of sexism and society's repression of female sexuality in general.

If *Desert Hearts* seemed old-fashioned, it was because it was a marvelously self-conscious attempt to create a bit of cinematic "affirmative action." Its setting is timeless, except in terms of the classic Hollywood conventions it follows. It is a no-holds-barred melodrama of the Clark Gable and Joan Crawford type. Only this time we have women in the romantic leads. In fact, this film—like the two mentioned—is not about "sex," but romance. This, and its classic Hollywood happy ending, with the couple riding off toward a blissful "ever after," are its glory. Lesbians, after all, have been allowed little eroticism, and even less happiness in the mainstream media.

The film's setting and characterizations are superb. There is the classic train ride, with the uptight, elegantly suited and coiffed Vivian stepping nervously into the heat and expansiveness of the desert. There is the ranch manager, played to perfection by Audra Lindley, who seems at first one of those house mothers of early "women's films," but gradually reveals herself, too, to be caught in a painful drama of sexual attraction and ambivalence toward the wild and free-wheeling Cay, as sexy and flirtatious a "cowhand" as ever hit the silver screen. Even the male hands are in awe of Cay. "Beats me how you get so much traffic with no equipment," says one.

That so many critics dismissed this film as badly done is understandable, if obtuse. It is broadly "coded" with Hollywood clichés. The morning after Vivian and Cay's first love-making, Vivian literally "takes down her hair." The "East equals repression/West equals sensuality" symbolism is played for all it's worth. The soundtrack, full of classic country and Western tracks by Patsy Cline, Kitty Wells, and Elvis Presley, is perfectly suited to the sappy, romantic, yet sexually unbridled style of the film.

But *Desert Hearts* isn't a study in Hollywood convention. The eroticism and subtly played out dynamics of sexual desire and romantic longing between women are beyond anything dreamed of in classic cinema of the 1940s. And the sexual explicitness is advanced even for contemporary heterosexual movies.

To experience this film in a neighborhood movie house, surrounded by typical moviegoers of both sexes, is to understand the power of its deceptive simplicity. As a female movie lover, I have spent my life in a state of mixed consciousness. On the one hand, it is impossible not to identify with most movies' male protagonists, since the point of view is implicitly male, and the male is the dominant, active figure. On the other hand, as a woman caught up in the romance of the medium, there is a strong identification with the female object of desire: the beautiful, often passive image of all that is delightful and longed for.

Straight men who see this movie will experience the same split consciousness, if they can keep their homophobia in check. For Cay is as sexy—and proficient in the arts of courtship, seduction, and sexual technique—as any leading man. And she knows "what women want." *Desert Hearts* is as pleasurable to watch as an old Greta Garbo flick, and as consciousness-tampering as Jane Rule's lesbian cult novel *Desert of the Heart* upon which it is based.

Madonna's
Feminist Challenge

Watching *Truth or Dare*, the amazing documentary of Madonna's "Blond Ambition" tour, I thought constantly about Bob Dylan. That's not as weird as it sounds. In 1965, at the height of Dylan's equally fantastic, culture-changing career, D.A. Pennebaker made a very similar documentary, *Don't Look Back*, about Dylan's concert tour of Great Britain.

The films are too similar not to evoke comparisons. The theme of both is the nature and meaning of celebrity in an era of radical cultural and political change. The structural strategies are also identical. Both follow their stars around, moving jumpily from backstage "reality" to on-stage performance. Both films construct an image of the star that is informed by similar characteristics: mystery, danger, personal charisma, and a sense of absolute control over everything in sight, from personnel and entourage to stage production to relations with the media, management, and public officials.

Finally, and most importantly, both Dylan and Madonna reveal a serious and radical artistic agenda. Both self-consciously recognize the powerful role they play in the politics of their times. They are—often obnoxiously, always aggressively—disrespectful of every official moral and political belief of their day. Madonna says, late in the film, that her goal is "to push people's buttons" and that her art is essentially "political." Who could deny that Dylan, while he would never say anything so revealing, had the same mission?

The differences between Dylan and Madonna, as seen by comparing the two films, reveal much about the changes of the past 25 years of U.S. cultural politics. Three things stand out: the always problematic relationship between serious popular artists and the media, the main issues that define the times, and the changes in gender relations. Dylan became a superstar in spite of his almost religious refusal to give interviews, appear on television, or follow any of the gambits every celebrity must engage in to ensure even a shot at success. Looking back, Dylan's stance toward stardom—his insistence upon an absolute separation between his "private," "real" self and his "art"—seems unbelievably innocent and romantic. It is rooted in a time long past when a celebrity could actually see her/himself as "outside" the industry parameters and as having the power to thwart the media's efforts to define her or him by simply refusing to play the game.

Truth or Dare, by comparison, shows the end of such romantic innocence, and the acceptance of the postmodern truism that there is no more inside/outside distinction for major media figures—although Madonna does not reveal her "real" person any more than Dylan did.

Madonna knows that she exists within a powerful all-encompassing media world, and she aims to beat it at its own game by playing its rules for all they are worth. Unlike Dylan, she flaunts herself and lures the camera shamelessly.

Warren Beatty chides her for filming a throat examination. Sarcastically, he comments upon her narcissism, "If it's not on camera what's the point of saying anything at all?"

But it's not these bits of trivia that make her relationship to celebrity so different from Dylan's. *Don't Look Back* shows similar moments demystifying stardom and humanizing the star. But no one in Dylan's 1965 entourage would have accused him of courting celebrity. The whole point of *Don't Look Back* was to track the artist as he thwarted and confused the mainstream media.

Don't Look Back was itself a countercultural film; it was Dylan's deconstruction of the *Time* magazine version of Dylan. In a great scene, the 25-year-old singer insults an older *Time* reporter by explaining, in the most contemptuous terms, why he wouldn't bother to say anything to a publication like *Time* because it is so clearly a lying, immoral magazine.

Madonna wouldn't dream of doing that. She doesn't deconstruct media; she's a major player, producing her own very mainstream version of her own heartily embraced celebrity. She doesn't want to knock the media; she wants to bend it to her own ends from within because she accepts its terms entirely.

Charged with narcissism and self-exploitation, Madonna answered that she wanted to show the "real" side of celebrity in juxtaposition to the staged version, that *Truth or Dare* is a film "about celebrity." So, of course, was *Don't Look Back.*

But whereas the earlier film stressed the conflict between the artist as person and the artist as star, *Truth or Dare* elides the distinction utterly. Both artists created mere constructs of their supposedly "real" selves. But Madonna's self-construct stressed celebrity as her quintessential feature; Dylan's denied it entirely. And this difference says volumes about the massive changes in the contested terrain of media politics since the 1960s.

In *Truth or Dare*, the issue is obviously sexuality. We see Madonna in bed with everyone, exposing her breasts, simulating oral sex on a bottle of Evian water, calling Beatty "pussy man," and generally being as "lewd and lascivious" as imaginable, not only on stage but off.

Her on-stage performance is as sexually daring and aggressive as anything I've seen short of actual porn. Watching the "Blond Ambition" concert in its entirety on Home Box Office recently, I was so overwhelmed by the woman's physical intensity and sexual aggressiveness that I could not get her out of my head for days.

She and her dancers challenge every "normal" sexual convention, belief, and value. Men and women change sexual identities continuously. Madonna simulates sexual intercourse while singing "Like a Virgin," all the while switching positions in a way that defies all standard, sexist notions of sexual propriety. She makes fun of U.S. censorship advocates, curses like the toughest of tough guys, and masturbates on stage.

Of course Dylan—the politico of 1960s rock—would never have done such things for the camera. Nor would he have cried on screen as Madonna does often. This is not only because of differences in Madonna's and Dylan's personalities or in their film strategies. It's because the feminist and lesbian, gay, and bisexual movements with which Madonna identifies have changed our political priorities.

In the 1960s we were mostly concerned with the economic and political corruption of our institutions and national policies. Dylan's targets in *Don't Look Back* were bosses, racists, and masters of war. Now there is a different, or at least an enlarged, agenda. Sexual identity, power relationships, and the boundaries of "good taste" in public expression comprise the forefront in our community discourses.

Madonna pushes the limits of what is allowed, emotionally and sexually, while Dylan didn't need to. This is because the media are so much more ubiquitous and powerful today, and because one of their major agendas is setting the rules for sexual and emotional representation and behavior.

I have saved the issue of gender relations for last because, once mentioned, it tends to override everything else about the significance of Madonna and her film.

In the 1960s it was impossible to imagine a female performer as the subject of a film like *Don't Look Back* or playing the role in U.S. culture and politics that Dylan played. His counterpart in artistic importance and celebrity was Joni Mitchell, a performer who has yet to receive a fraction of the appreciation she deserves, although in the 1960s she was clearly "the queen of rock and roll," as *Rolling Stone* magazine put it.

When you see *Truth or Dare*, you will see a public female presence so powerful, so self-contained and authoritative, so sexually assured as to be frightening. The woman is truly scary, whether you like her or not. She's scary because she stands there—out on her own—facing down most of the Western world and being absolutely and obviously comfortable about it.

Madonna's sense of humor, irreverent and lusty, celebrates female freedom from sexist constraint of all kinds. Her sexual bravado, seen in her live performances, as opposed to in her videos, cannot possibly be misunderstood as the behavior of a sexual object. In the tradition of male rock stars, she exudes an unbounded sexual energy and aggressiveness.

She is so at ease with her sexual power, so fearless of its effect on others, so outrageously candid and open that she stands as a living symbol of the liberating power of breaking social taboos.

If, however, this film was meant to comment on the nature of celebrity and (implicitly) on how much women can achieve, it failed. Critics commented on the sense the film gives of a "lonely, lost child in a storm." This strikes me as a hackneyed repetition of the "it's lonely at the top" cliché. This has nothing to do with the down side of feminine power and success that the film reveals. It has to do with the place of men in the film and in her life.

Madonna is surrounded by men who adore her, lust after her, sycophantically and opportunistically bow at her feet. She mocks most of them and mothers some. She and a friend have a hilarious conversation about the inadequacies of their lovers. When a friend suggests she read Susan Forward's *Men Who Hate Women and the Women Who Love Them,* she says, "I think I could have written it." And when asked, in the game that gives the film its title, who the great love of her life was, she replies with obvious emotion, "Sean, Sean," referring to her ex-husband, actor Sean Penn. Herein lies a truth about how far we've come and what's still left to deal with. Let me explain with a personal anecdote.

I left this film almost walking on air, exhilarated by its sense of female pride, power, and progress. When I got home, I got a call from a friend. Before I could start raving about the film, my friend began her own story, her reason for calling. Her promising relationship, with a man who seemingly could relate to a self-sufficient, tough woman, had ended. The guy was returning to his much needier, more traditional wife.

Hearing this story yet again, in the midst of my "Madonna high," I shifted my take on *Truth or Dare.* Men find Madonna troubling; they like her less and criticize her more than most women do; and, in a weird irony, they worry publicly about her "sleaziness" and object to her on "feminist" grounds. I think this personal anecdote points to why. Madonna represents the ultimate challenge, which feminism has made to men from the start: "This is what the future is gonna look like, baby, and if you can't take the heat, get out of the kitchen."

Most male reviewers were cautiously, almost fearfully respectful of this film, but none credited it with the kind of sexual and political power it has. To do that would have been to face up to this ultimate feminist challenge. That so few—even in 1991—were willing to do so signals the darker political message beneath the almost blinding light of *Truth or Dare*'s feminist euphoria.

Hollywood's Year of the Woman

The announcement, in the winter of 1992, that the Academy of Motion Picture Arts and Sciences planned to dub their 65th annual awards ceremony "Oscar Celebrates Women and the Movies" nearly knocked me off my chair. It was bad enough that the rest of the media created the illusion that 1992 was "The Year of the Woman" primarily because (as far as I could tell) we had elected a president who admitted he valued his wife's abilities, and defeated a vice-president who couldn't win an argument with a sitcom heroine.

At least in the realm of electoral politics and television drama, we had taken some strides, in at least a few places. The movie industry, by shocking contrast, has rarely had a worse annual record for its treatment of women than in 1992. And that is really saying something for an industry that is—even compared to such less-than-egalitarian institutions as Congress and television—

a veritable dinosaur in its retrograde, masculinist policies and its near blindness to the rising tides of consciousness among women audiences. Talk about guys that "don't get it"; these guys have never heard about it.

In Hollywood today, women play only 34 percent of the roles and earn 33 percent less than male counterparts for comparable industry jobs, from the most illustrious to the most mundane. One reason, of course, is that most Hollywood movies these days target children, men, or morons. The week the nominations were announced, for example, the top 10 box office draws included only one film, *The Crying Game*, that wasn't a cartoon or an action/adventure.

At a time when women hold many important jobs, as writers, directors, producers, camera operators, and so on, even in television, it is still possible to name on a single hand the number of women allowed to direct Hollywood films. And of those few, the most prominent—Penny Marshall, Barbara Streisand, Jodie Foster—gained their clout through their long-standing bankability as stars, hardly a necessary apprenticeship route for men.

This has all been true for some time, of course. The Oscar nominations themselves made 1992 the most bizarre choice for a year to celebrate women. Of the five films nominated for Best Picture, the two with strong female roles, *The Crying Game* and *Howard's End*, were foreign. (It is worth noting, now that anyone who might care already knows the "secret," that in *The Crying Game*, the juiciest, most politically daring feminine role went to a man.)

The other nominated films, the ones with the huge budgets and promotional campaigns—*A Few Good Men, Scent of a Woman*, and *Unforgiven*—were old-fashioned, macho genre pieces produced by, for, and about the most traditional male audiences and heroines: a western, a military drama, and a silly star turn for an aging superstar. In fact, there were so many "men only" features last year, starring lots of men and boys supported mostly by marginalized females and animals (*Glengarry Glen Ross, A River Runs Through It, Hoffa, Malcom X, Chaplin*), that there weren't enough nomination slots for them all to fit into.

As for the women's roles, the comparison invited tears of frustration. Two of the five nominees for leading actress came from foreign films, *Indochine* and *Howard's End*. The others played in small films with such limited distribution and promotion—*Passion Fish, Love Field, Lorenzo's Oil*—as to make them negligible. Some industry apologists took to exclaiming, in this regard, that it was "just wonderful" that "at last" the Academy honored independent and art films. Don't bet on that interpretation. The truth is there were so few major roles for women in big budget, blockbuster, highly promoted films that year that the Academy was forced to dig into the dregs of the commercially viable to find any women at all to nominate.

The industry's real attitude toward independents and art films was loudly heralded in the Supporting Actress award. It went to the only nominee who played in a mainstream Hollywood feature—the young, inexperienced Marisa Tomei—over a slate of accomplished, remarkable actresses in far meatier, mostly independent or foreign roles: Vanessa Redgrave, Joan Plowright, Judy Davis, and Miranda Richardson. That the Academy passed over all these actresses in favor of a relatively unchallenging performance in a really trivial film was enough by itself to make the awards ceremony a travesty.

It got worse. The ceremony itself was an exercise in sheer tastelessness and gall. As the celebrities were ushered into the sumptuously appointed hall, the orchestra played a rousing rendition of "Thank Heaven for Little Girls." The people who put this thing together were so confused and desperate to find female role models, on screen or off, that they actually chose editing as the role in which women, historically, supposedly shone. They subjected us to an embarrassing montage of women slaving over editing machines, over several decades, cutting and splicing images of cowboys, gangsters, and Marines. If they had gone on to show the women who ironed the costumes, typed the scripts, and mopped the floors, it might actually have passed as a political statement about industry sexism.

And so it went. Only Barbara Streisand, who had a personal axe to grind for being passed over the year before in the directorial nominations, even dared suggest that the hype about honoring women was premature. Geena Davis, on the other hand, who delivered the opening thematic statement, didn't even balk while reading lines that described women's roles, in the most positive tones, as "to tease, to seduce, to flirt, to..."well, you get the picture.

Which brings me to the matter of the famous "Hollywood

Left" that the mainstream media have been so agitated about. According to *The New York Times* and its lesser satellites, we are in the grip of a wave of "Politically Correct" popular culture orchestrated by powerful Hollywood activists such as Geena Davis, a prominent member of the Hollywood Women's Political Committee and ardent crusader for the Clintons.

The claim that Hollywood movies reflect "Left" political biases is preposterous. The behavior of the stars themselves, these much-touted radicals, at this so-called feminist event raised questions about the seriousness of their activism. To be sure, many stars spend much money and energy on progressive causes, some of them feminist. Their cash and visibility are commendable and should not be underestimated. These people carry great weight with fans and their endorsement of left-of-center positions, such as reproductive and gay rights, no doubt helps shift public attitudes.

Nonetheless, as the Oscar debacle made clear, these "Leftists" and "feminists" have a far more marginal role in progressive politics than one might assume from all the hype they give out and receive; the little influence they do have may, in certain instances, do more harm than good. The momentous pronouncements from the stage, jewel-encrusted lapel pins, and after-hours parties to benefit animals and other oppressed creatures show that the Hollywood Left believes its own PR; it sees itself as noble and heroic. But when called upon to do something even marginally threatening to the industry that pays and glamorizes them so excessively, by calling attention to the treatment of women in Hollywood, these "Leftists" were neither noble nor heroic.

To be sure, they delivered impassioned political speeches. They urged power brokers in the hall, and the one-billion-plus-global TV audience members to consider the downtrodden of Haiti, Panama, Tibet, and other far-flung sufferers. But in doing their "political work," they never let on that the streets outside the hall were filled with feminist activists protesting.

Except for MTV (which deserves more credit than it gets), no media outlet even hinted that members of WAC (Women's Action Coalition), a national 4,400-member organization, were out in good numbers, all day, demonstrating against the idiocy I have just described. The protesters had called for support from the very women so prominent in the nominations and ceremonies, as well as from the many others who were caught and interviewed by the E! entertainment network (which ran continuous coverage for twenty-four hours before the awards, and substantial promotional coverage at least a week beforehand). They asked, at the very least, that stars wear a WAC lapel pin symbolizing support of women in the industry.

Well, I looked and looked, and listened and listened, but I did not hear a single word nor see a single pin on any of the scores of prominent "politically active" women seen and interviewed that night. In fact, Jodie Foster, Geena Davis, and Susan Sarandon bent over backwards *not* to answer questions about the issue. Sarandon and Foster thought it "nice" that women were honored and hoped for "better roles" for all. Davis did even better by admitting *she* had no complaints since "a lot of the good roles come my way."

Of course, every celebrity, Left or Right, wore a red ribbon for AIDS victims, and black celebrities added a lavender one to show they opposed urban violence. So important was it, I suppose, to be unequivocally on record as opposing death and disease, that any other issue, even one related to the theme of the evening, took a back seat. Not a one could find space for the little WAC pin.

Professional women of all kinds—even female corporate executives and public officials—network, organize, and share information, clout, and skills. Meanwhile, the Hollywood Left women, among the wealthiest and most culturally influential in the country, choose to maintain their outrageously token positions, at the expense of the thousands of actresses, script "girls," wardrobe workers, secretaries, and would-be directors, writers, and producers who serve them.

The truth is that about five women—Jodie Foster, Susan Sarandon, Geena Davis, Meryl Streep, and Glenn Close—are offered every good role (and they are few and far between) that comes along. To get better roles, more roles, more opportunity, more decision-making, and equity throughout the industry, they need to organize on behalf of the other women in the industry and against the existing order on screen and behind the scenes. And that, it seems, is too risky for them.

In the wake of this embarrassing attempt to "honor women in film," the media yet again made fun of "Political Correctness," activism, and progressive people generally. Sarandon, the most visible female politico, was singled out as a "pampered celebrity" indulging in fatuous "do-goodism" in the interest of her own "smug, self-satisfied" ego. Yet again, we heard the dangerous rightwing propaganda about politics as yuppie "lifestyle," about "bleeding heart liberals" running Hollywood.

But as angry as I was at the press for pushing such nonsense, I was even angrier at Sarandon and the others. They have so much visibility that what they define as "politics"—meat-eating and fur-wearing are very big these days—are widely accepted as crucial political issues. And so, the truth about movie industry sexism and about political activism itself—which involves commitment, risk, and personal sacrifice, not to mention collective, strategic planning to achieve some actual social change—was seriously distorted, to the delight, no doubt, of rightwing misogynists everywhere.

Centralizing Feminism: Thelma and Louise

I liked *Thelma and Louise*. I enjoyed sitting in the comfy new East Village cineplex one hot Manhattan evening and joining a theaterful of cinematically savvy strangers in a good laugh at the genre/gender revenge taken on a string of assorted male bozos by a couple of tough white chicks on the lam. So did my male companion.

I don't think it's a particularly serious movie. I certainly don't think it's a feminist movie, in any theoretically coherent sense of the term. I don't believe it was meant to be either, and therefore the ideological and aesthetic nitpicking of some progressive/feminist commentary seemed to me misplaced and inappropriate. While I'm willing to throw in my two cents about what's right and wrong about the movie, it's not the movie itself—as text—that most interests me. The most interesting thing about *Thelma and Louise* was the media hullabaloo that followed its release and the passionate public discourse it engendered rather than the merits of the film itself.

I accept the statements of writer Callie Khouri about her motives and intentions in writing the movie, and the widespread critical discussion of it as a gender-bending genre film—a female-driven outlaw movie in the tradition of *Butch Cassidy and the Sundance Kid* and *Bonnie and Clyde*. What works in this movie, what audiences respond to, is that it takes a popular, emphatically gendered (and, of course, sexist) format—the good/bad, lovable but naughty outlaw duo on the run from the forces of authority and repression—and makes it work with women in the lead.

The not so subtle socio-sexual ramifications of this device are developed with a light enough touch to make for good entertainment which leaves no deep or painful feminist bruises (at least for most viewers). Thus the surprisingly ebullient critical response and subsequent box office success. But, while it certainly avoids making any clear political statements, it attends to details of genre convention and contemporary gender issues seriously enough to make people committed to the sexual and cultural status quo very uneasy.

The off-hand presentation of stereotypical male bimbos, most of them young, hot babes in tight jeans, from the point of view of the female gaze as it concerns itself with more pressing business, is only one cute example of cinematic and gender savvy. More impressive is the gradual shift in landscape—maneuvered through details of "mise èn scene" and shifts in depth of focus from the traditionally female claustrophobic clutter of the early spaces the women inhabit, the kitchen and diner, to the vast expanse of the open deserts and canyons, which allow them to breathe and act naturally and freely (and thus fatally) later.

On the other hand, the plot gimmick behind the cross-country flight makes little sense on any level. A real political tract would have focused on the attempted rape issue. That Louise shoots after the danger of rape passes muddies the political waters hopelessly. From that moment on, the point is generically preordained. Mythic heroes like these two, who are after all real criminals, albeit sympathetic and attractive ones, always die, preferably with the melodramatic fanfare we've expected since Jimmy Cagney tumbled down those famous stairs to the urban gutter that spawned him. The strategy of allowing audiences to vicariously rebel against constricting norms and then accept their "just" and inevitable punishment is ultimately containing and conservative.

So what's the big deal? What got everyone from Liz Smith to *The National Review* so terrified about female "fascism" and unbridled violence against males?

The effect of this film must be understood in terms of the enormous impact feminist thinking about sex and gender issues has had on public discourse in the last two decades. Anyone alive in the 1950s and 1960s knows that a movie like *Thelma and Louise* could not have been conceptualized then. The gimmick upon which the plot revolves, date rape, had not yet been conceptualized. Before Second Wave feminism burst on the cultural scene, the idea of force in sexual relations was not talked about. Married women, until recently, had no right to say "No." And women who wore Thelma-type outfits, got drunk in sleazy truckstops, and flirted to the point of sexual foreplay, essentially gave up their right to a voice. You can't count the number of hit movies that reinforced that point, from the 1920s on.

Feminism problematized traditional thinking about this issue. Popular culture has traditionally reinforced the masculine assumption that female sexual desires are irrelevant, not credible, and easily ignored. Only 10 years ago the soap opera "General Hospital" made it into the media big-time with a storyline in which the hero first raped and then married his sweetheart. This union was celebrated—and unquestioned—everywhere. Today, on the contrary, soap operas, made-for-TV movies, and daytime talk shows nearly beat us over the heads with sympathetic, feminist-informed narratives of sexual and domestic violence. Anyone daring to go on "The Oprah Winfrey Show" and defend the creep who attacked Thelma and was shot down by Louise had better be prepared to be yelled down by audience, crew members, and the loud-mouthed hostess herself.

Thelma and Louise simply brought ideas that have long been taken for granted in less "respectable" media forms, in classrooms, and in private conversations to center stage. It (perhaps inadvertently) pitted the gut sentiments and beliefs of a growing number of people who don't normally get heard against the longstanding assumptions of classic Hollywood genres, which have always reinforced the gender inequalities upon which this society depends. It publicized how very fragile and contested many of these old assumptions have become, how little men can depend—in any area—on women's silent, smiling acquiescence to male desire. No wonder so many in the establishment press that serves the status quo attacked so ferociously.

I don't think this film represents a trend in moviemaking. Controversy doesn't sell in the meetings and packaging deals of Beverly Hills. Arnold Schwarzenegger needn't fear that Susan Sarandon will chase his ubiquitous face off magazine covers for long. Nor should Kevin Costner be concerned about losing his place as reigning king of Political Correctness at the Oscars. Guntoting waitresses and housewives pose no danger to sappy white male liberalism.

Still, the furor that surrounded this movie pleased me. Especially because it *wasn't* an explicitly feminist movie, produced by politicos as an "intervention." Rather, it simply takes for granted certain notions first expressed by feminists, which now, apparently, are part of an oppositional way of thinking shared by a majority of women and lots of men. That's a good thing.

Hollywood's Families

The American
Family and the
American Dream

Until recently, Hollywood has relied on a set of themes, conventions, and genres to dramatize the myth of the American Dream in which the poor, working-class immigrant rises, through great effort and ambition, to a position of success, respectability, and happiness. The story has had two separate versions, one for girls and one for boys. For girls, the quest was for a Cinderella-style bourgeois marriage to someone destined for wealth, success, and power. And for boys, the quest was to get into the world of capitalist opportunity and become that someone.

In movies, these two aspects of the American Dream were portrayed not as related and interdependent, but as two different levels of reality. From the 1930s to the late 1950s they were dealt with in separate genres and dramatized by extremely different views of human nature, social relationships, and family life. The domestic issues were acted out in two genres: the melodramatic "women's films" of conflict, sacrifice, and tragedy; and the cheerier musical and romantic boy-meets-girl/loses-girl/marries-girl comedies. The "men's films," on the other hand, dealt with heroism and adventure. They portrayed an aggressive, self-sufficient male who must make his mark in a dangerous world of plenty and plunder. Although there were several such genres, the most popular, even today, has been the "urban crime film."

The distinction between the "women's world" of security, warmth, and love, and the "men's world" of corruption, violence, and betrayal persisted through the 1950s. The social upheaval of the 1960s, however, and its aftermath of political cynicism and personal confusion, presented a challenge to filmmakers. Increasingly, the separation between "love" and "work" seemed artificial and hypocritical. The political truths that came out of Vietnam and Watergate, and the issues raised by the student, women's, and gay and lesbian movements, drew connections between economic and political policies, and the pain and injustice suffered by people, especially women and children, within the family. In the early 1970s Hollywood began to look at the American Dream to see what had happened to it. What it saw was a family in crisis, a family whose values had been exposed as hypocritical and whose positive, meaningful aspects could be viewed only through a haze of nostalgia.

In this social context, the 1972 appearance of Francis Ford Coppola's *The Godfather* was clearly a landmark in American film history. It is the ultimate film about the bourgeois family. More importantly, it bridges the gap between female romance films and male crime films, showing them, once and for all, to be connected and interdependent. The establishment of the nuclear, and extended, patriarchal family, in the process of the working-class rise from poverty to wealth and power, was seen to fit more properly into the world of Scarface and Little Caesar than Ozzie and Harriet.

From that time on, filmmakers have been no less at a loss than the rest of us to know what to do about the "family" and the positive emotional and spiritual values it was supposed to foster.

Lighthearted, "happily ever after" romances rang hollow. But the human needs that these films addressed were and are quite real.

Perhaps the most telling observation about Hollywood's attitudes toward the family is that its romantic, "happily ever after" movies stopped short at the altar, while its grimmer, more problematic treatments portrayed the ongoing marriage itself. Courtship was all for Hollywood; the family itself was left to be managed in the dullness of the real world.

There were many reasons for this. For one thing, marriages were nothing more substantial than sexual attraction. Young people didn't build their lives on family or class traditions, and had few taboos against divorce. It was thus necessary to endow the romantic chase itself with enormous drama and excitement. Courtship, in movies, became an intricate "pas de deux" of twists, turns, and near misses, ending unambiguously with a wedding finale. The "happily ever after" convention thus became a kind of secular replacement for the earlier, traditional church wedding between persons bound together spiritually, economically, and culturally. Like a Jane Austen novel of manners, the romantic comedies and musicals dramatized the process by which civilization reproduced itself.

Because of the emphasis on sexual attraction as the moving force toward marriage, and the need for reconciliation of so many conflicting personal factors, the idea of romantic love took on two striking characteristics in the movies. First, sex was always palpably in the air, creating a sense of erotic tension, which was never acted upon. And second, the process of courtship itself included a series of increasingly standardized conventions involving enormous difficulty, confusion, and distress. The songs of the day, many written for films, emphasized this painful aspect of romantic love. Cole Porter and others wrote of the "rocky road to love," the "fine romance with no kisses," the "fine mismating of a him and her," and the obligatory "You say tomahto, and I say tomayto/Let's call the whole thing off" episodes, before the two straightened things out and tied the knot. Such songs and witty verbal exchanges became recognized substitutes for the erotic interactions of real romantic love.

Media theorists have suggested that the taboo against sex acted in women's interests in the 1930s. This taboo required them to be more interesting and active heroines than the later, purely sexual heroines, in order to give the necessarily sexless chase excitement and drama. In the end, however, the marriages they entered represented the "democratic" smoothing out and reconciliation of the "best" of each partner's qualities. The poor man became wealthy, the aggressive woman domesticated, and the traditional sexist family was established. The formula was most simply embodied in films like *Holiday*, *It Happened One Night*, and *Philadelphia Story*, in which wealthy women marry penniless or unsuccessful, but up-and-coming lawyers, reporters, and so on. In other variations, the problems to be resolved included the woman's career, or a previous engagement to a socially acceptable, but romantically dull, other. Irene Dunne gave up her career as mayor to marry Charles Boyer in *Together Again*. Rosalind Russell played a woman executive domesticated by her own male secretary in *Take a Letter, Darling*. And Katharine Hepburn played the uppity, but ultimately softened career woman to Spencer Tracy's lower-class but ultimately triumphant character in several films in which the rejection of a stuffy, socially prominent fiancé also figured.

In many ways the musical comedies of the 1940s presented the most sophisticated reconciliation of the difficulties encountered in the consummation of the democratic "melting pot" marriage. In them, the "career woman" was presented as a performer, among the most "feminine" of careers. The working class was represented by show business (the business of the moguls themselves), a profession that was presented as "deserving" of integration into middle-class respectability because of the enjoyment it brought to life. Ginger Rogers and Fred Astaire, Dick Powell and Ruby Keeler, and Betty Grable and Dan Dailey were among the couples who sang and danced their way to marriage, and up, up, up the ladder of success.

The melodramatic "women's films" of the 1940s dealt more realistically with the fates of women who lived for love and were destined to become caretakers of hearth and home. These films portrayed the sacrifice, disappointment, and compromise that were women's true experiences in marriage. Husbands failed to climb the social ladder; children failed to live up to expectation; love presented itself outside the constraint of marriage, demanding sacrifice or damnation of the unlucky woman for whom love and duty were in constant conflict. The movie heroines inevitably paid for their sins and ended up suffering. The audience was thus sent home smug and satisfied with its duller but more stable lot.

The stars of these films—Bette Davis, Joan Crawford, Barbara Stanwyck—were larger than life, full of energy, passion, and drive. Believing in the promise of the American Dream, they wanted love, money, and position for themselves and their children. But since they were women, their efforts on their own behalf doomed them to tragedy. Ambition, drive, and competitiveness threatened family harmony and stability. In films like *Beyond the Forest* and *The Postman Always Rings Twice*, women trapped in stifling marriages are presented as evil villainesses whose desires for escape and self-fulfillment appear as crimes against nature. In *Stella Dallas* and *Mildred Pierce*, sacrifice for one's children on the part of the aggressive woman is rewarded with rejection and betrayal by the children and perhaps the loss of true love. The husbands in these films, needless to say, are either absent, short-lived, or of little consequence.

Mildred Pierce, made in 1945, is a classic female tragedy. Its dark *film noir* vision of bourgeois family life is filled with passion and damnation. Mildred, played by Joan Crawford, is a woman who takes things into her own hands when she realizes her passive husband will not. She rises from waitress to owner of a chain of restaurants, achieving wealth and position with difficulty, drive, and sweat. Crawford sends her two daughters to the finest schools and spares them all hardship. Still, one of her daughters hates and condemns her for her unsavory, unladylike rise to fortune. She becomes sexually involved with her mother's lover, kills him, and allows Mildred to take the blame.

Clearly this is the dark side of the American Dream of domesticity and social mobility. Ambition becomes consuming; love smothers and cripples; sexual desire is not the cement but the destructive force within families. The smooth transition from working-class poverty to middle-class affluence creates intense conflict and hatred between generations and sexes within the family. It would not be long before the castrating, neurotic female stereotype of the late 1950s would appear, ensuring once and for all that the failure of the Dream—should it ultimately prove a failure—would be blamed on the woman, the wife and mother, who like Eve refused to submit to patriarchal law and stay "in her place." And so, until *The Godfather*, it was.

Mean Streets

The contrast in style between the romantic comedies in which love led to eternal domestic bliss and the dark women's dramas in which love was hopelessly (often tragically) pitted against it, was extreme. But the contrast was no more extreme than the difference between those same "love and marriage" vehicles and the more popular dramas of urban crime and violence. Indeed, the eerie conventions of film noir—the contrasts of dark and light, the off-center or distorted framing, the use of double images created by mirrors and shadows—were often used in both urban films and tragic women's films. In both cases they served to symbolize the social and emotional realities of life under capitalism in ways that made the romances seem increasingly fabricated and false.

The gangster and crime films presented the same sense of passion, greed, incipient violence, and spiritual isolation felt in *Mildred Pierce*. But in these male-oriented films, family ties were virtually nonexistent. Far from suggesting that families such as Mildred Pierce's produced gangsters and criminals, they held on to the myth that family love and support was the only force operating to save these men.

The gangster films of the 1930s and 1940s invariably included a scene or two in which the gangster/hero returned home to his family in order to show the softer side of his character. The implication was that he had somehow gone bad in spite of his mother's efforts. James Cagney, in some of his best-known films, such as *Public Enemy*, made such a ritual visit. In *Dead End,* Humphrey Bogart's mother slapped his face when he visited her, to make clear the difference between what he learned at home and what he chose as a way of life in the city.

The city itself, especially after the Depression, came to symbolize a force far greater than family values, a force responsible for molding characters into hardened, unregenerate criminals. It became a subtle metaphor for capitalism itself, a way of life that offered opportunity and riches but increasingly implied pain, injustice, cruelty, corruption, and violence for those who tried to win its prizes.

In 1932, *Scarface*, subtitled *Shame of a Nation*, was the first movie to introduce the idea that poverty might be responsible for crime. Far from being a progressive idea, however, it was a mere rationalization that explained nothing. It was empirically obvious, by the 1930s and the Depression, that crime and poverty existed side by side. There was never any attempt to link this observation to capitalism or, more to the point, to look critically at capitalism's way of distributing income with an eye to changing it. Rather, the connection was treated as an explanation for something permanent and unchanging in human nature and the human condition. There would always be poverty; there would always be crime.

Because of its focus on the lust for money and power, the crime drama became the most fascinating movie form for Americans socialized to dream of great wealth and power. So attractive were the gangster heroes of the day that civic leaders became alarmed at their appeal. The obligatory violent death at the end was not enough to undo the glamorous impression of movie criminals. Eventually, Hollywood solved the problem by projecting the same qualities of brashness, individualism, and toughness onto the private detectives and policemen who were on the "right side of the law" so that heroes need not be the "bad guys." Now, good guys and bad guys were all alike. They were all loners, free of the influence of family and its softer emotions, and cynical, suspicious, and hostile to everyone. Personal relationships all but disappear in the urban crime film, leaving a residue of paranoia, suspicion, and hostility, and demanding a violent resolution to every conflict.

It is the urban crime film and the image of human nature and human relationships it produced that survives and rings true today, while the idea of family harmony and "happily ever after" romantic love has increasingly faded from the screen. It is not surprising then, that it was a gangster film that absorbed and redefined the "family movie," rather than vice versa. *The Godfather* made the first clear connection between the values of the family and those of the city. It was the first "men's film" to portray what was really going on in kitchens and parlors where the women "presided," albeit with little power or influence over children, husbands, or even their own lives.

The Family Transcendent

That the *Godfather* movies are primarily concerned with the myth of the family, rather than "crime" or gangsters, is obvious. As I have shown, the director had before him endless models of Hollywood crime and gangster films. He chose to do something entirely different: he tried to explore the emotional and ideological links between the bourgeois "family" and capitalist "business." Here are director Francis Ford Coppola's own words from an interview, shortly before the release of Part II:

> I feel that the...juxtaposition of the father's rise and the son's fall come together when the film is viewed in its entirety;...and that it makes an extremely moral statement regarding the self-destructive forces set loose when evil acts are performed for the alleged preservation of good (i.e., the family).

The centrality of the family theme is made clear from the start of Part I, which opens with an elaborate, 30-minute family wedding scene. From that point on, the film develops a set of contrasts in a world of dark and light, business and family, violence and love. Family scenes, which take place in bright sunny rooms and flower-filled gardens, are photographed in soft-edged, nostalgia-flavored pastel shades. Family ceremonies, the preparation and consumption of food, and the care and nurturing of children figure prominently. The business scenes alternate dramatically with the family ones, taking place in dark, nocturnal settings and often containing a degree of violence that contrasts dramatically with the style and tone of the home scenes.

The family scenes are a far cry from the wit or melodrama or romance of "women's" drama. The Corleone family is a patriarchal, man-centered one in which women and children play their traditional subordinate roles. They are the warmth and comfort to which men "return," a respite from the grimmer activities of the day. They serve as the justification for that grimness.

The structure of the film dramatizes the extreme contrasts between the men's and women's worlds and their ideological incompatibility. The Corleone women have no say in business or family decisions. They are seen and not heard. Indeed, they are ignorant of what is really going on in that other, foreign world. They are lied to, patronized, "protected," and abused. They have no autonomy.

The Corleone men love and enjoy their families. Vito, in Part I, is almost always shown thinking of his children. He delights in a child's card "made for Grandpa." He is shown buying fruit for the family on the day he is shot. His death takes place among the sun-bathed tomato vines, while he is playing affectionately with his grandson. He lives and dies for the concept of family. And by the time of his death he has built an entire empire, which is, in fact, a patriarchal extended family.

There is an enormous irony here, however, because of the con-tradiction between the sense of love, warmth, and community which the family represents, and the sinister world of violence and greed with which it is dialectically intertwined. Over and over, Coppola in-tercuts scenes of violence with scenes of family love and renewal. A christening takes place, to welcome new life to the family, at the very moment the child's godfather has arranged for a brutal killing.

In Part I, Coppola reveals the connections between violent crime and values. In Part II he goes further and shows that the very forces that have built the Corleone empire and its corresponding ex-tended family are responsible for its ultimate destruction. "Business" values—greed, individualism, deceit, ambition, self-interest—are the seeds of the Corleone family's demise, because they are ultimately in-compatible with the values of love, loyalty, and community.

By cutting back and forth in Part II between Vito's success and the rise of the Corleone family, and Michael's tragedy and the family's destruction, Coppola dramatizes this process. He portrays the crisis of the family as an inevitable result of the growth and logic of capitalism itself. The needs of business, in the end, change the nature of the family and turn members against each other. The family becomes increasingly respectable and assimilated, dealing with senators and corporate heads. And as Michael becomes the "normal American" he hoped to be, the family ties break down. Ethnicity is replaced by assimilation, as Michael moves the family from New Jersey to culturally sterile Nevada. Loyalty, trust, and mutual concern turn to suspicion and betrayal. Fredo, in his own self-interest, turns against his brother Michael. Connie, now wealthy and free to live as she chooses, becomes an irresponsible mother and tramp. Michael becomes smaller, harder, and more isolated with each frame. By the end of the film, in Coppola's own words, Michael is "very possibly the most powerful man in Amer-ica, but he is a corpse." From Coppola's point of view this is a trag-edy of heroic proportions. But to see Michael as a tragic hero is to sentimentalize the crisis of capitalism and the family.

The Godfather is a wholly and thoroughly bourgeois film. It is told from the point of view of the bourgeois male hero. And if it speaks of the decline of the American Dream of family love, community, and social mobility, it does so in a haze of nostalgia for those who wòn the battle only to lose the war. If the family doesn't work, then we're all lost; if Michael is a monster (as Coppola believes), then human nature must be monstrous. From a Marxist perspective this is obviously false. From a feminist perspective it is even insulting. Told from Kay's point of view, the story would look different. Told from the viewpoint of those whom the Corleones exploited and hurt through their "business policies," it would not be recognizable.

The issue of point of view—especially with regard to sex and class—is crucial to any discussion of Hollywood's treatment of the family crisis since the *Godfather* films. *The Godfather* made clear that the family was not made in heaven, but was the end result of an historic process whereby the immigrant working class rose to bourgeois wealth and assimilated to American culture. While it is true that the patriarchal family traditionally had been the only source of nurturance, connectedness, and meaningful personal values, the question remains—is it, in its conventional form, the only possible source? And, more important, is its positive aspect enough to justify the evils done in its name to those inside and outside its protective roof?

Liberalism: The Processing of the Dream

The most optimistic Hollywood approaches have stuck closest to the traditional definitions of family issues. *Kramer vs. Kramer, An Unmarried Woman,* and *Ordinary People* all start from the same point of view and use the same stylistic techniques to pursue the question of post-crisis family survival. They assume the family must go on as an institution for the reproduction and socialization of the family. What is missing from these films is a sense of purpose within the family. Gone is the struggle for money, power, and social advancement that added drama and intensity to the early romantic and melodramatic women's films. Gone is the sense of historical mission to provide opportunities for one's offspring. Marriage and divorce come cheap. Money comes easily, or rather, is always there.

Compare a statement by director Paul Mazursky about his idea for *An Unmarried Woman* with the opening of *Mildred Pierce,* for example. Mazursky says, "I wanted to do a movie about the middle-class women who have very happy lives, a lot of opportunities, for whom things are good—but who are...psychological slaves." In contrast is Mildred Pierce, narrating her own story in a flashback. In a police station, she waits, dressed in furs, to be arraigned for the murder of her lover, a crime her daughter has committed. "I was always in the kitchen. I felt as though I'd been born in the kitchen and always lived there except for the few hours it took to get married...I never knew any other life. Just cooking, washing, having children." And later, when her business is doing well, "Everything I touched turned to money. I needed it for Vida. She was growing up." The tragedy of Mildred Pierce, like the tragedy of the Corleones, grows out of the enormous, but debilitating, quest for money and social position. The drive to move from poverty to wealth "for the sake of the children," and the superhuman effort put forth to achieve this goal, triumph over emotional needs.

In *Kramer vs. Kramer, An Unmarried Woman, Ordinary People,* and other films about the family, there is no such energy or drive, no struggle to achieve great things, better oneself and one's family socially and materially. The characters in these films are already where they want to be, and have achieved without visible struggle. They are the sons and daughters of Mildred and Michael who have rejected (or forgotten) their parents' grubby struggle for power and money. They believe that they can preserve and improve—morally and humanly—the legacy of their parents, without acknowledging or dealing with the realities of that legacy. *An Unmarried Woman* and *Kramer vs. Kramer* accept part of the feminist critique of the patriarchal family structure and try to present alternatives to it. But they fail to confront the economic and social dynamics that made that structure appropriate to the status quo.

Kramer vs. Kramer and *An Unmarried Woman* both start with the fact that women are stifled within the family because of rigid and unfair sex roles. Joanna and Erica are neglected and betrayed wives whose marriages fail primarily because of their husbands' failures. Both films are determined to show that happiness and good parenting can go on without the classic family structure, and in spite of the breakdown of traditional sex roles and moral codes.

Two ideas are central to these films: that women living alone and male parenting are acceptable options. At the time these films were made, these ideas were very much on the minds of young, educated adults. Divorce, "consciousness-raising," and "two-career families" were part and parcel of the post-1960s upheaval of cultural and sexual values. Why then did these films fade so quickly from memory? Why did the characters become flatter and more wooden with time while those of Mildred Pierce and Michael Corleone reverberate with energy and passion still? The answers lie in their stylistic techniques and their limited social context. These films tried to impute meaning to a view of family that has no bearing on and no relationship to the social and economic world in which these families exist.

Kramer vs. Kramer and *An Unmarried Woman* are done in a style that does not represent social realism so much as scenic verisimilitude. They both have a look of smooth perfection about them. Every detail of clothing and furniture is beautiful, expensive, and brand new. Each restaurant, each art gallery, each Manhattan jogging route, is exactly right for people of this privileged class. Indeed, class in these films is clearly a matter of style and appearance rather than work or values.

Replacing emotional and economic struggle with changes in consumer habits is a perfect solution to the problem of meaning in these films. The audience vicariously enjoys the surface attractiveness and is manipulated into accepting this visual and material perfection as a substitute for the far more difficult spiritual issues raised by the characters and their situations. The audience is lulled into assuming that Erica in *An Unmarried Woman* never grieves for her broken marriage, and Ted in *Kramer vs. Kramer* never misses his wife or feels guilt or anger at her, or at his demanding, but deeply hurt son, because these people somehow "manage" their lives more smoothly, more tastefully and "correctly" than the rest of us. These larger-than-life movie figures judge all who fail to see "themselves" in these films because they managed less well, felt more empty, confused, or inadequate. But, in reality, the films are hollow, obscuring the emotional vacuum they dare not face with material things and transformations of lifestyle.

Ordinary People, made a few years later, takes the crisis of the family more seriously than the two films just discussed. It does not paint every family member as wholesome and decent. It shows the tension of family life and its devastating effects on those bound together in intimacy and dependence within it. But it creates a world of affluent suburban perfection very similar to the other films. Social and economic factors have as little to do with the Jarretts' problems as with the Kramers'. As in the older women's films, *Ordinary People* puts the blame on the woman. This time the mother's fault is not her tragic ambition to escape her female role. Rather, it is because she is entrusted with the role of "keeper of appearances" in the contemporary family that she errs. She allows the need to "keep up appearances" to take precedence over her emotional responsibilities to her husband and son. Far from wanting more money, power, or status, Beth, like Michael Corleone, needs to control and limit the actions of her family. She is a narrow, cold-blooded ghost of her earlier models. But, like them, her crime is taking her social role too seriously and neglecting her emotional role.

Guilt, possessiveness, jealousy, and anger are all dealt with openly here, but they are resolved most unrealistically: first, because the father effortlessly takes on the dual role of parent and breadwinner, replacing the flawed and exiled mother; and second, because the Jarretts are rich. Again the question of class is key. Jarrett is a well-to-do businessman or professional of some kind. But his hands are clean: no blood, no sweat. The signs of his moral and material success are a beautifully furnished home full of polished oak, Creuset ware, napkin rings, and shetland sweaters.

All three of these essentially uplifting and intelligent films take human relationships seriously. All are respectful of human life and human potential. The use of close-ups framing emotionally meaningful expressions and gestures, and the straightforward, conventional narrative structure and camera technique, serve to give solidity to these characters. They emphatically suggest that human nature is enough, that even without the help of political or spiritual structures, we are up to the job of rebuilding the American Dream for our children.

Their solutions, however, depend on a very narrow, class-bound view of life. We don't need to take the whole system down, they suggest, if we can just learn to be decent, caring, and rational to each other. These new, overhauled families are free of the extreme evils of patriarchal abuses of power. The men undergo emotional surgery to rid themselves of the taint of the political and economic life "out there." The women, too, are pale shadows of their unliberated forerunners. They have no social responsibilities now that they have won their "independence."

Much about American life and the true nature of the family crisis is left out of these films. Their emotional distress, even the very serious trauma suffered by Conrad Jarrett, smacks of class privilege. Guilt, anger, divorce, adultery, emotional "collapse," and psychiatric care reflect a very insular version of the "breakdown of the family." Other fundamental social problems integral to family life—domestic violence, child abuse and neglect, alcoholism, drug abuse, single parenthood on welfare or low wages, lack of day care, etc.—are all beyond the realm of experience of these sheltered characters. The requirements of their brand of "verisimilitude" preclude the portrayal of such unredeemable ugliness and hopelessly messy, emotional chaos.

The Underside of Affluence

Looking at the post-family crisis from a different stylistic perspective, one finds oneself in a more emotionally vivid, if unsettling, world. The films that have had the greatest impact on our collective consciousness and sense of national self-image are those that have accepted the challenge of investigating social and moral decay and have pursued the implications for domestic life. Hollywood directors with a recognizable body of work who address such issues can be counted on one hand—Altman, Scorsese, DePalma, and Coppola.

Of these, Scorsese and DePalma in particular have created an expressionist film style that captures the contemporary sense of paranoia, menace, anxiety, and social anomie. Both *Taxi Driver* and *Blow Out* present nightmare visions of a social world in decay: a world of restlessness, random violence, and hostility in which human beings do not communicate or cooperate, but edge around each other with animal-like cunning and caution. These qualities haunt us with their riveting aggressiveness. They are characteristic moods of our time. Like *The Godfather,* the films of Scorsese and

DePalma link their visions of urban violence to a corresponding domestic realm. They express a strong "anti-family" sentiment; they portray the breakdown and dissolution of family life as a result of, and as a factor in, the breakdown of society as a whole.

Raging Bull, for example, is—among several things—a film about family relations. It describes a family reduced to aimless violence, suspicion, and brutality. Moreover, it comments quite explicitly on this situation as an outcome of the death of the American Dream. *Raging Bull* mimics, and ironically compares itself to, the classic boxing films of the 1940s, where a poor immigrant boy works his way up to become champ, only to lose his world and the love of a good woman. The film begins and ends with the corpulent, has-been LaMotta doing readings from *On the Waterfront* and other dramatic classics. In between, his career follows a course ruled not by ambition or love, but by unharnessed violence, aggression, and sexual obsession.

It is as if Scorsese were saying that boxing and marriage—violence and sex—have no purpose beyond themselves anymore and so become their own excuse for being. The boxing scenes are so raw and explicit that they almost constitute a pacifist critique of boxing. And, as in *The Godfather,* they are intercut with domestic scenes, portraying a sexual obsession verging on violence. Thus, the rage and violence that motivate Jake in his "work life" are clearly shown to carry over into his marriage as well. His sexual jealousy and possessiveness toward his wife Vick is irrational and out of control. There is no point to their relationship beyond sexual attraction; they have no children, no future plans, no values of any kind in any sphere of activity. His psychotic concern that she be exclusively "his" sexual property dominates their entire domestic life. Thus, in both realms, we have a vision of human life lived at the edge of destruction for the sake of a single, all-consuming physical and emotional passion.

The style of the film is designed to exaggerate and emphasize this abstract sense of emotion cut off from reason or value. There is slow motion and speed-up during the fight scenes, to draw out the impact of the blows and heighten the buildup to a climax. Scorsese uses dramatic framing techniques to emphasize the emotional excess in the characters. At one point, Jake's unfocused rage collides with a neighbor and he threatens to kill the neighbor's dog and eat it. In another, Jake bangs his head wildly against the bars of a jail cell in helpless, uncomprehending frustration at finding himself a caged animal (his crime is statutory rape). "This is stupid!" he bellows. "I'm not an animal!"

Along with the expressionist scenes of rage and violence, there are also scenes of detailed realism, showing the working-class neighborhood in which LaMotta grew up and lived. But where the films of the 1930s and 1940s suggested that it was working-class poverty that "caused" crime and violence, *Raging Bull* emphasizes the hollowness of this "liberal" attempt at superimposing an artificial patina of "redeeming social value." Scorsese shows the detailed reality of working-class, ethnic life with no comment. The setting resembles that of the older 1940s' movies, but the content of the film is deliberately different. Where John Garfield's driving ambition in *Body and Soul* grew out of his working-class Jewish family background and was thus integrally related to the myth of the American Dream, LaMotta has no such past to explain his behavior. We see nothing of LaMotta's family or youth, nor is his passionate drive to fight a matter of social or financial ambition. LaMotta's violence emerges spontaneously, as does his related sexual obsession; no causal factors are suggested for either.

It is as though Scorsese were cynically luxuriating in the end of "social responsibility," the end of the American Dream of positive, progressive values and upward mobility. He can peel away the phony layers of civilized social thought and reveal the sheer brutality and destruction beneath. Now that no "future" exists to warrant personal growth, discipline, and responsibility, we see human nature left to its own devices, developing into lower and lower forms of bestiality. Far from the narrative structure of beginning, middle, and end in films like *Kramer vs. Kramer* and *Ordinary People*, *Raging Bull* is a static film, burrowing deeper into endless human corruption.

It may seem a far cry from *Raging Bull* to DePalma's *Dressed to Kill*, but they are, in fact, closely related. They both relentlessly portray the demise of middle-class morality, ambition, and the excessiveness of self-justifying violence. ("Sex and violence lend themselves uniquely to the cinematic form," said DePalma cryptically in an interview.)

Like *Raging Bull, Dressed to Kill* is a cinematic tour de force of emotional and visual power. Like *Raging Bull,* it takes as a model an older movie form—this time Hitchcock's thrillers. And like *Raging Bull, Dressed to Kill* takes the decadent urban setting as a given, and projects it onto the realm of domestic life.

Dressed to Kill is composed of two segments. The first deals with the world of wealthy housewife Kate Miller, a world remarkably similar in style and content to that of *An Unmarried Woman.* Like Erica, Kate lives in a gorgeous and fashionable high-rise apartment and has a less-than-adequate husband; a single, precocious teenage child with whom she shares a chummy rather than parental relationship; and a generally slick, expensive lifestyle. She is always elaborately and perfectly groomed and dressed. She sees a therapist, holds chic dinner parties, and is pleasant and cultivated.

But unlike Erica, Kate's quest for a "better man" and a freer, more liberated sex life leads, not to a fantasy-fulfilling artist-lover, but to sexual humiliation, terror, and grotesque murder by a sexually confused transvestite (in fact, her own therapist). DePalma precedes Kate's "punishment" for acting out her desire for freedom with a scene in which a small child stares accusingly at Kate as if in judgment for her just-completed adultery. This tensely staged scene serves as a moral judgment on the wife and mother, and a justification for her thus "deserved" slaughter. The message is explicit: if the middle-class wife and mother ventures outside the safe world of the home and enters the street world of violence, hatred, and insanity, she will get what she has been "asking for."

Like Scorsese, DePalma creates a social setting that is bizarre and expressionist in its impact. Trick camera angles, sophisticated cutting techniques, and the dramatic use of lighting make DePalma's New York City, like Scorsese's, a world of mean streets; glaring neon; ghostlike, menacing store-window mannequins; vapors rising eerily from manholes; and distorted shadows lurking around each corner. It is a world of human refuse in which no productive work goes on, no human emotions exist except rage, lust, horror, and fear of survival. Everyone is a potential fraud or enemy, and all symbols for American political institutions and values are ironic jokes.

The explicit politics of these filmmakers come through most

clearly in *Taxi Driver* and *Blow Out,* two remarkably similar films about isolated male heroes. In both, the plots revolve around the tragic and grotesque fates that befall the heroes, largely because of their moral conviction, concern for others, and commitment to justice and personal integrity. Jack Terry in *Blow Out* and Travis in *Taxi Driver* are drawn to symbols of the now-dead American value structure.

These two films are particularly interesting from a political perspective because in both cases the isolated heroes are the moral centers of the films. *Taxi Driver* and *Blow Out* are seen from Travis's and Jack's perspectives. These characters attempt to act upon the sense of horror and impotence most of us feel about the increasingly aimless violence and moral anarchy of urban life. Both heroes want things to be different. They dream of a better life. But they are weak, cut off from contact with the world in which they move, and helpless to act in any way that would make a difference. Both men work at jobs that allow them to roam aimlessly, and in isolation, through the dark city streets, observing and "recording" the nervous, explosive nocturnal life. And each, in the end, performs an act of orgasmic violence that changes nothing but is emotionally cathartic.

Although Travis and Jack are "workers," they can hardly be said to represent "the working class." Nor are they in any way related to the degraded creatures they move amongst. Marxists stress the damage done to working people by capitalist productive and social relations, while Scorsese and DePalma supposedly present the view of the "people" on the street. This view is, however, a projection of middle-class anxiety and fear at the breakdown of law and order. There is a tangible sense of dread in these films that the underclasses—not workers but idle, purposeless, malign "riff-raff"—are lying in wait for an unsuspecting target for their malice and resentment. The sense of middle-class anxiety that Travis and Jack both project is rooted in a paranoia at least partly born of guilt and shame. The American Dream has failed to deliver the goods and those who "got in under the line" are barricaded in their expensive high-rise cages.

These films, which are stylistic continuations of the gangster films and film noir, have replaced and reinterpreted the themes and images of the standard family films, the romantic and musical comedies. The images of social anomie, paranoia, and violence are the ones that dominate the screen today, while the sunnier, "happily-ever-after" images are rarely seen and more rarely remembered. These urban films reflect more clearly than their producers and directors would perhaps admit, the tragic contradictions that have always been at the heart of the American Dream.

Beyond the Dream: Toward a New Vision of Family

All these films—*The Godfather, Kramer vs. Kramer, Blow Out, Raging Bull*—express a sense of crisis. Some are nostalgic; some are full of rage or self-pity; some are escapist. But none goes beyond the limits of the middle-class worldview to challenge its hegemony and seek some other perspective from which to approach the problem. They all assume the universality of capitalist values and social structures. Each in its different way loudly and clearly announces the same hopeless message: if the social order and productive relations have disintegrated, then we have reached the end of civilized history. It is this lack of perspective that leads American filmmakers to such depths of cynicism and/or self-delusion. They cannot see that things could conceivably be different.

With the rise of the Right, Hollywood's efforts to maintain its favorite themes and conventions led to even more reactionary (and untenable) visions of family and society. What was healthiest about *Kramer vs. Kramer* and *An Unmarried Woman*—their acceptance of women's demands for a fuller, less constrained emotional and work life—became increasingly passé. In Alan Parker's highly acclaimed drama of family crisis, *Shoot the Moon,* the "Earth Mother," isolated in suburbia and surrounded by a brood of well-behaved children, returned.

The crisis of mass culture in the United States reflects a deeper crisis in the entire social order. It is not merely the family, but the possibility of meaningful relationships of any kind that is in question, from simple friendships to the larger emotional/social ties we call "community."

We on the Left and in the feminist movement have had to rethink our ideas about the family. The demise of the traditional family does not necessarily "liberate" women, nor does it come with a ready-made formula for a superior way of establishing meaningful bonds. The solution to Hollywood's problem will only come with the solution to our own. We are sorely in need of a new social vision, a vision of post-capitalist, post-bourgeois family relationships that bridges the gap between public and private values and experiences, and reintegrates the realms of work and love in a shared, humane communal life.

The current crisis cannot be patched up. It will not be wished away with fantasies of apocalyptic violence and destruction. It will only be changed by people who want something different and who know, at least vaguely, what that something might feel like, and what they will need to do to bring it about. The role of the media in communicating such visions (or their opposites) and portraying human nature as capable and desirous of living them (or not) is increasingly apparent. So far, the view from Hollywood isn't encouraging.

Youth Cult Films

Much as we might like to ignore it, the cult of youth has taken over the local movie screen. If you live outside the four or five urban cultural centers of the nation, it can be near impossible to find a serious adult film on a Saturday night. From the Steven Spielberg-style kid's-eye view of the joys and terrors of suburban childhood, and the *Animal House/Porky's*-type raunch marathons, to the Coppola-cum-John Hughes "sensitive" and "misunderstood" misfit sagas, to the Sean Penn-style *really* bad-boys-who-come-to-bad-ends tragedies, it's mostly white, male teenagers who dominate the screen.

There are complicated social and economic reasons behind this trend. The privatization of adult life, which started with home television, was a blow to theatrical filmmaking. By the mid-1980s, this techno-sociological phenomenon had reached only dreamed-of heights. We now own or are encouraged to lust after and save for a mind-boggling variety of home video entertainment equipment. The temptation to consume media privately, at one's convenience, is hard to resist, unless one has compelling reasons to go out.

Teenagers and young adults have such reasons. Dating and peer group socializing, done largely at shopping malls these days, under the marquees of multiplex, small-capacity movie theater chains, are the stuff of teenage life. Malls have become the community centers of the white middle classes who fled urban decay and its problems. From 10 in the morning until 9 at night, couples, older people, and young mothers stroll past the fake palms, waterfalls, and stone benches, under the enclosed, climate-controlled, security-sale auspices of the mass marketplace. They often seem semi-dazed absorbed in the spectacle of endless consumer goods, displayed in numbing repetition.

Off to the side, near the theater complex, are the eating plazas: huge areas filled with picnic-style tables and enclosed all around with dozens of pseudo-ethnic fast-food emporia, which now feed young America an average of four to five times a week. Pizza, hoagies, gyros, tacos and burritos, fried fish and hamburger sandwiches, iceberg lettuce salad bars, and sodas are served up in infinite abundance. This is where kids hang out when they tire of the escalators and shops.

This setting or its revolutionary precursors provides the social context within which youth films and youth itself must be understood today. It is an integrated and self-sufficient community in which kids meet, work, eat, and consume endless commodities—mostly records, clothing, and movies. It has little relation to family or home life. It replaces them.

Young people's displacement from the larger community of adult concerns and responsibilities is the dominant, if unstated, theme of youth films today. The very idea of being a "teenager"—neither helpless child nor self-sufficient adult, but in some kind of developmental limbo—perhaps began in the early 1950s. Before that there were films about "youth gone bad" and Dead End Kids, but they were largely sociological studies rooted in Left-liberal ideas about environment and reform. Films like *Scarface* and *Public Enemy* pointed a finger at government and social agencies and implicitly demanded programmatic solutions.

That was before McCarthy and Freud put an end to the dominance of Leftist social theories. James Dean, very close on the heels of the older, but equally tormented, Marlon Brando and

Montgomery Clift, largely shifted the cinematic discourse on troubled youth from the street to the home. Dean, the angry, white, middle-class kid who longed to belong but abhorred the family and society he was meant to belong to, spoke to kids everywhere whose lifestyles anticipated the coming crisis of American values and the accompanying "breakdown of the family."

Dean was, truly, a rebel without a cause. He really longed for an authoritative family, for a father to proudly model himself upon, and a world to proudly enter as an adult. He was caught up in an era in which the struggle to preserve the traditional nuclear family was fierce, but ultimately doomed. Mass culture and mass consumption were destined to replace the faltering fathers of TV sitcoms.

Dean's three films, compared to modern teen flicks, show a startlingly intense battle, inarticulately waged, against the direction of American life. The tension in his mannered performances—half self-centered neurotic baby, half heroic martyr in the battle against social and emotional hypocrisy—is real. Like the tormented, doomed women played by Bette Davis and Joan Crawford in 1950s melodramas, the Dean character exposed the contradictions and cruelties of the American Dream. Integration into the family and corporate world of 20th-century America necessitated giving up one's dream of a meaningful, authentic life as an individual and (implicitly) as a social and political being. For middle-class men, the payoff was a modicum of status and money. For women and kids, the costs of fitting the stereotypes of mother and son or daughter were exorbitant, the rewards merely shams.

The Dean films always conclude with a phony resolution. The utopian family formed by the three misunderstood delinquents in *Rebel Without a Cause*—Dean (the drunken vandal), Natalie Wood (the near-streetwalker), and Sal Mineo (the cat murderer)—cannot survive. Mineo is tragically sacrificed and the others reunite with fathers—one weak, one overdominant—who finally understand and care enough to be "real fathers" capable of authority and love. In *East of Eden*, Dan, son of a prostitute and cursed with her "immoral," un-Christian instincts, wins sweet Julie Harris and the love of his dying Christian father.

Only Jett Rink, in *Giant*, lives to old age and acts out an emotionally and politically more plausible ending to the rebel son's tale.

As the working-class kid who strikes oil on Rock Hudson's —the good liberal millionaire rancher's—"pure" land, he acts out the rage, contempt, and revenge upon liberal capitalism's smug hypocrisy that implicitly fires all these teen rebels. Like the other Dean heroes, he longs for acceptance into the perfect family, Hudson's and Elizabeth Taylor's. Like Cal in *East of Eden,* he tries to win the father's love and respect by making money, but those fortunate enough to have inherited wealth without dirtying their own hands hypocritically rebuff him as crass. He ends as he starts, a loser, an outsider, and a loner.

In merely three films, made before he reached adulthood really, Dean reached the stature of Brando, Monroe, and Elvis Presley as a 1950s symbol, and for good reason. Social and political themes filled his films, and were either not developed, or artificially sabotaged to allow for the false happy ending Hollywood required, as was so common in 1950s domestic melodrama.

In subsequent decades in which teen films rose to cinematic (or at least box office) dominance, the subversive undertones of these early models have been almost entirely eradicated. The current youth film bonanza reflects the fate of the family itself—physically intact in the walls of suburban ranch homes, yet culturally and emotionally fragmented and drugged out on media and chemicals. The image of James Dean lives on in the malls that he himself would have drunkenly trashed, but his spirit does not.

The 1960s and 1970s

In the 1960s, socially oriented youth films experienced a brief, understandable run of popularity. *Bonnie and Clyde, Easy Rider,* and *Alice's Restaurant*—drawn from a bunch of mushy exploitation films about hippies and protesters—posed social questions against which their heroes' antisocial acts were sympathetically judged and portrayed. Nonetheless, the level of dramatic and social integrity of these films generally could be gauged by the tragic, violent endings that befell their heroes. Only Benjamin in *The Graduate* lived happily ever after, with a good wife and job, destined to produce little Tom Cruises and Ally Sheedys.

In the 1970s, when the social prophesies of 1960s youth proved false (or at least premature), youth films began to showcase variations on easily cloned themes, which even today fill screens with regularity. Two films, George Lucas's *American Graffiti* (1977) and Terrence Malik's *Badlands* (1974), tell us most about the two main categories of youth films in the 1970s: the tragedy of working-class social rebellion and the comedy of middle-class accommodation. Both stem imaginatively from aspects of James Dean's characters.

Looking back, one recognizes a class struggle implicitly at the heart of *Rebel* and *Eden* and spelled out in *Giant*. In the first two, Dean is obviously, if symbolically, a renegade from middle-class respectability, with his black leather and boots, his prostitute mother on the wrong side of town, his inarticulate mumblings and public displays of emotional excess, and his "chickie" races with the town hoods. In *Giant*, of course, this class identity is explicit. The aspect of the Dean hero that represented working-class (or dissident) anger and disaffection from the Dream was embodied in a minor, largely unpopular subgroup of working-class bad boys who are not saved. The other aspect of the Dean hero, who wanted to belong more than he wanted to destroy middle-class life, is the aspect that has spawned the dominant image of youth in movies today.

American Graffiti was an enormous hit. Watching Lucas's mash note to American mediocrity, today, it is hard to understand why this film was taken so seriously. Only its form, rambling and episodic, showed originality. Its characters and their problems were as one-dimensional and lacking in social or emotional resonance as its bubble gum, teenybopper rock soundtrack. The "punch line" of the film, the fact that deejay Wolfman Jack is not black but white, tells it all. This is a movie made by and for a bunch of privileged white kids who rip off both black culture and white capitalism in the interests of "fun." There is no hint of the cultural or political contexts in which rock music or capitalism developed and now exist. The two heroes, played by Ron Howard and Richard Dreyfuss, make easy choices for safe, conventional futures. The Paul LeMat figure, the working-class kid rightly angry that his middle-class pals are ending the good times by doing what white middle-class kids do—getting married and going to college—is a jokey, supporting character. So are the Pharaoh gang members who mildly terrorize Dreyfuss on the night before he "goes East," and leaves this artificially integrated social world for one in which gangs and workers will become "them," or "the problem."

American Graffiti set the guidelines for almost all the big box office youth films that followed. Cruising high schools, hanging out in town centers (which soon became malls), and avoiding homes and parents as insignificant forces in teen life characterize virtually every teen "party" film and most serious teen growing-up dramas.

Whether it's *Valley Girl*, *Porky's*, or *Ferris Bueller's Day Off*, these films take place in a claustrophobic world inhabited and negotiated entirely by kids, and informed by their very shallow, very limited sense of emotional and social reality. Parents are either wholly absent—at work or on vacation—or hopelessly out of it, giving dated, barely tolerated advice about things they don't understand in any way. The anger of James Dean is as foreign to these kids as is the rebelliousness of the kids in *Blackboard Jungle* or *The Wild One*. The sexual tension in Dean's films that created electricity between the young people, and even between parents and kids (Natalie Wood's Oedipal thing with her father and Saul Mineo's almost openly homoerotic attachment to Dean in *Rebel*), is also dead.

Badlands, on the other hand, which was a box office flop destined for cult status, continued the saga of rebellion from family and society. It took it to its logical conclusion and so set the tone for the other recent (albeit rare) tragedies of working-class youth. Martin Sheen, doing a terrific James Dean, plays a version of the mass murderer, Charlie Starkweather. He takes Sissy Spacek away from her authoritarian father, more cruel and irrational than Raymond Massey was, by murdering him. They go off, much like Bonnie and Clyde, on a binge of wholly remorseless robbery, betrayal, and murder until Spacek leaves and Sheen is caught.

This film is poetic and powerful in its portrayal of a working class kid who wants to "be somebody" and achieves his goal. The end he achieves, media celebrity, and the means by which he achieves it, psychotic random violence, are wildly out of sync. The film lets the irony stand. It is "arty" and dreamlike compared to the overwhelmingly unimaginative "realism" of the party/high school films. It is as though James Dean's legacy of rebellion had drifted off into aesthetic, cinematic heaven, leaving his co-opted alter ego to plague us. *Badlands* is a film buff's film. Its hints of political and social truth about the unregenerate descendants of Dean are deliberately transformed and transported out of the realm of social discourse, to be savored in the rarefied atmosphere of "pure art." This was a dream, the film says, much as Warren Beatty, in *Reds*, told us that American communism and the inspiration for the Russian Revolution had been a dream.

The 1980s

James Foley, who claims Dean's films as his model, continued the teen outlaw/family conflict genre in *Reckless* and *At Close Range*. The first is too absurd to discuss. The second is an interesting film, however, and a classically grim and tragic one. Sean Penn plays the son of a true outlaw/robber. Searching for a bond with his absentee parent, Penn joins a gang and finally is forced to kill his father, as he discovers that the outlaw values James Dean tried unsuccessfully to locate and live by are actually far worse than straight society's. The tension between father and son—the love/hate, intimacy/betrayal knots that bind them—is real enough. The downbeat ending and grim feel of the work doomed it for the same box office oblivion that the idiocy of *Reckless* actually warranted.

The strand of the James Dean heritage that thrives today can best be seen in the two most successful teen comedies of the 1980s, *Fast Times at Ridgemont High* and *Risky Business*. Here, the gang from *American Graffiti* is reborn, a bit wiser but hardly sadder. Only the shallowness of these films surpasses their cynicism. The films reveal the scary implications of parents' and social authorities' absence as significant aspects of middle class kids' lives. These kids utterly disdain straight adults. They deceive and mock parents and school officials with a broad wink, to which audiences—even adult audiences—respond knowingly. No longer troubled by adult hypocrisy or emotional absence, they have learned to live without love or moral or social values. They mean to get theirs, like Daddy, and enjoy it to the hilt—unlike Daddy.

In *Risky Business*, Tom Cruise plays a straight suburban kid who ends up hosting a party that supplies hookers to all his friends, and eventually even to the Princeton recruiter who happens in, has a ball, and thanks Cruise by getting him into the Ivy League. Cruise makes a bundle, guarantees his Wall Street future, thoroughly snows the folks, and blithely continues his sexual and financial arrangements with the hooker/heroine. This new generation of kids takes what's most fun from the outlaw and subculture worlds (the rock soundtrack is on the money, this time). They also take the moral bankruptcy that characterizes advanced corporate capitalism—where their Daddies now work—while discarding the Puritan ethic that originally fueled it.

Ridgemont High is more typical than *Risky Business* in form. Its kids live in the high school and local mall and spend time hustling, surfing, and having, talking about, or fantasizing sex. The houses they inhabit consist, for the audience, of poster-covered, album-lined bedrooms in which the telephone is continuously in use. They venture into family space only when the folks are away, which is most of the time. Sex is easy and, when one girl actually has an abortion, it is handled with the zombie-like emotional aplomb typical of all of these kids. Much more traumatic, in terms of dramatic and narrative emphasis, is her anxiety over her oral sex skills, a matter that receives much attention, including instruction from an older friend who demands arduous practice of her protégé.

Both these films, among the very few that are sophisticated enough in their humor to warrant critical notice and adult audiences, are really in-jokes by and for the yuppie/preppy world. Parents and kids probably don't see such films together, but for each group they speak sugar-coated, but serious, truths. The legacy of corporate liberalism is total corporateness on the economic and social levels, and ultra-liberalism—what Marcuse called repressive tolerance—in matters personal.

The one filmmaker to have developed an actual body of work, such as it is, in this genre is John Hughes, who has become a one-man teen film generator of apparently endless resources. His films synthesize all the various thematic strands introduced in the 1950s and resolved in the 1980s. More or less, they are alike. Kids' culture is the only culture. Parents, to the extent that they figure at all, need parenting from their emotionally and socially more together offspring.

The Breakfast Club is classic in its emotional and narrative implausibility and flagrant youth stroking. It tells of five kids, each representing a teen stereotype, all locked up for detention together. They grapple with the big issues—the double standard, the "in" cliques and the outcasts, the insensitivity and stupidity of parents—

and end up the best of unlikely friends and lovers. The jock and the troubled, vaguely punk girl get together; the Valley Girl and the vaguely longhaired rebel get together.

Once more there is no larger world beyond the classroom/bedroom/mall orbit. Personal relations and social life are all-important. In *Some Kind of Wonderful*, the sensitive hero is actually supported against his blockhead father when he blows his entire college savings on a pair of diamond earrings for a special girl. It's worth it, in teen-world, because he ends up giving the gems not to the Class Princess but to his loyal, somewhat butch, working-class best (girl) friend who has silently loved him for years.

It would be unfair to dismiss the positive elements in the Hughes universe. It would be even worse, however, to take them at face value. Hughes's kids do have moral values. They have social consciences even. Invariably he pits working-class integrity and responsibility against rich kids' obnoxiousness, cruelty, and snobbery. Invariably the nice, poor kids are into something creative—quirky, personally designed and sewed clothes, music, art, and so on. Invariably they behave well, hold jobs, honor their hopeless parents, and disdain designer labels and trendiness of the more meticulous (as opposed to punk) varieties.

These kids always end up knowing and choosing the right path. They are self-respecting, strong, loyal, and certain to stand up to bullies, snobs, and other cruel people. They are, in fact, a very marketable, very processed blend of the best and worst of James Dean and Natalie Wood. Destructiveness or any other form of antisocial acting out, such as streetwalking or cat-killing, are impossible to imagine in these films. They take place in the declawed world of the other suburban mall-based movies. Where *Ridgemont High* and *Risky Business* flaunt their cynicism and hedonism, however, Hughes's films are sexually and economically antiseptic. They are much closer to Spielberg's world of childish wonder and decency than to *Animal House*.

How does Hughes manage to put decency, even class consciousness, into this fast-lane setting? It's easy. He has no sense of humor, for one thing. He seems to really take his kids and their problems to heart. He seems to have dreamed himself into a fantasy world not unlike the wasteland of Saturday-morning cartoons. His kids are more like Smurfs and Care Bears than human beings. His world is more like theirs, too. It is static and one-dimensional. No one will ever grow up here. No one will ever experience rage; aspire to greatness; be laid off, murdered, or abandoned. In fact, the waif in *Some Kind of Wonderful* has no family or visible means of support. Like the Smurfs, or the denizens of Winnie the Pooh's forest, these kids are *sui generis* members of a self-sufficient, mysterious universe that operates not by the laws of capital but by Good Magic of the kind practiced by Linda, the Good Witch of Oz.

It might seem that Hollywood has, with Hughes, come up with its ultimate "Happy ending/Nice and tidy," to use Brecht's phrases. But such a conclusion would—thankfully—be premature. The most riveting and provocative film about American youth so far produced is *River's Edge*, written by Neil Jimenez and directed by Tim Hunter. No film has better captured the social and political implications of the generational trends just charted. Based on an actual incident in which a 16-year-old boy strangled a female friend and bragged openly to his friends, who waited two days to "narc" to the cops about it, *River's Edge* explains, to those with the stomach for it, what became of the real James Dean, the real Sal Mineo, and the real Natalie Wood in a world unworthy of them. It is not a pretty picture but it is essential viewing, in spite of its problematic political conclusions.

The kids in this film are all very different, but each is terrifyingly believable. Like the classic Dean character, each is both hopeless and likable, each bears the burden—spelled out in the most intelligent script ever written for teenage actors—of America's political hypocrisies and contradictions. Even the killer, a cold-blooded, affectless boy-monster who acted, without hesitation nor remorse, on the first urge that ever promised any kind of power, is recognizable as an element of everyone's neighborhood hang-out gang.

Hunter and Jimenez manage to transcend the phony liberal/conservative limits of the media-generated debate on "what's wrong with these kids," but, once they've done it, they find themselves floating in ideological outer space. They take as given, and treat with compassion and respect, the total disaffection of the self-sufficient, asocial world of youth culture. "I don't give a damn about your goddamn laws," says one kid early on (in the spirit of James

Dean himself). The rest of the film spells out the moral abyss that opens from society's refusal to hear or take seriously this heartfelt statement.

These kids really mean it; they have no emotional nor social reasons not to mean it; and they live it out with utter truth to its "radical" principle. The trouble is that there is no political context in which such disaffection can make sense. What there is—and here the film is most brilliant—is a mass media-produced hodge-podge of ideological/emotional non sequiturs that seem to be about feeling, about value, but are only about images. The unkindest cut in the film is its amalgamation of 1960s' radicalism with the most vicious 1980s' reaction. The "good kids," Matt and Clarissa, can love and feel and ultimately act morally. But this is in spite of the confusing messages they've gotten from their liberal role models. Matt's mother is an ex-Flower Child who bought the message of the counterculture and, because its egalitarian utopianism was so vague and dreamy, is left with no way to be a parent, to provide discipline, values, structure, or meaning to her kids' lives. She cannot tell Matt not to smoke dope in the house, for example, because she knows no reason not to.

Easy Rider and the spirit of the 1960s figure as alluring but dangerous myths for these kids. Their teacher, an old 1960s radical, tells them—in a worst-case version of 1960s politics—that if they cared about their dead friend they'd be in the streets hunting down the killer with guns. That scenario is no more comforting than the speed-freak rightwing dramatizations of the most frightening character, Layne, who is determined to protect his murderous friend as a schizoid gesture of "all for one" loyalty. Mouthing bits from every militaristic scene the local mall and late-night TV has provided, from Chuck Norris to John Wayne, he orders his ragged troops on. Clarissa, knowing something is skewed in this concern for the killer, not the victim, can only judge by the weird fact that she cried for the "guy in *Brian's Song*" (the first blockbuster made-for-TV movie) but not for her lifelong friend. Media characters are truly more real and compelling to these kids than their adult models. They suggest courses of action that are more emotionally compelling, but not more morally or rationally satisfying.

River's Edge is most disturbing in its conclusion. When Matt and Clarissa renounce both rightwing and leftwing heroics to "do the right thing," they implicitly choose the path of law and order, although that's not how it seems. What else, after all, could they have done? Still, the cop that they now treat with excessive politeness and respect is the same fool that James Dean turned to when his parents' generation failed him in *Rebel*. He is a worse fool, really, as Matt—way ahead of Dean—knew from the first frame. Like Dean, Mineo, and Wood, these kids are way too good, too deep, too smart, to be helped by the law—whether in liberal or conservative incarnation. But Jimenez, child of the 1970s, disaffected and disappointed equally by 1960s' and 1980s' "bullshit," as he put it in an interview, has no other way out.

In failing to put his film in a broader political context, to see his way clear of the options Hollywood and the rest of the media so firmly put forth as the only political possibilities, he has linked himself, sadly, with the nihilist impotence of the kids he so understands and loves. Those of us with more hope for our own kids' futures can only hope that the next treatment of youth will take the truths of this film, its sense—in spite of everything—of youthful decency, intelligence, and strength, and find a less barren political context in which to arrange it.

Yuppie Horror Films

The white, professional classes—at least that outlandishly fortunate 1 or 2 percent who enjoy rising six- and seven-figure incomes while the rest of us slide down the slippery slope of diminishing means—are not sleeping well these days. Tormented by guilt and anxiety over their obscene good fortune in the face of so much social misery, they suffer terrifying nightmares of violent retribution. They dream of monsters invading their homes and brutalizing them; they dream of being cut down by random, and not-so-random, violence as they make their Guccied, limousined way through the streets and avenues where the dispossessed struggle to survive.

Three films in particular—*The Hand that Rocks the Cradle, Cape Fear,* and *Grand Canyon*—are intriguing in their use of horror conventions and themes. In each case, we have a well-off set of protagonists terrorized by external forces of chaos and destruction.

And in each case, by film's end, the "good guys" are reestablished in their "rightful" positions of comfort and authority, while the "evil" intruders are banished. Thus, life goes on and white, middle-class authority retains its position.

On the most obvious level, then, these films reassert (to a population getting less and less convinced of it) that the system and its class hierarchies are "natural," beneficent, and operationally effective. Still, in each case, there is a subtle, rather subversive subtext that explains their popularity with those who are doing a lot worse than the actual heroes we are supposed to be cheering. Listen closely and you'll hear an updated version of "Sympathy for the Devil" played softly in the background.

The horror film has always been one of the most socially revealing pop genres. Dreamlike by its very nature, it allows filmmakers to break the rules of realism and allow their most terrifying fantasies to come to life. And since we are social animals whose desires and terrors are to a great extent born of common experiences and values, horror films of every era tell a lot about what is bothering us as a culture.

Of course, those who control the production of culture will tend to create it in their own image. And so it's not surprising that today, when the gulf between the Haves and Have Nots is growing by outrageous leaps and bounds, Hollywood is producing horror films that reflect the specific fears of that small, infinitely pampered group of thirty- and fortysomething baby boomers who get to make movies and live in luxury for their efforts.

This class angle explains the hokey way each of these films manages to get the heroes—created in the filmmakers' images—off the hook and out of harm's way. It also explains why, in each case, the real roots of social anger and resentment against the fortunate among us are disguised and mystified. Violence and terror appear as manifestations of supernatural or random evil. They are never presented as socially understandable manifestations of rage at an unjust world. Of course not. These are self-interested myths whereby Hollywood justifies its own place in the world.

But in these films the dominant message is shakier than usual, the subversive subtext louder and clearer. While most of us will, on one level, identify and sympathize with the heroes and heroines, like good little Americans, there's always at least a bit of sympathy and admiration for the bad guys, too.

The Hand that Rocks the Cradle is the most straightforward. The media insisted on labeling it an "anti-feminist tract" in the tradition of *Fatal Attraction*; that is a red herring, since the media are obsessed with feminist-baiting and oblivious to class nuances. The only feminist aspect of the film is the McGuffin that sets the action in motion. The Good Girl, Claire, is molested by her gynecologist; she reports him; he commits suicide; his pregnant wife Peyton is left dishonored, impoverished, and childless. Peyton, understandably upset, is transformed into the Bad Girl—the psychotically monstrous Bad Girl—and, going to work as Claire's nanny, maniacally sets out to destroy her.

The nightmare aspect of this film is obvious. The principals are as wimpy and one-dimensional as cartoon figures (I'm thinking of the Care Bears). They live in a dream world of luxury, beauty, and wonderful servants (a mentally deficient black handyman defends them with his life!) who keep their lives and considerable possessions shirring and humming. Their house looks like a picture from a storybook. They trust everyone. And Claire—like a character in a classic anxiety dream—literally can't move or breathe when trouble arrives since she has debilitating asthma.

As in a dream, the horror stops before the monster actually catches them. We are told to wake up; it was just a bad dream; she's gone and life really is as picture-perfect as we remember it. But the spirit of Peyton—angry, dispossessed, almost attaining the American Dream only to be stripped of everything and made to work as a domestic, cleaning up after a bunch of ninnies—lives on. Played by Rebecca de Mornay, she represents all those people who are getting madder and madder by the minute, and her feelings, the only ones that are honestly represented and felt in the film, are valid.

The filmmakers know it, too. They have so little sympathy for their protagonists that they barely give them any life at all. But Peyton—racist, manipulative, greedy, pathological—now that's a woman who has lived through the 1980s and been transformed by them. Her ugliness is the ugliness of the Reagan-Bush era with its nasty way of pitting us all against each other—especially the poor, women, and minorities—as we scramble for the few crumbs left after the lucky top dogs finish their gargantuan meal of imported delicacies.

Cape Fear is a much classier version of the same story. Made by Martin Scorsese, it is way too wise to create any real good guys. The beautiful yuppies this time are obviously tainted and, at least in the case of the father hero, Nick Nolte, corrupt and ignoble. This is apparent at the outset.

The family itself comprises people who despise themselves and each other because, in fact, they are not even close to living up to the "Father Knows Best" model upon which the family in *The Hand that Rocks the Cradle* is absurdly based. In *Cape Fear,* the father sleeps around, the mother is neurotic and bitter, and the young daughter struggles on her own to grow up in a household in which both parents are hypocritical and self-absorbed.

Moreover, the nut case that terrorizes them and haunts their version of undeserved bliss actually has a valid grudge against them. The father, a lawyer, once defended him against rape charges but suppressed evidence because he knew he was guilty. As a result, he helped send his own client to jail.

As the nightmare avenger, Robert De Niro is the kind of monster that might actually haunt you after a night of debauchery. Like the Terminator, he just keeps coming. Fueled by fire-and-brimstone fundamentalism and righteous rage, he flirts with Nolte's wife, nearly seduces the daughter after turning her on to dope, and brutally rapes the hero's mistress. And that's just for starters.

The sexism in this film is grotesque. De Niro's Max Cady, like Hannibal Lecter in *The Silence of the Lambs,* is a vicious psychopath who takes delight in toying with and then brutalizing women. The rape scene is one of the ugliest bits of misogynist mayhem you've ever seen through half-covered eyes. And Scorsese unquestionably endows Cady with an unsettling amount of charm and charisma.

But even here, the class angle puts a somewhat different light on things. Cady exists as a larger-than-life nightmarish mirror image of Nolte himself. What Nolte does to every woman he touches—wife, daughter, mistress—is a classier, more clean-handed version of Cady's far more physically brutalizing woman-hating. And Cady knows it: that's his hold on Nolte. With every nasty leer, Cady seems to be saying, "You're no better than I am. You just have a smoother way of being a bastard. And the World lets you get away with it while it locks me up."

Think Clarence Thomas and Mike Tyson.

Again, of course, Cady gets killed and the family—finally—gets its "Leave It to Beaver" act together. But the message, just as in *The Hand that Rocks the Cradle*, is loud and clear. The 1980s ride is over. The vandals are at the gates, and they've got a grudge that's been building for a long, long time. It won't be long before they come for you.

Grand Canyon is not a horror film. But it is certainly somebody's nightmare of class and race guilt and violent retribution. Its way of handling those feelings is just more disingenuous and offensive. Rather than create a real monster filled with understandable anger, *Grand Canyon*—made by Lawrence Kasdan, who also made *The Big Chill*, about the decline and fall of 1960s idealism—tries to buy safe passage out of the bad dream by making the hero a Friend to the Black Man and pretending that social violence is random and impersonal.

In this well-made film, all sorts of people get shot at and nearly done in, rich and poor, black and white. It's a matter of "urban decay," "the breakdown of the social fabric," and so on. Nothing specific is to blame here. We're all in it together. Beverly Hills shoppers get shot at just as often and senselessly as the kids in Watts. (Yeah, right.)

The "hero" is the white, educated professional, a liberal for our times. Lost in a bad (black) neighborhood, he is saved from gang violence by his black, "good" counterpart—a poorer, less educated, but equally middle-class version of himself. Suddenly realizing that he is vulnerable to social violence after all, the white liberal forms a bond with the black guy and more or less buys his way to heaven by doing wonderful favors for this guy and his family, allowing them to escape from the ghetto and become just like the hero. His wife does the same thing: She finds and adopts an abandoned Latina baby. Life goes on.

Too sophisticated, too much an "artiste" to make a sappy horror film in which the nightmares of the rich and famous are dramatized in all their emotional "Sturm und Drang," Kasdan chooses instead to be rational about it. The trouble isn't some wild-eyed lunatics at the gates of Eden. That's too juvenile, Kasdan is saying. But it's not social injustice and class anger, either.

"No, no," says the good, enlightened liberal, "these are just crazy times. We must pull together and lend a hand."

Treating the social breakdown as though it were just another of those natural disasters so common in southern California, where everyone's house slides down the hill or something and people reveal "their best sides" by helping each other out, Kasdan obscures the politics of the times as fantastically as do the other films.

Well, fellas, it's not working. Out here in the real world, where real-life stories don't resolve themselves Hollywood style and troubles just keep growing, people are fed up with the excesses of the 1980s and the grief and injustice they spawned. But you know that, don't you? That's why these films, each one of them, expresses below the surface so much angst and dread.

If *Grand Canyon*, the most "serious" of these films, is the least convincing, it's because it's ironically the least honest and realistic about what's going on. There's a growing rage among all sorts of people these days—at Congress, at the President, at the media, at the corporations and banks that are costing people their jobs and homes and savings. The faces of Robert De Niro in *Cape Fear* and Rebecca de Mornay in *The Hand that Rocks the Cradle,* those are the faces we recognize and relate to. The real world may be getting scarier than fiction.

Family Troubles: Woody Allen and Rachel Kingsley

There's something mysterious about the current obsession with "family values." The focus, predictably, started on "unfit" mothers like Murphy Brown, who "glamorizes" single motherhood and thinks "fathers aren't important"; and like the impoverished Rachel Kingsley, whose son "divorced" her on grounds of neglect and abandonment to foster care; and mothers like Mia Farrow, whose mental health is in question because she took in too many neglected, abandoned children. Why has there been no discussion of the role of the men in these bizarre situations?

The family, admittedly, has broken down. But the view, so favored by prominent rightwing males, that this situation has been caused by feminism and must be cured by putting the reins of domesticity back in the hands of fathers, is a strange one. If, as implied, strong, solvent, good-hearted males are crying in their beers because women have banned them from domesticity, where the hell are they? Most women with children don't have guard dogs and "No Trespassing" signs on their doors, fending off armies of Ward Cleavers desperately trying to get in and take charge.

In fact, as Barbara Ehrenreich pointed out in *The Hearts of Men,* it was not women, but men who used the excuse of women's growing economic independence to run in cowardly, irresponsible droves from the responsibilities of family life, leaving whatever children there were behind. Many of those who did stay around did so on their own terms and for their own reasons, not a few of which were less than caring or responsible. Domestic violence, incest, and child abuse on the part of fathers and father figures, and the failure of fathers to support children, whether living with them or not, are national scandals.

When the media seek to discuss or analyze what's wrong with families, these material realities become invisible and irrelevant. The truth about men's role in this crisis is obscured behind fantasies of the old patriarchal homestead, with good old Dad keeping the kids in check and wayward Mom off the streets and in the kitchen. This is true both in fictional and nonfictional media representation. Whether it's a well-meaning movie like *Boyz 'n the Hood,* which creates a fantasized Black Super Dad and paints every mother as almost criminally selfish and negligent; or the sensational cases of Woody Allen's sexual behavior or 12-year-old Gregory Kingsley's maternal divorce trial in Florida; the media twist things around so that men are heroized, or at least let off the hook, while women, no matter how blameless or in what circumstances, are demonized.

I confess, I followed the Allen and Kingsley stories with mesmerized fascination. These cases were in many ways as telling and disturbing as the Thomas/Hill hearings and the William Kennedy Smith trial. The issues were even more vexing and confusing than sexual violence: What is a parent and what is a family? What are the roles and responsibilities of women, men, and government toward children in a post-industrial, postmodern, post-feminist world?

The coverage of the Kingsley case was a first heartbreaking, then heartwarming melodrama of the American Dream at work.

There was the mother, unkempt, mascara running, a litany of bad jobs, welfare, bad relationships, sexual improprieties, and substance abuse charges against her filling the airwaves. There were her two younger sons, one testifying in an ill-fitting suit, nervous and gawky, mistaking his left hand for his right.

Across the room was the Russ family, led by the father, George Russ, a prominent attorney representing himself in a perfect TV drama. He had noticed Gregory while inspecting a boys' orphanage and singled him out to take home as a foster child. There was his smiling blonde wife and her well-scrubbed brood of poised and handsome children. And there was Gregory himself, an almost frighteningly unemotional and articulate boy who testified about his neglect and abuse, his lack of feeling for his natural mother and brothers, and his desire to sever all ties to the Kingsleys, take the name "Sean," and be adopted into the Russ family. Throughout the trial, Gregory's voice never wavered from its firm, confident monotone. His face betrayed no trace of emotion. Had the context been different, he could have been auditioning for one of those creepy horror movie children from *The Bad Seed* or *Children of the Corn*, so inhumanly controlled and unfeeling did he appear.

In the framework of the media spectacle this trial became, Gregory's behavior and attitudes toward his demonized mother seemed just about as American as Norman Rockwell and cherry pie. Even the judge's obvious prejudice (he actually called the boy "Sean" throughout the trial) seemed noble and touching in this mediated context. The evidence against Rachel Kingsley was truly damning, and her *pro bono* attorneys were powerless to tip the balance even an inch toward their client. I was torn as I watched the proceedings. Children have the right to safety, ongoing care, and emotional stability. Rachel Kingsley certainly had failed (for whatever reasons) to consistently provide that. Let the kid decide, I thought, and to hell with Pat Buchanan and Dan Quayle.

Except that was not really the point. Ultimately, the suit had much less to do with the rights of children than the rights of wealthy, white men to select and appropriate whatever children they like. (And, by implication of course, to get rid of whichever ones they don't want, leaving them to the care of impoverished women and social service agencies.)

The fact is that few responsible, solvent white males, who, like Russ, actually do function as active, eager fathers, can take the pick of the genetic litter, and apparently do. Gregory, especially compared to his physically and emotionally troubled biological brother, was clearly a male prince among men—handsome, precocious, assured. Nor could one fault him for jumping at his good fortune in being "discovered" and transformed from underclass riffraff into the ranks of the privileged.

But if George Russ and Gregory Kingsley are anomalies, Rachel Kingsley certainly isn't. She had been abandoned by the abusive father of her children (who nobly "agreed" to the adoption since he was no longer interested in being a father), and had struggled to keep herself alive and fed ever since. What does the new progressive family law say about the rights of mothers to material sustenance and emotional stability? Why didn't someone, like the state, "adopt" Rachel Kingsley and her other two, far less promising or attractive children? One thing is certain: the political nuances of such gender/family issues are far too complex for the simple conventions of television.

The Woody Allen case was even more confounding. For a long time I resisted the idea that this sleazy scandal deserved any political analysis at all. But that's because in this case it has been not only the media, but most of the "Left"—broadly defined as everything from the Democratic Party on—that made it hard for many to see the real sex and gender issues involved in this case.

My first response to the messy affair was anger at the Republicans' efforts to politicize what seemed a tawdry personal incident. As Quayle aide Bill Kristol put it, "Woody Allen is a good Democrat." But as time went on, I began to feel more and more that the Republicans just might have a point. Allen's behavior toward both Mia Farrow and her daughter Soon-Yi Farrow Previn is really the flip side of the Kingsley/Russ case. If conservative males want women as desexualized servants, and children as investment property, liberal males—even in an age of lip service to feminism—often want something equally odious: the freedom to use both women and children for sexual pleasure without the burdens of patriarchal responsibility.

"The heart knows what it wants," says Woody in his cinematic whitewash of the matter, *Husbands and Wives*. But as every male child should be told early, "That doesn't mean the heart is supposed to get what it wants; or that it comes without strings." Like a lot of men, Woody Allen never had to grow up. Rich and famous, Allen was able to maintain a 12-year relationship with Mia Farrow without ever living with her and her children, or even spending a single night in her apartment! Indeed, Soon-Yi's startling rationalization for the wholesomeness of her affair with her mother's longtime lover was that Allen was "in no way a father figure" to her. In all the years Allen was involved with her mother, Mia, "he barely ever spoke to me or noticed me," says Soon-Yi. Well, there's a prince of a guy for you.

The moment this situation changed was apparently when Allen noticed Soon-Yi as an object of sexual desire. Never fear, though, the deal with Mia was already dead. "Almost immediately" after she gave birth to their one biological child, Allen explained to *Time* magazine, their "romantic relationship" ended. (You know what a sexual turnoff motherhood is to a lot of men.) While women bask in the glow of sexual liberation—which makes them more demanding but men less likely to put up with it—men have a whole lot of trouble staying with women as they mature, develop, and become more difficult to manage. It's a lot easier to simply replace women who become "high maintenance" with newer, easier-to-handle models.

(Anyone who thinks physical beauty is the issue here should consider again. Older men—even when they look like Woody Allen—have no trouble remaining sexually desirable to beautiful young girls. The reason women don't retain the same erotic lure—especially as they gain experience, poise, and social power—has to do with a lot more than mere physical changes.)

It is here that the thorny matter of incest, emotional and actual, comes in. Of all the young, malleable girls Woody could have hit on, he chose Mia's daughter, and according to *Newsweek* he never thought for a moment that what he did posed a moral problem. But as strange as that may seem, it is not—based on what we now know about incest—an unusual situation. Every day men choose to make sexual partners of their children and stepchildren and nieces and nephews because they are there; because they are relatively vulnerable and powerless; because these men haven't the foggiest idea of what a parent is, or what an adult man's responsibility is toward the children in his life. It doesn't help that so few public discussions of sexual matters in the media, even the so-called "progressive" media, have anything sensible to say about male responsibility toward their families.

The Right says that it is women who cause men to misbehave sexually, and it is women who—like the "bad" and "fallen" Rachel Kingsley—cause the family to "break down." Liberalism says, implicitly at least, that once women got "liberated," all bets were off, and we were all on our own, no matter what our ages or kinship entanglements.

Obviously, this doesn't apply to all liberal males. But just the fact that so many of us—male and female—had trouble deciding whether the Woody Allen affair was politically relevant at all, much less what the "correct" take on it was, speaks to a real vacuum in the development of the Left's position on "family values." Maybe Dan Quayle isn't so wrong about that at all.

When I finally saw *Husbands and Wives*, I was surprised at how little the film actually reflected the issues raised by Woody Allen's personal life. That's because Allen, like his mainstream and tabloid media counterparts, has a way of twisting and obscuring gender issues in his films. If Russ was playing a Ward Cleaver-like patriarch on Court TV, liberal Allen was playing his usual put-upon, victimized, morally anguished schlemiel to the art house crowd. Although no reviews mentioned this, *Husbands and Wives*, like TV in the Kingsley case, demonized the "bad" women and whitewashed the male hero. The young girl in the film is aggressive and experienced. She controls the sexual flirtation she engineers, while saintly Woody of course demurs. Adding insult to injury, the Mia character is portrayed as a passive-aggressive manipulator who subtly maneuvers to replace aging Woody with a young, attractive colleague.

In light of all this, *Murphy Brown's* life is looking better and better. Rich, mature, secure in her person and her work, she has a kid and the option to choose a bunch of media-made men, good friends, and responsible colleagues, to help her raise him. She doesn't have any sexual strings attached, so she is free to get on with her independent, socially meaningful life. I can see why Dan Quayle was so distraught about this. It could definitely give women some dangerous ideas.

Hollywood's Men

Romanticizing Male Violence

Everywhere you look, there are books, movies, discussions, and news reports about male violence. As traditional assumptions about gender, sex, and family relations go by the board, all sorts of heinous crimes—rape, incest, aggressive sexual harassment, even certain forms of murder that patriarchal mores and myths have excused or kept hidden—are now being exposed and named.

What was once dismissed as "Boys will be boys" and "She asked for it," "No one will believe you anyway," and "If you tell, you'll go down with me," is now a matter for the courts, the press, and Thelma and Louise.

Men are being called on the carpet, so to speak, and the media and social theorists have their work cut out for them trying to renegotiate the terms upon which we, as a society, must deal with these acts. From what I can tell, they're not doing too well. Faced with the deadly serious question, "Why are men such creeps?" they have—so far—come up with two dramatically contradictory and equally inadequate answers.

This realization came to me by chance. While perusing a stack of books from the "men's movement" (you know, howling in the woods, mourning the lost father, demonizing the all-too-present mother), I happened to catch the 1991 Academy Awards nominations on the news. I found this a very weird conjuncture. I was reading statements by and about men who had committed horrendous crimes against women and children. At that very moment on the TV screen, current cinematic versions of such criminals were singled out for artistic honor by the film industry.

Reconstitutive Tom-Tom Beating

The contrast was startling. On the TV screen, Robert De Niro (*Cape Fear*) and Anthony Hopkins (*Silence of the Lambs*) looked— in typical Hollywood style—at once charismatically sexy and incomprehensibly evil in their roles as psychopathic killers. The "men's movement" books described these types as "wounded inner children," "co-dependents" in "dysfunctional family systems," and as "abused little boys" whose mothers inflicted "inappropriate dependence" upon them.

So which is it, guys? The omnipotent Evil Demon, not really a part of the human condition or community and therefore easily expunged? Or the weak, helpless victim of social or psychic disease/addiction for which "treatment," "re-parenting," or perhaps some good old reconstitutive tom-tom beating are recommended?

From a woman's viewpoint, both images are outrageous. They elide the real issue—that men in sexist societies have social power and, therefore, must assume responsibility for their actions. Male crimes against women and children are, after all, profound breaches of social responsibility for which men must be held accountable—in *this* world and in *this* lifetime. But, in both current representations of the matter, all that is denied in favor of one or another fantasy removed from all social context.

Take Max Cady in *Cape Fear*. He is so clearly deranged and maniacal, so outside the realm of "normality" (his physical prowess is

so superhuman as to be cartoonish) that even his considerable cleverness and charm are pure camp. As in all classic horror films, the villain is painted in colors that distance him from the real men in the
audience, and the real women and children whom he terrifies. "It's
just a movie," says Hollywood, slyly, as though some of the men are
not going home to act out their own scenes of violence and terror.

The conventional horror-film version of male violence obscures
the place where Dr. Jekyll and Mr. Hyde intersect. There, one's own
father, husband, senator, or even postman does monstrous things for
reasons explainable as part and parcel of "normal" U.S. masculinity.

Blame "Mommy"

But nowadays, the "men's movement" contradicts the classic
image of male violence. Look at *Bugsy*, an anomaly among gangster movies if ever there was one. Bugsy Siegel, as Warren Beatty
plays him, is clearly not a monster. He's just a dreamer who's a bit
insensitive, a bit undisciplined in controlling his temper. He's not
too smart and far from grown-up. He gets outsmarted by his partners and his lover, Virginia Hill (Annette Bening), who is one of
those tough, domineering women who—in "men's movement"
language—tend to foster "inappropriate dependence" in boys (and
boyish men). He's more Peter Pan than Scarface.

What Bugsy does—shoot people in cold blood and walk
away, make discussion of murder a form of sexual foreplay—is as
evil and monstrous as the behavior of any movie maniac. But he—
unlike Cady—isn't held responsible because he's such a baby. He
can't keep track of his money. He gets sidetracked from business
by a boy's dream of a "Never-Never-Land" desert playground
(which became Las Vegas). Even his relationship with Hill is pure
Robert Bly. She is the Mommy who controls and betrays him.

This revisionist, or alternative, view of male violence is as
slippery as the old "monster" version and still obscures the truth of
male social power and its effects upon others. Now we get a crazy
fantasy in which somehow men have all the power, status, and
charisma and yet—paradoxically—they are not in control, not responsible, not really the ones who are doing what they are—visibly—doing. Even while they are beating up women, raping the

children they are charged with protecting, and so on, they are really as much victims as the, umm, victims.

Men's Movement Double Talk

Reversing power relations between the sexes achieves this sleight of hand. In talking about sexual violence, for example, "men's movement" guru Terry Kellogg says, "We missed the fact that...the victim and the offender are in the same line and that they have the same issues...a basic victimization." "Power is the illusion," adds comrade Terry. "See, women's co-dependency is their power through powerlessness...Men's co-dependency is their powerlessness through power." Yep, that's what the man said.

Now let's get this straight. The woman who is bleeding, crying, having lifelong nightmares of being raped by her father is really exercising power through weakness. And the perpetrator, who is walking out the door to have a beer, close a deal, buy some sex, is really a co-dependent victim. Right.

Personally, I prefer the old-fashioned monster movies to the new, more devious ones that let men off the hook for their vicious deeds. But in the end, they are two sides of the same coin.

We have no imaginative representations that fuse male acts of violence with the real circumstances in which they occur, that show male perpetrators of violence—and they are everywhere—in their psychological and institutional contexts.

In the real world, the results of this imaginative void are everywhere apparent. To use the most dramatic case, two-thirds of the population found it impossible to believe that Clarence Thomas—obviously no superhuman monster nor frightened "inner child"—"could really have done those things."

They just "couldn't picture it," and for a very good reason. We have no public "pictures" of men like Thomas—responsible, sober, mature husbands and fathers, pillars of the community—"doing those things." And so the social schizophrenia goes on, and men, literally, get away with murder by common consent of a society blinded by cultural hocus-pocus.

The Fantasy
Boys of Summer

Somewhere in mid-July in 1991, as I watched *Point Break*, the story of a young FBI agent who becomes a surfer in order to catch a gang of surfer/bank robbers—a movie I'd never dream of seeing between September and May—I realized that I had been watching some version of this same dumb movie at least once a week. In fact, I came to look forward to these boy-bonding fantasies of endless summer games. I was intrigued by their obvious, if puzzling, appeal.

It took me the rest of the summer to figure out why. These films—all of which project a "juvenilized" version of American manhood, in which the heroes and villains are stuck, Peter Pan-like, in a never-never land of boyhood fun and games—are Hollywood's answer to a real political crisis in the meaning of masculinity. They project a nostalgic, romanticized vision of a state of masculinity fixated in adolescence—in those days (which many in the audience now inhabit and others must recall wistfully) when boys could be boys and questions of "what I want to be when I grow up" could be indefinitely deferred.

That Hollywood puts forth such bloodless, dreamlike male fantasies these days is both depressing and encouraging. On one hand, it means that the official rhetoric about the American renaissance of pride and political health fools no one, not even the guys who run the Dream Machines. On the other hand, of course, it leaves American males pretty much paralyzed and impotent, deprived of a destiny or purpose in life.

And why not? Neither public nor private life looks all that meaningful or inviting these days. There isn't anything much a red-blooded male could honestly aspire to in mainstream America. We live in a world that has made old-fashioned heroism hard to believe in, whether we're talking business, politics, or daily life. The idea of Frank Capra-style populism and decency (don't even mention honesty or nobility) just doesn't wash these days. Nor do American males, young or old, see much in the way of integrity or contentment anywhere around them. We've got corporate crooks like Donald Trump and Michael Milken getting their comeuppance, and a lot of frazzled, burnt-out corporate slaves struggling along in mid-life crisis.

A column in the business section of *The New York Times* was telling. Steven Berglas, a therapist who treats successful corporate types, explained why he has so many powerful yet desperate clients. "Achieving career success has nothing to do with achieving psychological gratification," he says. "It may actually impede the process." The reason is obvious: Corporate values make it impossible to sustain relationships or engage in gratifying work.

That's always been true, of course. But now that the rewards of 1980s yuppie greed and dishonesty are gone, the whole rat race looks less inviting. If you can't dream, anymore, of mastering the art of the deal and stealing Trump Tower, Boardwalk, and Park Place away from the current king of the hill, why subject yourself to the strain, isolation, and long hours of a CEO, much less one of his underlings?

One might have thought, after the Gulf War, that military heroics would look good. But it seems not. The most interesting thing about the cultural scene these days is the total absence of rightwing military culture in the wake of the Great Victory. Where's John Wayne? The new version of "Green Berets?" Maybe they're coming, but I don't think so. I don't think a blood-and-guts version of the Gulf war, complete with real soldiers and geography, would work. The euphoria was too short-lived, too emotionally contrived to be put to the test of lifelike drama.

There weren't any realistic films about heroic white cops in urban America in 1991, and for the same reason. Where would they be? In Los Angeles? Not likely. The black community has cornered the imaginative market on that topic, clearly. Law and Order would be as hard to sell as Manifest Destiny these days. Better stick with futuristic cyborgs and forget Sergeant Friday for now.

So what's left for the white male here? Politics? Wall Street? As Paul Simon so eloquently put it, speaking for a generation of white males: "Who'll be my role model, now that my role model is gone?" To realistically answer that question would be a bummer. And so the producers of summer movies didn't even try.

The Boys of Summer they created fall into two categories, both informed by an essential component: they make no pretense of being realistic. They present fantasies of male journeys toward success and/or happiness which, when you look beneath the surface machinery of adult actors and recognizable landscapes, are straight from such childhood literary models as "The Hardy Boys" and "Terry and the Pirates." Bent on avoiding any and all triggers to audience anxiety (and reality these days makes that quite a challenge), they make no compelling reference to anything in our actual social, moral, or political landscape.

The first and least effective group involves doctors and lawyers, refugees from the greedy, callous 1980s who "see the light" and are transformed into simple, down-to-earth "good folk." The only one that comes even close to working is *The Doctor*, starring William Hurt as a hotshot, bloodless surgeon who gets cancer and learns to "live and love and care" from a terminally ill young saint of a woman. This is basically a disease-of-the-week vehicle (the director, Randy Haines, has done many TV movies) and it is only Hurt's brilliant acting that holds it together. The idea that Hurt could, in fact, become the person he's supposed to become and still operate successfully in a cutthroat, bloodsucking den of doctor-criminals ripping off, deceiving, and killing patients is absurd. But then, that's why even this "serious" drama takes place so far from any believable American setting. The beach houses resemble playhouses and the hospitals become kindergartens. The key scene of emotional rebirth takes place on a romantic desert at twilight.

Doc Hollywood does better as a "grown man as child" escape fantasy by choosing a sillier TV formula. The hero this time is also a hotshot surgeon, but his salvation comes from being stranded in Sitcom City, a tiny town full of bumpkins and one gorgeous law student. Well, that's one possible answer for young men today. If only we could all find a sitcom to grow old in.

The dopiest but most revealing of the Superman-to-Clark Kent transformation films about 1980s types adjusting to the grim 1990s is *Regarding Henry*—also about a hotshot who gets traumatized into reformation. Henry gets a bullet in the brain, reducing him to an imbecile. He remembers nothing of his villainous life as a philandering, gouging corporate lawyer and—infantilized as he is—he has become too pure and innocent to continue with his evil ways. What no critic seemed to notice in the reviews I read was that Henry had been reduced to a mental incompetent, a child-man with the brains and emotional development of a grade-school student. His daughter becomes his friend, his wife becomes his nurse, and he becomes Christopher Robin. And, since the family is loaded and Henry is still good in bed, they live happily ever after in an Upper East Side version of Pooh's Forest.

This movie provided me with the clue to what is really going on here. It's a fantasy of returning to childhood in middle age, a way out of trying to find meaning in traditional male success models. Get lobotomized, it suggests, and you'll regain your moral purity and be able to have fun again. You'll return to the last good times you remember, in grade school.

Regarding Henry was a flop, though, because it didn't go far enough. It assumed that personal life was the answer. But it's not, of course. Staying home and being looked after by Mommy, even when sex privileges are included, just doesn't cut it as a life-style option for a red-blooded male.

In the 1970s, when feminist thinking held sway in the media, it seemed that it might be the answer. Dustin Hoffman in *Kramer vs. Kramer*, John Voight in *Table for Five*, and Alan Alda in just about everything found fulfillment in the newly discovered joys of parenting and domestic responsibility. Even male coming-of-age films involved learning to resist the bad values of the snobby, sexist guys and developing meaningful relationships with decent, intelligent, mature young women. It was definitely growing up and settling down time, and the operating concept was shared domestic emotional responsibilities.

It's hard to imagine selling that package now, though. Two-career families are not fun and games. Unless you have the money and household help of a movie daddy, you end up with the same headaches working women have always had, and precious little time for romping freely in the twilight desert, or wherever. Domestic life, for all its gratifications, is no free ride to Sesame Street. The economy and social-service cuts make the fantasies of the happily-ever-after househusband as hard to sell as any other version of male fulfillment.

So what's a fella to do? The good wife in *City Slickers* knows. She generously sends her burnt-out businessman hubby off to a dude ranch where he can hang out with cows and cowboys doing all sorts of neat male stuff, just like the guys in "Bonanza." "Go and find your smile," she tells him. Like the unconditionally loving, understanding, undemanding mommy every boy longs for. And he does. Dude ranches actually became big business that summer as a result of this film. There are clearly a lot of guys out there who are frantically searching for their smiles.

Which brings us to *Point Break, Mobsters, Robin Hood, Bill and Ted's Bogus Journey*—the rest of that summer's films in the back-to-boyhood genre. What all these films have in common is a preposterous premise, setting, and general relationship to reality. They all star actors who, a few years ago, would have been relegated exclusively to teen films, mostly by John Hughes, where rites of initiation took place at the mall. Christian Slater and Keanu Reeves, whose perky faces were everywhere that summer, don't look more than 17. Their pals in *Mobsters, Point Break*, and the *Bill and Ted* movies are even younger looking. Even *Robin Hood* is basically a Saturday morning cartoon caper. Kevin Costner really should have skipped the whole thing. He comes off as way too long in the tooth to be rough-housing, pushing people in the water, and sitting around the campfire boasting about the number of inches he's got hidden behind his fly. And that, in one way or another, is what passes for honest work in all these movies.

In *Point Break*, Keanu Reeves, as an ex-football star now in the FBI, finds himself caught up and changing loyalties in the hippie-esque surfer culture. Well, who could blame him? Especially because the sport looks like such great fun. Toward the end, five surfer/crooks, including Reeves, skydive, grabbing hands in midair, and then seem almost to fly to the ground. This scene—the best of my summer fantasies—definitely looked like it was worth blowing your career for. Especially if your career is something creepy like the FBI. There's simply no contest. I mean I could see that, and I'm a girl.

When you compare these white-boy adventures with the movies that got most of the attention that summer—*Thelma and Louise, Jungle Fever, Boyz 'n the Hood, New Jack City, Straight Out of Brooklyn, V.I. Warshawski*, even *Terminator 2*—the spiritual and political crisis of the white, middle-class male becomes apparent. Women are portrayed as having moral authority and the missionary zeal to be the outlaws and avengers. Black inner-city males are now seen as the appropriate heroes of serious urban drama and classic Horatio Alger tales of rags to riches.

"So what can a poor boy do?" Mick Jagger asked in the rebellious 1960s. For him, of course, the answer was "to sing in a rock-n-roll band," and wait until "the time is ripe for palace revolution." It seemed reasonable at the time. Now, of course, we have Axl Rose drunkenly spewing out racial slurs and lunging viciously at his own audience, while Paul Simon, a voice from the past, searches mournfully for his lost "role model."

Rich White Men of Fiction

What do men want? This question began to preoccupy me recently when I realized how long it had been since I had read a novel written by a white, North American male. I and most of my women friends had spent most of our post-graduate lives practicing a kind of literary affirmative action, passing around and avidly discussing the many feminist-inspired novels that told about our lives, our dreams, our glories and tragedies.

But maybe I was missing something. Maybe the middle-class male hero had shaped up. Curiosity sent me to B. Dalton. Having dutifully made my way through the current sampling of acclaimed novels, I chose Bret Easton Ellis, Jay McInerney, and Robert Stone, representing three generations of hero/authors, typical of this genre's tones and themes.

Times have neither changed nor improved much for these men;

they are still lonely, isolated, and misunderstood, and taking it out on the women that haplessly cross their paths. They are still pursuing the Great White Whale and missing it at every turn. Little wonder, since they spend virtually all their waking time in drug- and alcohol-induced stupors.

Less than Zero, written by Bennington College senior Ellis, is the latest darling of the literati: "an updated *Catcher in the Rye*," "a West Coast *La Dolce Vita*." And indeed, talent is not what's missing from these books. A short summary will explain most of what is. A young man returns to L.A. on vacation from a Vermont school. His girlfriend hangs around throughout, nibbling at his jacket tails. Our hero mostly ignores her to hang out with his rich, handsome male pals, doing and dealing every kind of drug and sex imaginable. Young Galahad cannot talk to his parents. He's too strung out on angst, drugs, and the soul sickness of the rich and lazy. At summer's end he returns to school, more jaded and debilitated than ever.

Perhaps I should have begun with "Stop me if you've heard this one." The book begins, "People are afraid to merge on the freeways in Los Angeles. This is the first thing I hear when I return." It ends, "Images so violent and malicious that they seemed my only point of reference for a long time afterwards." And we have heard it before. What was fresh and socially meaningful in F. Scott Fitzgerald's 1920s, in J.D. Salinger's 1950s, was lazy, irresponsible, and depressing in the 1980s. And yet, the spirit of classic American authors rings through the pages of all these books—much to their posthumous embarrassment.

Jay McInerney is a Hemingway man. His first novel, *Bright Lights, Big City*, chronicled a rich magazine writer's substance-saturated travels through the nighttime Sodom that is New York. *Ransom* takes another such fellow, this one trying to save his soul and escape the burden of having been born to a TV producer (you wouldn't believe how the rich suffer today), by leaving the United States to spend his days in the Kyoto dojo of karate sensei, trying to achieve spiritual wholeness.

What's most galling is these authors' presumption that there's some benefit besides style in spending several hours inside the petty, self-pitying hearts and minds of these poor little rich boys.

There is, of course, much to be said for viewing the deepest heart of capitalist darkness through the eyes of an imaginative, insightful social observer. But these books are so thin and narrow in scope that they serve only to illuminate the most parasitical inhabitants of that darkness.

Children of Light, by Robert Stone, perhaps the most praised of all these books, is also the most whiningly self-indulgent. Its hero is a middle-aged Hollywood screenwriter who predictably stumbles from page to page in search of a line of coke followed by downers and a Chivas chaser. He is pursuing his particular salvation in the form of a screenplay he wrote long ago, now being produced and starring his schizophrenic long-ago lover.

The last straw for this "equal opportunity" reader is that the film in the novel is based on Kate Chopin's early feminist masterpiece, *The Awakening.* Stone sees the book's heroine, Edna, only as a pathetic 20th-century-style basket case. He ignores the entire body of the book leading up to her suicide—a symbolic act by a woman unable to live any longer in the restrictive female world of 19th-century bourgeois America. The only scene he describes is the final one, in which Edna walks naked into the sea. This act, out of context and robbed of Chopin's sensual, symbolic style, makes bathos of a courageous act of political significance.

Children of Light gives us another crazy, fey Fitzgerald heroine who nearly drags the hero down. Once more, we have the lures of Mammon from which few escape. The trouble is that such wealth and decadence are as foreign to most of us, as irrelevant to our lives, as Southfork Ranch. But while "Dallas" and "Dynasty" invite fantasies for tainted pleasure, these books sell us the song and dance that being rich is a tragic business.

They also sell a song and dance about the political and economic realities of sexual relations, personal responsibility, and meaningful activity. It is obvious that none of these men has been reading the books I read. While the heroines of Alice Walker, Toni Morrison, Grace Paley, and Bobbie Ann Mason toil away in their kitchens, raise children alone, get beaten, abused, and cut off welfare, all the while trying to figure out the meaning of their social and political environments and maybe change them, these guys are dreaming of anorexic beauties wading into the sea with their rubies on. Give me a break.

Outing Hollywood

Three major films of 1982—*Making Love, Personal Best,* and *Victor/Victoria*—featured gays and lesbians in central roles. The fascination with homosexuality and its implications in these films reflected the public's deep concern and confusion over the "sexual revolution" and the spread of "alternative lifestyles" in recent years. Sex roles, sexual identity and "preference," monogamy, the family, and last but never least, male supremacy itself, are up for grabs. How could Hollywood resist taking a stab or two at reassuring order?

Thanks to the quick and militant response of the lesbian and gay movements, we were spared the vulgar, exploitative gay-baiting of films like *Cruising.* But the two most "serious" of these films manage to hide several homophobic thorns beneath their rosy camouflage of "enlightenment."

Although both films are about homosexuality, they are at least as revealing of Hollywood's class and male bias as its homophobia. Just look at the difference between the treatment of gay males in *Making Love* and lesbians in *Personal Best.*

Making Love follows the antiseptic model of *Kramer vs. Kramer*: take a complex and disturbing social issue; feature the nicest, richest, prettiest couple in town; have them skate elegantly over the surface of the issue, creating a lovely, painless ending.

The men involved in the film are rugged and studiously firm of wrist. The hero is a doctor, married to a beautiful TV producer. He falls for a young male novelist who comes for a check-up, and his marriage ends. Everyone behaves admirably. No one is diminished; no one grows. Weary of criticism from the gay male community, the film is careful to avoid offense. In the end, however, its caution is itself a gross offense.

The film's hero suffers no trauma over coming out in middle age. He suffers no economic loss, no loss of prestige, friends, family. Ditto, his wife. You needn't suffer, says the film, if you're a gorgeous charmer who brings in a hundred thousand a year as a self-employed professional. No need for support groups, demonstrations, or the gay rights movement (without which of course, Hollywood would never have produced even this plastic package). Few gays, in or out of the closet, can take comfort from this "solution."

Personal Best, about women, not men, is a very different film. It received better reviews and seemed, on the surface, to be more realistic and less focused on sexuality as the primary quality of all gay men and lesbians. But this is because it's not really about lesbianism. It's a male fantasy in which women make love to each other, among other things.

The plot concerns two female track and field stars who become lovers, quarrel when they start to compete with each other, and part. The main character, Chris (Mariel Hemingway), is the one who "grows up," in writer/producer/director Robert Towne's words. This means she grows into a superior athlete and out of "infantile" same-sex "infatuation."

The film is full of subtle and not so subtle sexist stereotypes. Tory, the one who remains a lesbian, is the heavy. In typical sexist-relationship style, she begins by helping the younger, more feminine, more vulnerable woman improve. When her partner begins to surpass her, she becomes possessive, and is perhaps even responsible for Chris's injury from a badly timed jump.

There is a woman-hating coach who dominates and bullies

the women. He calls men who fail "Pussy" and successfully destroys the women's relationship when it interferes with their performances. The ultimate heterosexual finale, when Chris finds a male lover, is preordained. Cinderella is saved from the wicked Dyke by Prince Charming.

There is no social context whatever for the lesbian aspect of the film. No guilt, no anxiety, no sense that it's really not okay for women to kiss in the middle of a mixed party while all the guests look on emotionlessly. Come on, guys. Tell it to Billie Jean King.

Since the film is patently not about lesbianism in any serious or believable sense, why bother to put it in at all? The answer can be found where it belongs, in a *Playboy* interview with Towne. "The film was in part a dream I wanted to have," he says. "I love the way women move...The movie has everything I was ever demented about in women."

This is standard for the porn circuit. Pictures of nude and semi-nude women doing all sorts of things in all sorts of poses, and most especially making love to each other, abound in pornography. And this is classy, soft-core pornography. It has almost no plot because its real subject is visual. It abounds in shots of women jumping, running, falling, exercising, and a good 75 percent of them seem to focus on the crotch.

The only question left, then, is why the great reviews? First, the film finesses the sexual issue by seeming to be about "sports." More importantly, though, it plays on the widespread public ignorance and trivialization of lesbianism. Where *Making Love* bent over backwards not to offend the gay male community, *Personal Best* ignores the lesbian community. If anything, it's an attempt to reclaim lesbianism for male voyeurs. *Making Love* is about grown-up, autonomous men; *Personal Best* is about schoolgirls dominated and manipulated by a male keeper. That, in a nutshell, says it all.

Having had it with Hollywood's efforts to be serious about sexuality, one turned to Blake Edwards's wholly farcical *Victor/Victoria* with relief. The plot is absurd. It concerns a starving chanteuse in 1930s Paris who, with the help of an also unemployed gay male entertainer, impersonates a female impersonator and becomes an international sensation. There is little attempt to suggest the actual social and political overtones of pre-war Europe. There is less attempt to relate the subject to contemporary social or political realities. Nonetheless, the film manages, in its limited, laid back way, to ridicule traditional sexual stereotypes and present a wholly liberatory, good-natured perspective on the sticky question of sexual identity and preference.

The two leads are social misfits—failures at being a "real" man and a "real" woman. They are terrific at being human beings and friends, however. Both are strong, dignified, in touch with and unthreatened by their personal mixes of "masculine" and "feminine" traits.

When Julie Andrews becomes a "man" she comes into her own. Unhindered by the constraints of femininity she can't pull off, she is able to do the work she loves, and be "my own man" socially. There is no real effort to make Andrews seem "male." (She continues to wear lipstick, for example.) Rather, she is an abstract symbol of undifferentiated sexuality.

Remaining on the level of high farce, the film becomes even more outrageous when a thoroughly masculine gangster, played with deadpan aplomb by James Garner, falls in love with her/him. He suspects his love object is female but can't be sure. Finally, desire conquers inhibition and he plunges ahead, saying, "I don't care what you are." From that point on, the film becomes a zany mishmash of feminist and gay fantasy. Garner must appear publicly as half of a gay male couple in order to live with his lover, because her "career" demands it. His example gives his bodyguard (Alex Karras) the nerve to come out, and bed down with Preston. Everyone accepts everyone else with ease, and the principals set an uncommon example of decent behavior, given that the film refuses to be "serious" or "realistic." So far from any imaginable social reality is it, that it cannot even come up with a conclusion for itself, and simply fails to end. We have no idea what happens to this bunch of unlikely but likable lunatics. Having seen reactionary and demeaning "conclusions" drawn by the big-money boys in Hollywood, however, Edwards was probably right to leave it at that. He could have done a lot worse than to let U.S. audiences decide for themselves what to make of it all.

My Own Private Idaho
and Longtime Companion

After seeing *My Own Private Idaho*, Gus Van Sant's film about teenage male hustlers, I turned on the television and, quite by accident, found myself watching another film about gay male culture. The one I missed when it came out—*Longtime Companion*, directed by Norman Rene—is about the effects of the AIDS crisis on a group of friends.

The juxtaposition of these radically different approaches to the representation of sexuality and sex-related issues was startling. *Longtime Companion* practically comes within a plastic wrapper labeled "Kosher" and "Sanitized for Your Convenience." It deals with a group of squeaky-clean, white professional young men. It's a toss-up whether their good looks and niceness outweigh their professionalism and wealth or vice versa. Each works in the entertainment industry, dresses out of *GQ* and lives in the splendor of an *Architectural Digest* photo spread. They are all in monogamous relationships. The token (straight) woman is also yuppified, coupled, and chic.

The narrative describes the effects of the AIDS crisis on what can only be described as a "post-gay liberation" community. These people simply have no problems except the virus. Economic, emotional, social, and creative life is "What-me-worry?" terrific. Not only are they free of family tensions, they are free of families. As the plague hits one after another, there is not one friend or relation from outside their blessed circle at a single funeral service! Incredibly, they are a contained, separatist utopia with so much clout in the straight world that they are able to do even business exclusively with their own.

I could only assume that Rene and screenwriter Craig Lucas thought this assimilationist approach would endear gays to straight audiences. Instead, if my own response is any gauge, it is more likely to provoke resentment and hostility. How did these guys get it so good in a world in which most of us—gay and straight—are on the ropes one way or another, every day of our lives? Everyone dies, after all, but few of us will die surrounded by so much love, nurturing, and physical comfort. If that sounds crass, it is the film's dishonesty about both death and the gay experience that should be blamed.

Of course, this kind of class setting is standard for Hollywood, and *Longtime Companion* is pure Hollywood. *Making Love* was the prototype. Since then, we've seen a stream of movies, mostly made for television, in which beautiful professional young WASP men come out, live, and die in emotional and material comfort. *Consenting Adults* and *An Early Frost*, which also dealt with AIDS, are the best of these and are both much better than *Longtime Companion*.

That's because the TV movies have a specific goal: they are aimed at families, television's eternally assumed audience, in an attempt to help mom and dad, bro and sis, accept the gay sexuality of loved ones. Within the context of TV hegemony, this isn't a bad thing to do. The narrative strategy is unabashedly pro-family of course: it seeks to incorporate previously unacceptable elements— gay men (not lesbians, I should note)—into family life. But that's better than the traditional patriarchal response: expulsion from the nuclear family and the circle of love and acceptance.

Longtime Companion has no such clear purpose beyond the vague, generally unquestioned one of making gays seem "just like everyone else" except for their sexuality, which, in this kind of movie, is desexualized anyway. (They don't really do it; if they did, their hair would get mussed.)

There are two glaring problems with this well-intentioned approach. First is the question of "difference." To portray gay men as just like everyone else is nonsensical because there is no "everyone else." By default, the prototype becomes the standard Hollywood white, male professional. More tricky is the question of gay sexuality itself. Since there is no social or familial context within which to understand the characters' "preferences" or "lifestyles," the film—actually the entire liberal genre—takes an implicitly essentialist stance toward sexual behavior. One simply *is* gay, and that's what produces the behavior around which identity forms. There is no other way to understand why these guys aren't just like everyone else (and why they get AIDS) except for biology.

My Own Private Idaho, by reaching beyond propaganda, presents a far richer picture of sexual behavior and its significance and in the process manages—possibly by accident—to create one of the most moving and sympathetic pictures I've seen of sexual minorities trying to survive in a straight world. I say "by accident" because the film isn't really about gay men at all. It's about young men who work as prostitutes. The issue of identity is dismissed, and their behavior and how they got "that way" are seen as socially constructed rather than the expression of some biological "essence."

Two issues are at the heart of the film: dysfunctional families and class difference, and Van Sant's brilliance lies in his casual way of portraying sexual experience in terms of these two contexts. Mike (River Phoenix) is a working-class kid who's been seriously abused and abandoned; Scott (Keanu Reeves) is the rebellious son of the corrupt mayor of Portland, Oregon. The class and family circumstances that drive the two to hustling determine their very different trajectories.

Mike, who has known no other form of community or friendship, loves and desires Scott deeply. Scott, who has options and a ruling-class world to return to when he chooses, denies any gay identity and will only have gay sex for money.

The presentation of sexuality and "love" are particularly striking. Van Sant manages to "de-naturalize" heterosexuality in two ways. First, he naturalizes gay sex by presenting it as socially understandable behavior: it's just what people do sometimes.

As for love, it is as socially constructed as sex. Scott, when the time comes to return to his class position of wealth and power, begins a relationship with a suitable young woman. "I fell in love," he tells Mike offhandedly, as an excuse for abandoning his "best friend." This "love" he "fell" into is as socially constructed as the sex. It, too, is just what people do sometimes, for whatever reasons and with whatever feelings. The woman, for her part, says the same line to Mike, only for her it is a tearful, frightening admission. Rightly so. This guy is bad news as a love object in any setting.

It is interesting to consider that *My Own Private Idaho* was not meant for or marketed to a mass audience, while *Longtime Companion* was. And yet, River Phoenix's Mike is one of the most lovable and tragic figures in recent film memory. His appeal comes from how his life—all of it—reflects the pain, anguish, cruelty, and injustice that mark life today for most of us in one way or another.

Broadly speaking, it is simply a fact that families do not function and class marks the difference between choices and traps—sexual, social, and every other kind. In presenting this to audiences, Van Sant inadvertently paints a picture of "deviance" that is, in fact, perfectly normal in this weird world.

As a straight woman, my response to these films was heightened by personal circumstances. The day before I saw them, I attended the funeral of someone who had once been a member of my "family," someone whose life had been so intimately bound to mine in so many social, legal, emotional, and political ways that I didn't know what I felt from one moment to the next.

The mourners formed odd groupings of blended, layered family formations and political and social alliances that had crossed and shifted over time. Memories and emotions circulated among them tensely, painfully, lovingly. To mourn someone of this time and place, someone in any way implicated in the tenor of the era, is to feel all the conflicts, grievances, losses, betrayals, and regrets that love and desire bring with them.

In the wake of this experience I found *My Own Private Idaho* enormously comforting and moving. *Longtime Companion,* a disingenuous, bad-faith film if there ever was one, simply enraged me.

Tennessee Williams

Tennessee Williams—viewed by many as the greatest U.S. playwright—died on Feb. 25, 1983, at age 71, apparently by choking on a bottle cap. It was fitting, in a way, that the tormented life of this gifted, gentle, gay man came to an end in a lonely New York City hotel room.

Williams focused his many acknowledged masterpieces on human suffering and anguish through the experiences of society's victims and "misfits." His symbolic tales are full of visual fantasy and verbal poetry, but beneath the distorted lights and absurd affectations of his human "moths" and "unicorns," there is always the tortured soul of someone "different." His characters are twisted and crippled by the sexual tensions and rigidities of "normal" family life, and the demands of an equally rigid and cruel social system.

In "The Glass Menagerie," Laura Wingfield is unable to find a husband or even face the world to seek work because of a physical handicap. She is tortured by her equally pathetic mother's refusals to face their common truth: that they are sexual and economic failures. And in "A Streetcar Named Desire," Blanche DuBois wages a feeble struggle to live with dignity in a ruthless world that cares nothing for the gentle traits it has duped her into cultivating. Like DuBois, who ultimately can only survive through her sexuality, Williams's women are born victims who nonetheless manage to struggle along with a certain pride and wealth of self-deception. The figure of Stanley Kowalski, immortalized by Marlon Brando, is threatened by DuBois's implicit critique of his brutal, degraded life, and is compelled to destroy her "pretensions" by reducing her to sexual "meat" through rape. He is a symbol of Williams's understanding and compassion for those who are crushed by male force—economic and sexual—in U.S. society.

Born in Mississippi, Williams was the child of a classically cruel and hypocritical marriage between a "Southern belle," much like Amanda Wingfield, and an unfeeling businessman similar to the "Big Daddy" of "Cat on a Hot Tin Roof." He grew up in a crossfire of sexual and economic tension. A gay man, he came out late in life and never accepted the "sad" (in his words) fact of his "difference." He sought the help of drugs and alcohol, rather than Blanche DuBois's "strangers," to drown out the demons of guilt and loneliness.

That Williams is generally not accorded the honor he deserves is almost certainly related to his decidedly "feminine" perspective. Though he did receive many literary awards, Williams was denied the Nobel Prize—a slight he himself attributed to his known homosexuality. And indeed his insights into the tragedy of female economic dependence and emotional alienation grew directly out of his sense of identification with these problems.

Williams gave U.S. society much more than he got. Rising above the burden of shame and guilt—which for him took the forms of acute hypochondria and compulsive self-destruction—he created plays that let us see the beauty, suffering, and waste in the lives of the economically dependent and sexually oppressed. By daring to be both tender and truthful, Williams gave us a glimpse of a better world that is still only "lit by lightening."

Gender on Television

Made-for-TV Movies: The Domestication of Social Issues

When *The Burning Bed*—a made-for-TV movie about Francine Hughes, the battered wife acquitted of setting her husband's bed on fire—aired on NBC, it drew 75 million viewers, the fourth-highest-rated TV movie ever. With its downbeat theme and grim "video verité" style, the movie was an unlikely candidate for mass appeal. That it drew the rapt attention of much of mainstream America and was rerun on prime time only six months later points to major changes in the role and nature of TV movies.

The *Burning Bed*, and many other TV movies about social issues that have done well recently, mark the genre's coming of age. By presenting controversial issues in a way accessible to people of all ages, classes, and education levels, movies such as *The Day After, Something about Amelia,* and *The Burning Bed* became public events that huge numbers of people experienced and discussed. As a result, TV movies have gone far toward overshadowing theatrical films as a major catalyst for public debate on social issues.

It is always misleading to speak of TV programming in a social and economic vacuum. TV movies are produced and aired under very different conditions than are feature films. Television is now the dominant cultural form in America. It provides most of the information and cultural experience most people get. It is a near constant presence in most homes: 98 percent of us have at least one set, and it is on—and thus experienced in some way—an average of seven hours a day. Moreover, as the traditional socializing agencies in society lose power, leaving us with little spiritual, moral, or practical help in getting through our daily lives, TV has come more and more to fill the role of socializer and cultural unifier. As people move from job to job, city to city, spouse to spouse, feeling more and more disoriented and alone, it is the little lighted box that sits, literally, in the midst of their "living rooms" to which they turn for news of the larger world and for help in figuring out how to handle things.

TV movies, for various reasons, are an important element of TV's socializing and educational role. The current system of network broadcasting developed out of negotiations among the Federal Communications Commission (representing the government), the networks, and the major corporations. Each had special reasons for wanting to support TV, and, as a result, TV has several functions. It is primarily a business. Its job is to deliver audiences to sponsors, whose real need is to have viewers see their commercials, not the programs between them. TV is also regulated by the FCC in ways which require it to air a certain amount of "public interest" material, such as news and documentaries, and to present a "balanced" view of political issues. Finally, of course, the networks need to keep viewers entertained so that they can boast high ratings and charge sponsors high rates.

TV, which combines these three functions—information, entertainment, and commercial sales—is experienced very differently from theatrical film. We don't watch "a show" so much as we experience a flow of images and functions as we sit before the TV set.

News fades to drama and then to commercial break, news break, and so on. All of this is presented in a uniform style so that it is sometimes difficult to distinguish between fiction and "nonfiction" on TV. It is hard to tell actors from commercial salespeople or even from "real" people. In fact, the actors, the sets, and even the images and formulas symbolizing "the good life," "success," and "happiness," are identical on dramas, commercials, and even the news. All are based on a set of assumptions about good and bad, right and wrong, success and failure, which reflect the values of the institutions involved.

Theatrical movies are ideologically loaded too, of course. In the 1930s and 1940s they served somewhat the same role as TV movies play today, but the role of movies, even social-issue movies, has changed. Economic strain and the development of TV and home video equipment have made TV a feature of daily life for everyone. Movies, on the other hand, have become a "night out," something special, reserved largely for the 18- to 24-year-old dating set. The 1984 Academy Awards reflected the change. While the Academy continues nostalgically to award traditional, liberal social-issue films such as *Passage to India* and *The Killing Fields,* these are not the moneymakers, not the films everyone sees and talks about. Blockbusters such as *Indiana Jones and the Temple of Doom* and *Ghostbusters*, hardly thought-provokers, bring in the big bucks.

This change in the relationship between theatrical and TV movies developed gradually. As Douglas Gomery explained in a study of the TV genre, Hollywood tried for a long time to ignore TV, and didn't even rent movies to networks until the mid-1950s, when TV was clearly here to stay. Then, as TV ratings for Hollywood movies rose, so did studio prices. Soon TV executives decided to make their own features, and thus reap the rewards of high ratings without paying Hollywood's price. They were wise. By the mid-1970s, sensational TV movies such as *Cry Rape* and *Little Ladies of the Night* were outdrawing even first-run Hollywood features. *Roots* proved that even serious, downbeat themes could draw huge ratings. By the 1980s, serious TV movies had become national events, with news shows featuring special segments on them and publishers preparing study guides to send to high school and college teachers throughout the country.

Given the need to draw and hold mass audiences, as well as to satisfy the various needs of sponsors and government regulators, it is no wonder that TV movie producers are cautious to a fault, and follow formulaic guidelines religiously. In the better offerings, however, there is still room for intelligence, insight, and even depth. For one thing, since these movies are one-shot deals, dependent on huge promotional campaigns with inviting come-ons for ratings, they can risk unpleasant or complex subjects now and then. "TV isn't afraid of downbeat stories," says Lawrence Schiller, TV producer of Norman Mailer's *Executioner's Song*, "because it doesn't depend on word of mouth." *Executioner's Song*, in fact, was seen theatrically all over Europe, but only on TV here.

Even topics that seem primarily titillating can, in TV movies, be treated at times with sophistication and seriousness. "You need an idea that will grab an audience in one sentence," says *The Burning Bed* director Robert Greenwald. While this can be exploitative junk, it can also be a topic such as incest, which is too serious and demanding to make a big box office theatrical hit. No wonder many people believe, as does David Wolper, that "cinema today is popcorn fare, while TV has taken over the role of serious drama." Vastly overstated though this is, it bears a grain of truth.

This is not to suggest that theatrical features no longer treat serious subjects, or that TV can ever do what film, at its best, does. In fact, the most interesting and exciting theatrical films today, as in every decade, reverberate with social meaning, and in ways far too sophisticated and off-beat to draw large TV audiences. It is not old-fashioned, middlebrow movies that represent theatrical films at their best. On the contrary, these films in many ways resemble their TV counterparts. In both style and political stance they are safe, conventional, and pat.

A comparison of two above-average made-for-TV movies such as *The Burning Bed* and *Lois Gibbs and the Love Canal* to two serious theatrical features of the same period such as *Mrs. Soffel* and *Silkwood* reveals how TV, in general, handles social issues differently from film. Each of these movies deals with "women's issues" and features heroines rather than heroes. This is in keeping with TV norms, since TV, after all, is a domestic medium meant for family consumption. It has always favored domestic drama—

whether in soaps, sitcoms, or movies—because of its audience, and because of its social and commercial functions. Women buy most of the consumer goods sold on TV. Women handle much of the emotional and social negotiation and nurturing that comes with social and moral upheaval. And TV movies, like the products they sell, are often about this kind of activity.

Even a movie such as *The Day After* was presented not as political drama but as domestic crisis. Its settings were typical American living rooms. Its characters were straight out of "Father Knows Best" and "The Waltons." When the bomb fell, it disrupted a myriad of personal crises, and when the commercials came on they, too, were family oriented. "Are you worried that your kids may not make it to college?" asked the man from IBM ironically. "Well, get them a home computer." This lack of political or historic perspective fit well with the movie itself. Like most TV movies, *The Day After* allowed for no past, no public world, no class or race differences, at least not as significant social factors. Everyone was a member of a nuclear family, and no other group designation seemed to exist. The hero, a doctor, was a professional male and, of course, a father. Every household contained familiar furnishings and appliances, every character wore clothing and used grooming aids that mirrored their counterparts in the commercials, and the plot allowed for no dalliances that didn't obviously and immediately build the main action. In TV movies, as critic Stephen Farber said, "The purely transitional scenes that create mood and atmosphere...are inevitably rushed or abbreviated while the evocation of character through purely visual storytelling is less highly refined than in theatrical films."

The Burning Bed was a far better movie than *The Day After*. It managed to present domestic violence seriously and compassionately. The violence itself, while useful in drawing audiences, was not actually sensationalized in the movie, and the perspective was in keeping with feminist analysis. Still, it managed, with its distorted facts, its characterizations, and, not least, the ironic subtext created by the commercials, to limit and distort its feminist message.

The Burning Bed is told in flashbacks, as Francine Hughes (Farrah Fawcett), having turned herself in for killing her husband, tells her story to her court-appointed lawyer (Paul Masu). The

structure is spare and economical. Each segment relates a significant turning point in Fran's journey to desperation. We first see her
as a teenager in the early 1960s, smitten by the worldly Mickey
(Paul LeMat) with his Elvis pompadour. No one has ever seemed to
need her so much, and his every cliché brings stars to her eyes.

After the wedding, and the move to his parents' home, the
violence begins at once. The scene in which he first hits her is
loaded with sociological and psychological information. She has
bought a new blouse to please him and he reacts with jealousy.
Moments before, we learned that Mickey had no intention of finding work and was prone to booze. Fran, of course, is already pregnant, feeling trapped and terrified.

The scene is powerful. The setting, a shabby, overcrowded
house filled with too many people and too many problems, rever-
berates with tension, fear, and hostility. Having established Fran's
shock and fear, Mickey's irrational rage, and the elder Hughes's refusal to acknowledge any problem, director Greenwald allows the
inevitable blows to erupt wildly, and end as abruptly. The emotional atmospheric resonance of the scene, done with a rawness
unusual for TV, is nonetheless constrained—almost squashed and
flattened—by the structural and ideological requirements of the
form. There is information here, a lesson about male violence and
family and state complicity, but when the emotional impact threatens to stretch the boundaries of that ideological framework, the
emotional impact is cut off.

The movie continues relentlessly, portraying the key points of
escalation in Mickey's destructiveness and Fran's desperation. The
story is classic. Fran loves her children, even believes she "loves"
Mickey. How else could she have married him? Every agency and
family member corroborates this simple message: "You are a family," you belong together, you must "take the bitter with the
sweet." In the end, Fran's desperate act to save herself and her
children seems too inevitable to question, and, throughout, the
movie provides a lowkeyed sense of the ordinariness—the dreariness, really—of this kind of life.

The violence, and its larger implications about human nature,
sexual relationships, and the repressive role of the traditional family is
always muted and contained, however, because the movie has a sim-

ple, "one case at a time" approach. Fran's "solution" is a plea of temporary insanity devised by her white, middle-class lawyer, who wears his three-piece suit as though it were a uniform from another civilization. This plea was, in fact, used by the real Francine Hughes, but it was developed with the help of feminists who organized a defense fund and publicized the case as a feminist political trial. That the movie leaves feminism and the women's movement out, that it chooses to give credit to an individual—a traditional TV drama hero, at that—is typical of these movies.

In fact, the reason for the muted quality of the film's subject—violence—is that violence is not entirely what it's about. It's about solving the "problem" of violence by the use of methods that reflect the values TV always champions: the law, middle-class respectability, individual action. The Hughes story differs from most TV movies in focusing on a working-class family. But what a family it is! It's nothing like the "real" American families that smile out at us, again and again, in the soap and furniture polish commercials that sponsored this "women's" movie. These commercials reflect the world of Francine Hughes' lawyer, a world of order, reason, cleanliness, and the kind of joy that comes from having your husband notice that you used Downy—especially when your husband is doing the kind of important work that men in TV commercials do, the kind of work good lawyers, who care about women, do.

The Burning Bed has a contradictory message. It is almost rhetorically feminist in perspective. It is visually and emotionally powerful. On another level, however, because of its framing devices, it is a simple morality tale in which the solutions to women's problems lie in the bold actions of a soap opera hero representing a society that is all reason and heart.

Mrs. Soffel, another "true story" about a woman's repression within a traditional marriage, while obviously different from the Hughes story, affords some interesting points of stylistic and thematic comparison. Directed by a woman, the Australian Gillian Armstrong, it tells of a warden's wife (Diane Keaton) in 19th-century Pittsburgh who falls in love with a convicted murderer (Mel Gibson), helps him escape, and lives with him for three ecstatic days on the run, until they are caught and he is shot.

The similarities between *The Burning Bed* and *Mrs. Soffel* are in their evocations of a woman's repression and spiritual death within traditional marriage. Both women are presented as trapped in situations which require the breaking of a law for escape. Whereas Mrs. Soffel's prison—and this is a bit subtle for TV—is conventional middle-class marriage, Fran Hughes's escape is provided by that very same respectable world. Whereas Fran's oppressor is the brutish, working-class Mickey, it is just such a violent, common man—presented romantically, of course—that offers Mrs. Soffel escape.

A kind of Gothic fantasy of escape from middle-class repression to the fulfillment of a union with a rough young outlaw, *Mrs. Soffel* is subtly subversive of middle-class values, and so must end tragically. *The Burning Bed,* on the other hand, an odyssey of escape from male brutality to the safety of middle-class order and security, ends happily. Fran will no doubt finish school and get a job in an office, where she just may meet the right kind of man, one who will buy her the things the women in the commercials that sponsor her story live for. (That this is in no way what happened to the real Francine Hughes is just one more comment on the limits and distortions of TV movies.)

A similar sense of tragedy, and romantic longing for the sexual and worldly freedom of the outlaw, the sexual libertine, characterizes Mike Nichols's portrayal of Karen Silkwood in *Silkwood*. Here, too, the working-class principals are portrayed as sensual, free-living, and unrestrained by middle-class morality. Here, too, atmosphere and ambiguity of character, much of it a distortion of the facts about the real Silkwood, carry the film's deep meaning.

Meryl Streep's Silkwood is a sexually free, rebellious, dope-smoking runaway mother who shares her home with a sometimes lover and lesbian friend. The lifestyle issues, and the sense of social rebellion, more than political activism, are the film's major focus. As in *Mrs. Soffel*, such behavior, while attractive and emotionally justified, ends inevitably in tragedy and isolation. Karen lives, and dies, as an outlaw from respectable womanhood.

TV movies about women who become social activists, as Karen Silkwood did, are different. *Lois Gibbs and the Love Canal,* another "true story" directed by Bob Greenwald, tells of a working-class housewife's crusade to organize and fight the company polluting her community's water supply and killing its children. Like

The Burning Bed, Lois Gibbs's heroine goes from a passive, obedient wife and mother to a fighter, out to save her family's lives. While the movie is stylistically less impressive than *The Burning Bed,* the sense of consciousness-raising and organizing among working-class women is a rare and valuable thematic asset. Like Silkwood, Gibbs is set on justice at all costs, and like Silkwood, when her husband balks, she allows the relationship to end and continues to struggle alone. Again, there is no hint that Love Canal is anything but an isolated case, and no sense of general institutional responsibility. The villains are individual, mean men, and their flaws are personal, never broadly political.

Gibbs wins her case, of course, but her future is unclear. Like Fran Hughes, she is seen as acting primarily as a mother. There is a subtle subliminal message, too: if you get too serious about politics, you will lose your man. Most significantly, the movie shows that social problems, women's problems, no matter how serious, can be solved on a case-by-case basis. The system is rational: good men can be found to do the right thing; justice will out.

Whereas Silkwood and Mrs. Soffel end up dead, or as good as dead, Lois Gibbs and Fran Hughes are triumphant. This is the most marked difference between social issues as presented on TV and in most serious theatrical films. TV raises and resolves issues. It offers guidance, models, and hope. Life makes sense, follows a neat path from crisis to resolution, even if the world it creates is emotionally flattened and intellectually and politically simplistic.

In the more stylistically interesting Hollywood movies about similarly thorny problems, the message is different. In place of hope there is cynicism. The feelings of discontent and social repression are played on and explored with artistic flair and psychosocial suggestiveness. The viewer—whom the producers assume to be more intellectually and emotionally sophisticated than mass TV audiences—is not given a red, white, and blue message about things working out, about the American Dream being the answer to one's hopes and deepest desires. It is far too late for that kind of thing in the post-feminist, post-Vietnam years. Hollywood lately seems to acknowledge the depth of our spiritual and material discontent, the passion of our longings for all that middle-class security forces us to give up. But it doesn't offer any answers.

TV does offer answers. It is required, really, to offer answers. It is the voice of the American establishment reassuring us that it knows our problems and knows a guy we can call to fix them right up. It is often very good at laying out the dimensions of those problems, and even giving advice about some aspects. Its real concern, however, is not so much our problems themselves as the need to convince us of where to seek help, and how much we can reasonably expect to get.

A Family Affair

In the introduction to his book, "America at Century's End," Alan Wolfe lists "Seventeen Changes in American Life." Many items on his provocative list point to growing contradictions between the idealist rhetoric of traditional democracy and harsh realities of life in the 1990s. Particularly disturbing is Wolfe's comment about our relationship to our children. "America has long thought of itself as a child-oriented culture," he writes, "but hair-raising stories of sexual abuse, poor schools, latchkey kids, and an inadequate child-care system suggest otherwise. Even as we celebrate the innocence of childhood, we deprive children of the opportunity just to be children."

Indeed, if there is one thing that has characterized the American dream of progress, one vision that has brought the great influx of immigrants to our shores, it is the dream of generational betterment, of providing a better future for our offspring than we ourselves have enjoyed. In advertising and mass culture, however, the focus on youth has always had a double edge. Beneath the romantic Norman Rockwell sketches of doting mothers and proud fathers beaming at shiny-faced urchins marching off to church, there has always been an anxious subtext or two.

First, the focus on youth has had, from the start, an economic thrust. In the wake of industrialism and the breakdown of the patriarchal, farm-based family (best embodied for most of us in the images of "The Waltons" and "The Little House on the Prairie"), children—as future workers and consumers—became the symbols of potential economic growth. Early advertising stressed new roles for parents, especially mothers (some full-time housewives for the first time), in making sure children grew up healthy and properly socialized to fit into the new industrial order.

Where parents had previously simply raised their children to do the same home-based work they themselves had done, now things were different. Children were to be sent off into a brave new world of commodities and technological skills beyond the imaginations or understandings of their increasingly "behind the times" parents. And parents, for their part, were to devote themselves to the central task of "giving them every advantage."

Even as this new technology of parental self-sacrifice and obsessive, full-time nurturing (symbolized best by the rise of Dr. Benjamin Spock and the other "experts") stressed family solidarity as an almost religious principle, the strains of industrialism were tearing the family apart. The "Generation Gap" and the "Battle of the Sexes" were products of diverging roles, experiences, and values of individual family members. The "Breakdown of the Family" had begun.

Here, again, advertising and mass culture played a role. This time, however, the role was damage control. Having torn asunder the very bonds upon which family harmony had rested, it was now necessary to backtrack, to say "Whoa" to some of the horses of progress before they destroyed the family unit that formed the center of consumption and socialization.

By the 1950s, television had established its role in reinforcing the values of family life. The ideological function of the sitcom—then and now the dominant entertainment genre—has remained constant. From "Father Knows Best" to "The Brady Bunch" to "Family Ties," these scrubbed, well-functioning families have invaded our living rooms and challenged us to measure up. They have presented images of family unity and harmony to a nation deep in the throes of domestic chaos and trauma.

Well before the advent of home TV, the divorce rate was soaring, juvenile delinquency and youthful rebellion were rampant, emotional distress and domestic violence were on the rise. But week after week, Americans sat rapt before their television screens watching Ward and June solve the current "problem with the Beaver" and retire safely behind their cheerfully shuttered windows.

To watch American sitcoms, then and now, is to enter an "America" in which adults spend virtually all their time in their well-appointed, commodity-filled kitchens and dens talking to and about their children, worrying over and solving their children's problems, successfully teaching their loving, respectful offspring moral lessons about honesty, tolerance, charity, and compassion. It is a world in which violence, drugs, racism, and sexism barely exist, in which social issues of any kind, when they are raised at all, are quickly and easily solved in 22 minutes in the privacy of the family living room by fathers and mothers who still know best, with no help at all from government, schools, or social-service agencies.

But sitcoms are not, and never were, revealing of chinks in the social armor. If, as Alan Wolfe suggests, we are a nation increasingly ambivalent and hypocritical in our attitudes toward our children, increasingly unwilling or unable to provide for their needs and well-being, increasingly imposing domestic and social conditions that make it nearly impossible for children to thrive, it is sitcoms that most disingenuously deny these facts, that doggedly insist, against the growing contradictions of reality, that "America is...a child-oriented culture."

The other, more realistic side of the story is not invisible. Even popular culture has always provided us with more serious and troubling versions of family life and parent/child relations. The social-issue theatrical film is virtually extinct, thanks to the economics of the movie industry, but if you watch made-for-TV movies—the small-screen replacement for the family-melodrama and social-issue film—and read closely between the lines (after all, the sponsors are still watching), you will get a scary picture of how we really feel about our children; how, as a society, we are providing for them; and how we are dealing with these feelings and conditions. It is on "Movie of the Week" that such issues as teenage drinking, drugs, AIDS, pregnancy, prostitution, suicide, delinquency, and plain, old-fashioned alienation are addressed, often movingly. It is also in this genre that TV chooses to present its versions of more general "breakdown of the family" issues—domestic violence, divorce, incest, alcoholism, unemployment. In fact, in its better moments, "Movie of the Week" is TV's finest hour.

In the 1970s, when this form was invented, its generic conventions were established. A family was presented, usually at the breakfast table, cheerfully eating Cheerios and talking about homework or something. Then a crisis would emerge and build. The parents would be revealed to be Doing Something Wrong, obviously and glaringly wrong. The child would be shown to be increasingly troubled and skating on thin ice, socially and emotionally. Finally, the parents would be brought to their senses when Something Really Awful happened. The child was arrested for shoplifting or street-walking, hospitalized for drunk driving or a botched abortion, even attempted suicide. And then, in the denouement, a therapist was brought in and the family was "cured."

These films—*Sarah T: Portrait of a Teenage Alcoholic, In the Custody of Strangers* (about delinquency), *Consenting Adults* (about parents coming to terms with gay children), *Something About Amelia* (about incest), and *Minnesota Strip,* (about teen prostitution)—are among the best of the genre, and were hopeful and probably helpful. They took on the challenge of a world in which children were increasingly troubled and mysterious to their parents, in which the stresses of adult life—divorce, economic recession, emotional illness—were increasingly taking their toll on children and families. To be sure, the solutions were always private and always presented in terms of "holding the family together" no matter what. They presented lessons to parents in the trials of the day, pointed to common areas in which they were probably going wrong, and sent them to therapists or social workers for help.

The crux of these movies was the belief—still plausible, I suppose, in the 1970s—that families were, in fact, capable of "mending themselves" and functioning, at least to the extent that they could be expected to keep their kids dressed, fed, and out of jail. The films were addressed to white families (or an occasional middle-class black family), and while they portrayed working-class families quite often (another plus for the genre), they presented them with a model of middle-class goals and solutions.

The point was to become as much like the Cleavers and Nelsons as possible. If problems were acknowledged, they were seen as manageable because they were transported out of the larger social context that actually produced them and dealt with squarely in the privacy of the living room or the therapist's office.

And life went on. At least, until recently. In the last few years, the tone and agenda of the made-for-TV movie has changed ominously. While the thrust is still on family problems and solutions, the implications about what is causing the problems have changed since the 1970s and early 1980s. The liberal, "therapeutic" model of family healing has been replaced by a far more conservative model that seems to see the generational conflict as permanent and unresolvable. Its source is no longer temporarily "dysfunctional" families who need help in adjusting to social and personal changes. Increasingly, what we see on "serious" TV are narratives in which hostile, external forces of various kinds "invade" families and alter them irrevocably.

The earlier movies may not have acknowledged social and political causes in ways that pointed to social and political solutions, but they did present liberal ideas about adjusting to change, listening to children, respecting their feelings, taking seriously their need to be different from parents, and having parents take responsibility for their damaging attitudes and actions. The new ones not only take society off the hook, they take parents off the hook, too.

The shift I'm describing has been subtle and at first seems understandable. Take the treatment of homosexuality as a family problem. In *Consenting Adults,* a good movie about gay youth, we see Dad and Mom, with the help of enlightened Sis, accepting that their son—a brilliant, well-adjusted, handsome, confident pre-med student—is gay and happy, not "sick" or a freak. It takes time, but eventually they come around. The film ends with a Christmas dinner in which the son and his lover, another handsome pre-med student, are welcomed to the family. "Now I have two 'my-son-the-doctors,'" says Mom.

Within a year, however, we had *An Early Frost,* a similar film in which Mom and Dad adjust to the homosexuality of their apparently straight, professional son. Only this time the son (a lawyer) has AIDS and the conclusion is tragic. There is no happy ending in which the family circle expands to include a gay lover. There is, instead, a funeral. In one movie, we have gone from gayness as a healthy "alternative lifestyle," which the "backward" parents must learn to accept and incorporate into family life, to gayness as the condition that invites the invasion of a deadly, mysterious, fatal illness. In one way or another, ever since, we have had family TV movies in which some such external agent "takes over" a child's life and changes the family life forever, through no fault of parents or society and very much for the worse.

The sources of these family tragedies vary, but they are invariably presented as arbitrary, inscrutable, or the result of "evil" demons beyond the pale of normal human understanding. When the agents of crisis are human, they are always pathological or sociopathic, deranged murderers like Son of Sam or the Boston Strangler, or unbelievably monstrous characters capable of kidnapping, child molestation, selling drugs to grade-school students, and so on, because they are somehow or other "not like" the rest of us.

In these cases, the political implications are clear. Since the criminals are no longer seen as "curable" family members, or even members of the "normal" human race, prison and execution—the law-and-order solutions—are the only possible answers. A particularly moving example of this genre was the mini-series *I Know My First Name Is Steven*. This "based on fact" drama tells of a small boy, kidnapped by a sociopathic sexual deviant who keeps him for seven years, neglecting his care and schooling and constantly abusing him sexually. His parents and the police think Steven is dead. Finally, when he escapes and returns home, he is unable to readjust to family life and has to be let go, to live alone as a social misfit, more or less.

An equally interesting example, *A Stranger in the Family*, offered not a pervert but a drunk driver as the cause of the "loss" of a son. The boy, a star athlete and perfect child, becomes permanently amnesiac as a result of a car crash and must live out his days as a kind of zombie, lacking all memories of his family identity and all sense of normal love and affection for his perfect 1950s sitcom-style family. At one point the boy, unable to stand the pressure to become "normal," runs away and joins a group of street kids. Briefly, he finds a community among these other social misfits and aliens. But this idea is not developed. Instead, he returns home and his parents come to terms with the fact that they have a "stranger in the family" who will need constant care forever and who will never give them the love or gratification they had expected.

These two narratives provide important clues as to how the mass media, always committed to giving us directions about how to deal with the growing crisis of parent-child relations and the parallel crisis of teenage social alienation and delinquency, are now handling the issue. They are throwing up their hands and saying, "Beats us." They're telling us there are monsters out there—viruses, deviants, criminals, natural disasters, random violence, mysterious forces—lurking in the air and on the streets and infecting otherwise normal kids with social and physical diseases from which they will not recover. We may be able to catch some of the culprits and kill them, but the kids themselves will not be back.

The message is clear. And we don't actually need TV drama to tell it to us. The schools are collapsing and are not being repaired. Child care is nonexistent, yet most parents must work, and more and more of us are single parents. Drugs and guns are easily available, and no one in government is seriously interested in stopping them at their sources. Sexually transmitted diseases and addicted babies are rampant, but our courts are working hard to keep us from getting treatment, birth control, and legal abortions. And, most chillingly, we are raising a generation of kids who do not even consider the possibility of following the rules, obeying the laws, even respecting the sanctity of life itself, their own or others'.

We are, indeed, a nation of hypocrites, mouthing platitudes about childhood innocence, putting cherubic faces on posters and milk cartons, crying crocodile tears over specially selected infants who fall into wells or receive organ transplants. But our infant-mortality rate is outrageous and one in five of our children gets no medical attention at all.

TV has its work cut out for it. The sitcoms are already in a serious credibility crunch. The smiling faces of wealthy, apparently brain-dead families bombard us nightly on the 8 to 9 p.m. Family Hour, but they fool no one. The average child considers "The Simpsons" the most "realistic" sitcom on TV. And from 9 to 11 we are fed horror stories about why our kids hate us, why they are dying, why they are more like science-fiction monsters than Dick and Jane and Baby Sally, horror stories which offer two solutions: put more and more people in jail, or learn to live with science-fiction monsters. You'll get used to it, eventually.

The Year of the Young: Beverly Hills 90210 and Others

In what we like to think of as "the real world," 1992 was called "The Year of the Woman." In the world of series television, a kind of parallel universe that in some ways trails and in other ways anticipates the "real world," 1993 was "The Year of the Young"—the unattached, unmarried, unfamilied young.

At the movies, this has been true for a long time. The years after World War II ushered in the age of consumerism and home television—symbiotically linked developments, obviously. They also, for related reasons, gave birth to "The Teenager" as a cultural and economic force. When James Dean, accurately dubbed "The First American Teenager," took off his white shirt, coat, and tie—

the uniform of middle-class apprenticeship to the traditional Father/Citizen role—and donned jeans, jacket, and boots in *Rebel Without a Cause*, a new era of social and generational relationships (and, of course, fashion and consumerism) was born.

From then on, Hollywood has played "the Kids" theme for all it was worth, aiming its product at the world of dating teenagers. In the age of TV, when adults tend more and more to stay home, it is teenagers who are the movies' target audience.

Television, until the start of the 1990s, steadfastly ignored the social developments that produced this trend in movies and trudged on, against the grain of history, with its classic images of "The Family" and "Father as Hero," whether at home or out in the big, bad world of crime, law, medicine, or the media. Doggedly modernist in an increasingly postmodern world, television stuck with its myths of rugged individualism in the public sphere and patriarchal, nuclear harmony in the middle-American, domestic sphere, where everyone still lives in single-family dwellings complete with picket fences and tree-shaded yards.

This anachronistic insistence on maintaining retrograde images of a personal and social world long gone is understandable. From its inception, after all, TV had been the keeper of social stability and harmony, an instrument of reassurance in a world gone awry and coming apart at the seams.

Even in the 1960s and early 1970s, when authority was questioned with great intensity everywhere, the contested issues of war and peace, racism and homophobia, gender and generational warfare, were handled in the traditional settings of family and public life. Archie Bunker may have been a buffoon, but he was still the head of the household, and he managed to keep these explosive matters "All in the Family." The rising of the women, the falling of the military ideal, these too, in such shows as "Mary Tyler Moore" and "M*A*S*H," were carefully managed and resolved within the still-intact confines of traditional, male-run institutions like Lou Grant's newsroom and the Korea-based U.S. Army.

And then came cable, with its new breed of upstart networks determined to compete with the Big Three. These networks scoffed at the fuddy-duddy old rules set up so many decades ago by FCC commissioners, sponsors, and network executives, who were determined to win a place for the new medium in the post-war social order by being as socially responsible as was feasible. And the upstarts struck gold in both informational and entertainment programming.

Just as CNN has transformed television news, the Fox network has transformed the traditional family-based fictional series, first undermining and then doing away entirely with the whole notion—so dear to TV until now—that the family unit and its values still form the core of our personal and social existence. First came "Married with Children" and "The Simpsons," two iconoclastic series wherein it was revealed that far from Knowing Best, "Father" was an ineffectual bozo who could barely make a living, keep his wife sexually satisfied, or command his children's attention, much less respect, for more than a post-final-commercial instant.

So enormous was the success of these two shows that the networks didn't know what hit them or what to do about it. The classic 1980s sitcoms—"Cosby," "Family Ties," "Growing Pains"—almost immediately began to look, to one and all, like the corny TV-manufactured fakes they always were, and had to be retired to rerun heaven. From there, it's been downhill all the way for Dad, Mom, and the family homestead on TV.

The networks, still "in denial" after the shock of this cable-born sucker punch to the very core of their existence, continue to diddle around with possible new variations on the dead old form—households made up of single mothers and their younger siblings, single fathers, more-bumbling-than-usual regular fathers, and so on. But Fox itself has intrepidly followed the ideological implications of its original anti-family impulse, increasingly doing away entirely with parents and the worldview they symbolize—much as the movies did decades ago.

The reasons for this are economically obvious. The logic of consumerism, from the 1950s on, has always been to target ever-younger markets. All that stopped TV from doing this was its commitment to shoring up the old dead values of family and patriarchy. But Fox, the bad boy of the TV family, decided early on that its fortune would be made by openly thumbing its nose at parents and families and saying right out loud what the kids have been saying to each other for years: that the real scene, the real action, the real issues and problems that matter are to be found and resolved right there in the malls where the movies and compact discs turn over quickly, the Gap opens early, and the pizza and Pepsi keep coming, cheap and fast, like everything else in their postmodern world.

First came "Beverly Hills 90210," welcomed by kids because, unlike all the other shows about middle-class white teens, it dared to admit that kids today have sex, angst, and a private life filled with issues and worries and changes never mentioned or acknowledged in the pretty, hokey living rooms of network sitcoms.

These kids, to be sure, were incredibly rich, still in high school, and—not to be *too* risky too fast—there was *one* household in which traditional family values as TV has always presented them still thrived. The Walshes, transplants from wholesome old Minnesota, are as drippy and straight as any network sitcom parents. But they play an increasingly marginal role. Their daughter has already defied their command and moved out, once, to live with her boyfriend, and no one died or got canceled.

As for the other kids, they have hopelessly dysfunctional parents—convicted felons, alcoholics, New Age wackos, no-show weekend dads, and so on. And mostly, as is the case in the real world, they help each other deal with the disappointment caused by these inadequate, irresponsible grownups and get on with the real business of life: working out their own relationships and problems. These "really serious" matters of course turn out to be things their folks have no time for or interest in, so busy are they figuring out how to get through their own very different but equally complicated days and nights.

I consider "90210" a transitional show. The kids are eternally in high school—no career or money problems—and there is this vestigial ghost of traditional sitcom life to keep anything really scary from happening. But the shows introduced by Fox in the following season—"Melrose Place" and "The Heights"—are far more interesting.

In both cases, the characters are in their twenties, or at least finished with high school, and are into the phase of life in which figuring out what one is going to be when one grows up is central. "Melrose" is mostly about middle-class, college-educated kids in L.A.; "Heights" is about New Jersey working-class kids. Both focus on a group of friends that's racially mixed and mostly single. And in the L.A. setting, the group includes a gay man.

What is most poignant in both these shows is the very low level of expectation, hope, or ambition any of the characters has about any aspect of her or his life. In "Heights," the kids (except for one run-away) live with parents, for economic reasons, but there is no sense at all that the parents have anything to teach the kids about the future or how to navigate it. One is an abusive, drunk, Vietnam vet; the others represent a dying lifestyle in a world in which the industrial working class, and the family norms it supported, are finished.

In this world, one either tries to become middle-class through education or, if that's impossible (and it mostly is), one dreams—not too seriously—about becoming a rock star. To the extent that there is traditional TV glamour and optimism here at all, it's built on the dreams of these kids—social losers all—of getting their band together and getting on MTV. But the truth, represented by the one kid whose girlfriend is pregnant, is that learning a trade like plumbing is one's best bet.

In L.A., things are glitzier but no less depressing. This group lives in an apartment complex that—very sweetly, really—becomes the foundation for a kind of interim "family," sort of like a 1960s com-mune, for young people whose ultimate fates will take them in far-flung directions, some up, most down. The one solvent couple, a medical resident and his fashion-designer wife, have intense personal problems—Should she terminate her pregnancy because they're still broke? Should she sleep with the cute guy who gives her the attention her husband has no time for?—for which they turn to their same-sex neighbors, not each other, to discuss and resolve.

The rest of these nice young people have mostly dead-end hack jobs in advertising or entertainment, or they drive cabs, wait tables, teach aerobics, or repair motorcycles while waiting for their big break as "artists." The gay guy runs a homeless shelter. They all volunteer for "causes." They rarely mention or see their families. They grapple together with such issues as sexual harassment, abor-tion, AIDS, single motherhood, and the like.

Most critics have pounced on these shows for their excessive attention to physical beauty and fashion. Everyone here is gor-geous, in perfect shape, and up to the minute on what's pictured in this month's *Elle* and *GQ*. But these shows are not 1990s versions of "Dynasty" or "Knots Landing." Glamour is not what drives them. They are about a world in which one's appearance is one's only capital. The shows glam this up a bit, promising that good looks will buy more than is realistic, because there is no other optimistic message to offer. And because, perhaps more relevantly, the outfits help sell the 501s, Nikes, and other trendy fashion items that sponsor the programs.

There is a sad subtext here. The fact is—and the shows make this very clear—that for most kids, meaningful work, adult role models in family, politics, or the workplace, and satisfying relationships that last longer than the average 9.1 years are not likely to be part of one's life scenario. Friends are one's best asset but, again, the pace at which work and love relationships fade and change means that even this kind of stability is temporary. Talk to any typical college kid today, outside of Harvard and Yale anyway, and you will hear about this bad news in one way or another. For some, it's something they've thought about and can articulate; for most, perhaps, it's just a note of sadness and cynicism that belies their years and their hip outfits.

That TV tells these kids that *it* can offer them fame, fortune, stardom, and meaningful work as glamorous "artists" is cruel, of course. But any other suggestion makes no sense. That's why the traditional networks are having such a hard time figuring out how to deal with Fox's challenge. Stuck as they are with their traditional upbeat formulas about heroics and happily-ever-afters, they can't seem to come up with a show about young people that isn't hopelessly tired, corny, and preposterous.

The two network shows that tried to ape Fox's formula by presenting groups of single young people in dramatic situations—"Malibu 2000" and "The Round Table"—were canceled promptly. The first tried to do high soap opera melodrama along the lines of "Dynasty" and only succeeded in being laughably camp.

The second, a bit closer to the mark, was a sort of Washington, D.C. version of "Melrose Place." It centered on a group of interracial, mixed-class friends starting out in life, who gather at a Georgetown bar to work out their various personal and professional hassles. The problem was that, in typical network style, it insisted on clinging to the modernist myths about heroic, individualist quests for honor and truth. Using old plots and dialogue, it pretended that young Latina lawyers and African-American Secret Service agents could still, week after week, off-handedly perform great and noble deeds by which freedom, democracy, and the American Way would be maintained. The response of the twentysomethings was, "I don't think so. Switch back to Fox."

I don't think the two Fox shows mentioned above will last long either. The depressing subtexts are bound to overwhelm the cheery but phony fame-and-fortune promise sooner or later. I don't know what will replace them. But I do know that Fox has created a real crisis for series television, the like of which Dan Quayle has not even begun to glimpse or get nervous about. Murphy Brown, when you get past the single-motherhood gimmick, is still basically an old-style individualist heroine fighting for truth and virtue and liberal democracy—and winning. Every kid in America should be so lucky as to have a parent like her.

But as Fox well knows, and has only begun to start spreading the word about, Murphy Brown is history. The kids on the new shows have no elegant socialite mothers or statesman fathers to escort them into the big time and teach them how to become powerful, noble, and rich. They have parents whose cultural capital has expired, who have nothing to pass on, and whose ways of getting a home and paycheck don't work anymore, even for them. They are drunk, divorced, dysfunctional, and dazed. They are sitting home watching reruns of "The Donna Reed Show" and trying to figure out how to hustle their way through life, on their own fading good looks and dated lucky outfits.

I eagerly await Fox's solution to the problem they have created for themselves: now that the truth is out of the bag, how do we get through the next season with our make-up and hope still intact?

The Three Faces of Amy Fisher

Much has been made of the astounding fact that between 100 and 125 million people—roughly half the U.S. population—watched at least one of the three made-for-TV movies about 17-year-old Long Island high school student Amy Fisher's shooting of Mary Jo Buttafuoco, the wife of her 36-year-old alleged lover and pimp, Joey. They aired during the week of December 28, 1992 to January 3, 1993. (The CBS version ran twice more on the USA network.)

This, we were told, was proof that sleaze and idiocy are what "the people" with our mashed-potato brains and polyester souls "want to see" in the wonderful free market of ideas and images called commercial television. But while sleaze was certainly what viewers got that week, there is no reason to conclude that that is what they wanted.

The Fisher/Buttafuoco case raised several increasingly important issues, among them the sexual and economic exploitation of teenagers, incest, and, not least, the sexism of the media. Such issues, which have been put on the political agenda by feminists, cannot be dismissed as "sleaze." Those interested in such issues are not "sleazy."

If viewers expected at least one of the three Amy movies to provide some serious analysis of some very disturbing and very common kinds of social ills, they had good reason. That they got sleaze instead of seriousness was the fault of the sleazy networks.

The "Amy Wars" should be viewed in relation to what's been going on in nonfiction television in the past two years. Cable outlets like CNN, C-SPAN, and Court TV have brought more and more "real life" events to our living rooms—TV dramas that, in the best *Burning Bed* tradition, told some scary things about men, women, and sexuality. These stories—of Anita and Clarence; of Mike and Desiree; of Willie and Ms. "Blue Dot" of Bob and half the Capitol Hill female workforce—brought home more and more dramatically the gap between male and female attitudes and expectations on sexual matters.

And so, when the networks, in a rush to cash in on yet another tragedy, all decided to slap together whatever thoughtless, barely legal combination of pictures and dialogue they could manage in a few weeks' time, it was not surprising that what they came up with was far below the level of sophistication and insight of most viewers.

Good Girls and Bad Girls

These three movies failed to deal seriously with their subject matter, from any of the three points of view they chose. Each movie put forth—in its own bizarre way—an outrageously sexist, politically naive, and retrograde version of gender conflict. In each version of the story, the men were whitewashed and absolved of responsibility for what happened to the women in their lives, while all the women— Amy, Mary Jo, Mrs. Fisher—were presented as either dopey Good Girls or devil-possessed Bad Girls. And it was this that viewers not only refused to buy, but actually revolted against.

The NBC version, *Amy Fisher: Her Story,* presented Amy as a confused, misunderstood teenager seduced and misled by an older man. It also presented, at least briefly, a hint that she was sexually abused by her father.

Yes, in this version, her father molested her while her mother stood by. Yes, Joey seduced her. ("Deli sandwiches and a cheap motel?" she asks on their second date. "Simple pleasures," he smirks.) Yes, he went on to greedily and voyeuristically pimp for her. Yes, her boyfriend Paul set up a videotape for "A Current Affair." And yes, the media hounded and trashed her to the point of suicide.

But the movie makes virtually no judgment on any of this. It's trivialized and sensationalized, never addressed as a serious matter. It's "based on fact." Fade to commercial.

If NBC's version was the most insulting, since it actually raised all these issues and then ignored them, the CBS version, told from Mary Jo's perspective, was the most absurd. Sticking faithfully to classic TV-movie formula, it was one of those corny family dramas in which a Problem disrupts a good marriage and is resolved to happily-ever-after images of connubial bliss.

But in most TV movies (as in the televised lives of Hillary and Bill), some flaw in the marriage is diagnosed and corrected. Not this time. This Joey is the Mr. Rogers of marriage. He can never resist, upon entering his home, sweeping giggly little Mary Jo into his arms and dancing her around the room. Women attempt to tear his clothes off and he flicks them away to phone home.

So what about Amy? We don't know. She seems to be a mildly retarded space cadet who hits on Joey for no reason whatsoever. She then proceeds to devise a murderous scheme to do away with her fantasized competition, because...perhaps she's psychotic? Whatever. The audience will figure it out.

And then there was the "art house" version on ABC, in which the villain was the "bad media" and the heroine—the *New York Post*'s Amy Pagnozzi—valiantly tried to correct the misogyny of her male colleagues with cynical, feminist-tinged quips that no one ever responded to.

Of course, this "feminist" version was the one in which Amy herself—played by Drew Barrymore—was presented as the most stereotypically demonic, sex-crazed, and sociopathic. It got the best reviews because it gave "both sides," but in fact it fudged on every issue and exploited the "feminist angle," by negating it with the larger-than-life image of Barrymore as a She-Devil, stalking men with her irresistible wiles and leaving them dazed and destroyed.

Storming the Media

To claim that any of these movies was what viewers "wanted" is an insult not only to audiences but to producers of serious docudramas like *Burning Bed, Something About Amelia,* and *Off the Minnesota Strip.*

The most dramatic proof that viewers did *not* get what they wanted was the outrage of the viewers themselves. On the two-day slugfest that transpired on "Donahue" (January 5-6, 1993), audience members and callers revolted against the men with power, in front of the cameras, behind the cameras, and in print, who had so distorted the meaning of the case.

So insulted were these viewers by the sexism and silliness of the movies that they nearly shouted Phil Donahue, TV critic Marvin Kitman, Joey's lawyer Marvyn Kornberg, and—most amazingly—Joey and Mary Jo themselves (he for lying and betraying both women; she for being fool enough to support him) off the stage.

The teenage classmates of Amy Fisher were outraged at the media's portrayal of their community—and of Amy herself, who they insisted was "not the worst person in the world." As for who might actually qualify for that title, they were quick to list the many men—including Donahue—who had profited from the tragedy.

And so, it seems, the customers are storming the media marketplace demanding higher-quality goods for their (indirect) consumer dollars. Let's hope, as in the congressional scenario, some heads will roll, some acts will get cleaned up, and some feminists will get hired into positions of power in the network entertainment divisions. That's the very least women viewers deserve and demand.

Sex, Commercials, and Rock 'n' Roll

Since its inception in 1981, there has hardly been a kind, or dispassionate, word written about MTV, at least by "respectable," "responsible" adults. The round-the-clock, "all music" cable network, set up to entrap the hard-to-get 14- to 34-year-old consumer market, has, it seems, offended and alarmed nearly everyone in some way or other.

Commercial to its core, filled with images of sexy women and incipiently violent men, set in a mesmerizing time-space zone into which no social reality or cultural history dare intrude, it is, we are regularly reminded, the most menacing of cultural "beasts" yet to come slouching toward our already battered Bethlehem.

In spite of all this opprobrium, the thing keeps growing. No one denies that, having already transformed (and rejuvenated) the music industry, it has even, of late, given a shot in the arm to electoral politics. No less a lofty threesome than President Clinton,

Vice President Gore, and ABC anchor Peter Jennings made a point of showing up first and being televised at the MTV Inaugural Ball, the hottest ticket in Washington, D.C., during inaugural week, to press the flesh of the young video jockeys and fans who had been so instrumental in getting out the Democratic vote.

But wait a minute. If MTV is so apolitical, why was it at the center of national politics? If, for that matter, it's so hopelessly racist, sexist, and commercial, why has it been, more and more regularly, the platform for politically explosive rap and hip hop anthems from groups like Public Enemy and Arrested Development? If it's so unambiguously sexist, why has it produced the texts around which the most heated and vexed discussions—academic and popular—about feminism and sexual representation have taken place recently? (Whatever one thinks of Madonna and her academic supporters, or the many new all-female rap and punk groups yelling about sex and sexism in graphic terms, there is no doubt that MTV has been the site of an intense struggle over feminism and representation in which most women are somehow invested.)

And why, finally, in the greedy 1980s, when insider trading was the national sport on prime time and Wall Street, was it MTV that preserved what little there was of the culture of protest in the form of gala benefit concerts like Farm-Aid, Live-Aid, and the Sun City anti-apartheid event, which raised millions of dollars and at least some consciousness about the plight of those outside the glittery world of the Rich and Famous? (When I ask students to name one thing they didn't know about before TV brought it to their attention, the most common answer (followed by AIDS) is "the plight of the farmers," which they learned about through Farm-Aid. No surprise, really, when you consider how rarely poor, working people and their problems ever appear on TV news or drama.)

I'm not suggesting that MTV gets a wholly undeserved rap. MTV *is* most certainly commercial, often sexist, and a lot of other bad things. Its endless parade of half-clad women and fragmented female body parts; its scary glamorization of macho males, black and white, bragging about planned or past sexual exploits; and its driving need to valorize consumerism as the path to ecstasy; all these things are true and creepy.

But, for reasons I'd like to explore, MTV, more than most

forms, is also committed, for reasons beyond its owners' control, to promoting values that are far from conservative, politically or culturally. In fact—and this is why MTV is intriguing and important—it is the most contradictory of all successful commercial media today. MTV—rooted in the culture of rebellion out of which rock 'n' roll was born, yet committed to packaging and selling consumerism and the status quo—does a fascinating, sometimes dangerous little dance along the fault lines of corporate capitalism and reveals, in its often tacky way, just what we are up against when we talk about "cultural revolution" (if indeed any of us still do) in a postmodern, media-saturated world.

To get a handle on this textual kaleidoscope, we need to look at MTV in the context of the history of rock music. In fact, MTV, set up to deny the very concept of history (its famous man-on-the-moon logo boldly suggests to its viewers that history begins as a media event and then goes off in a chronology-defying spiral of endless, disconnected images), has evolved and changed quite dramatically and progressively in its brief 12 years, largely for political reasons its critics do not acknowledge.

Most MTV critics, members of the baby-boom generation for whom rock means the innocent 1950s and the counterculture 1960s (I'm not including here the many critics who simply dislike rock music for its "decadence" or whatever), assume that the serpent of commerce irrevocably tainted and corrupted previously pure culture and politics.

The most articulate, and moving, version of this narrative comes, not surprisingly, from Bob Dylan. A few years ago he said:

> The corporate world, when they figured out what [rock] was and how to use it, they snuffed the breath out of it and killed it. Used to be, they were afraid, you know, like "hide your daughters"...Elvis, Little Richard, Chuck Berry, they struck fear in the heart. Now they got a purpose, to sell soap, blue jeans, Kentucky Fried Chicken, whatever...it's all been neutralized, nothing threatening, nothing magical, nothing challenging...I had to see it, because you know it set me free, set the whole world on fire...There's a lot of us who still remember...

Anyone who came of age, politically, during the heady days of Woodstock, Vietnam, SDS, civil rights, and Women's Liberation knows what Dylan is talking about and, probably, shares his nostalgia. But this romanticized version of rock history is flawed. It ignores the importance of the social and political context in which rock, as oppositional culture, thrived, and the importance of mass, organized activism as a force that the corporate media have to respond to. Or, to put it another way, it idealizes the "purity" of the early days, as though, from the start, the industry and its values were not already central forces in the development of rock, without which there would have been no "rock culture."

Rock was never all that pure and virtuous; nor is it now a hopelessly crass batch of devil's candy. Now, as in the early days, it is a culturally and politically mixed bag. The current mass popularity of the alternative music movement called "grunge" is a perfect example of how the contradictions have always worked, from Elvis's and Dylan's times to ours. The kids who had been listening to Pearl Jam and Nirvana and the Red Hot Chili Peppers in garages and dinky clubs for years are now outraged that "their" music has been co-opted and commercialized by MTV and *Rolling Stone*—as outraged as Dylan is over his generation's earlier co-optation by Kentucky Fried Chicken. But co-optation is a misleading term. If one wants to be seen and heard in American culture, one must deal with agents, promoters, sponsors, and record and television companies. This has always been true of rock music, the bastard child of an illicit union between "people's music" of various kinds and industrial corporate capitalism.

From this perspective, MTV looks different. In fact, it is hard to sustain the argument that MTV "caused" the decline of rock as oppositional culture, or that it "caused" the total commercialization and degradation of that form. It's not as though, in 1981, the rest of the media were doing much better where commercialization, sexism, and violence were concerned. Those were, after all, the days of "Dallas," "Dynasty," "women in danger" slasher films, and the rise of blockbuster films about superheroes with special effects. What alternative music there was—mostly punk—was almost invisible to anyone over 20 and outside Manhattan. Those were dark days indeed for all of us, culturally and politically, and they only got worse as the decade went on.

Born in those dark and cynical days, it's no surprise that MTV reflected the most apolitical, commercial forces in the culture. It's founder, Robert Pittman, arrogantly and openly bragged of targeting a young, white male suburban audience and refused to air many videos by women or minority artists for commercial reasons. He hired VJs who were not allowed to say anything about anything, not even about the video clips they announced—which then were the only content aside from ads. The format of heavy rotation for very briefly popular songs fit the needs of the music industry, which gave the network free clips since they served as commercials for albums and concerts. It was, as critics said very quickly, an embarrassment to anyone who took rock seriously.

But—and I remember feeling this almost immediately when I saw it—MTV was also fascinating and exciting to watch, filled with bits of imaginative and creative visuals, both in the clips and in the irreverent, high-spirited graphics that changed as rapidly as the music. I couldn't take my eyes off of it for a long time, and there were some videos from those first years—Michael Jackson's "Beat It," Cindy Lauper's "Girls Just Wanna Have Fun," Tina Turner's "What's Love Got to Do with It?"—which seemed to me amazing, even then, for what they said about race, class, and gender, against the grain of the built-in structural forces meant to make these themes nonexistent.

As the years went, much has happened to change MTV for the better. As Lisa Lewis argues in her very smart book, *Voicing the Difference: Gender Politics and MTV*, women (like me) were watching, even if they weren't invited, and they began demanding more videos by and about them. Since their money was as good at the malls as their boyfriends', the network had to respond. Lewis charts the careers of Turner, Lauper, Madonna, and Pat Benatar and shows how each of these women was able to insert woman-identified, even feminist messages into a context of extreme sexism and conservatism because of the contradictions built into the structure of mass media: audiences matter and, in spite of much opinion to the contrary, they do not sit still for any old thing. Moreover, just as radical youth politics made it possible for groups like Crosby, Stills and Nash and Country Joe and the Fish to sing about protest and revolution on major labels in the 1960s, feminism—a force in the consciousness of almost every young girl today—made it possible for tough-talking, independent women to get on screen and rise to the top of the charts via videos.

That there are even as many politically conscious women as there are today is amazing, given the built-in sexism of rock culture. What is more understandable, however, is the amazing transformation of MTV where race is concerned. Almost blatantly racist at the start, MTV devotes whole programs to rap music and runs videos by black groups, including a growing number of feminist women's, like Salt 'n' Pepa, constantly. Pittman, culturally illiterate yuppie that he was, overlooked the fact that American popular music would not exist as we know it without the influence of black culture. To be a "rock" network and ignore black music would be suicidal. And so the network, built to sell jeans and acne cream, has been dragged kicking and screaming into the world of "Yo, MTV Raps!" with its vulgar (often sexually offensive and scary) tirades about life in the ghetto, complete with street scenes and graffiti that even Dylan would have to admit do a good job of "striking fear in the heart" of the white suburbanites Pittman originally courted.

For all the pressure to keep politics out, the fact remains that rock 'n' roll, as Dylan rightly notes, was born of rebellion and a utopian desire for freedom, and for the fulfillment of desires that this society represses. And MTV ultimately could do nothing to hide that fact that wouldn't also destroy it's own cash cow. That is what its critics either miss or ignore. As Andrew Goodwin observed in his study of MTV, *Dancing in the Distraction Factory*, the network was necessarily, from the start, "committed to the promotion of an alternative culture" (no matter how cynically or self-serving) and this commitment has forced it, in spite of itself, to "open up the political agenda on television, by using gatekeeping criteria that reflect the values of rock 'n' roll," values that are "romantic and oppositional" by definition.

Indeed, it is the logic of cable—from which MTV springs—to offer specialty programming for segments of the population not fully represented by network hegemonic images and ideas. That's why we have Christian Broadcasting and that's why we have MTV. It is MTV's success in rightly predicting a market for youth culture that has also caused it to expand and improve its original product. MTV was boring after a while. The endless stream of mindless, unanalysed videos could only sustain attention for a certain amount of time. This contradicts, to some extent, the "mind-numbing," "addictive" theories about TV that insist that viewers get hooked on the sameness of the format and can't break away. Today, on the contrary, MTV offers news; documentaries on issues such as race and homosexuality; a variety of 30 minute programs, among the most interesting of which is "Liquid TV," which airs some of the most creative animated features on television; and special features, including, of course, the charity/protest concerts mentioned earlier and the visits from candidates Clinton and Gore during the campaign, where they were questioned by college students.

Seen in this way, the model that presents rock as first "pure" and then "co-opted" is obviously simplistic. It is not so black and white a picture. Rather, MTV, like all pop culture, is contradictory and shifty, pushed and pulled by the forces of reaction and progress. And while the bad guys have most of the chips and veto power, they cannot totally ignore the demands of social movements and audiences. MTV matters, to my mind, not because it is "radical," or because it is "ours," but because it is the one place within media where the battle between "them" and "us" is most clearly being waged, and where we can measure how well we're doing.

If this seems like a crazy thing to say, I challenge you to watch the network—for a good long stretch of time—and note the presence of many things seen nowhere else on TV. Working-class and minority faces, voices, and scenes appear on MTV in ways which are positive and often rebellious; everywhere else they are shrouded in the ignominy of crime and servitude, or they are invisible. The news, around issues of prejudice and censorship especially, is read with a positive sneer of derision by MTV's Kurt Loder, while the Rathers and Jennings are telling the same sad stories with an authority-boosting tone of acceptance and inevitability. And the top bands—Arrested Development, Nirvana, Pearl Jam, and Red Hot Chili Peppers, to name a few of the ones worth listening to and thinking about—are as angry, as talented, and as culturally oppositional as the best new rock has always been.

But I am less interested in defending MTV than in reading a more serious message into its dubious strengths and obvious weaknesses. Rock and roll, or any other cultural form, is only as radical or oppositional as the social context in which it thrives. The corporate media hate opposition and suffer it only when they are forced to. It takes activism and empowerment to force the media to the left, and it always has. Kids today are yelling, "I want my MTV!" as the producers hoped they would. But they are also yelling a bit more than expected about what kind of MTV they want. And a lot of what they are demanding is less bleak than what we old New Lefties watch on VH-1 and PBS, with their sad-sack country and western revivals and tributes to Lawrence Welk.

Lifestyles, Trends, and Trash

Daytime Soaps: Where Time Stands Still

Those old enough to remember the tearful sighs and pregnant pauses of "Stella Dallas" and "One Man's Family" will feel that time has stood still on shows like "As the World Turns" and "All My Children." Here, premarital virginity, the nuclear family, and middle-class affluence are still the only acceptable, rewarding life styles, and Watergate, inflation, and the civil rights, anti-war, and women's movement never happened.

But while it's easy enough to laugh at the soap operas, it's not so easy to explain their popularity, which extends across age, class, and racial lines to include virtually every woman who has had to spend a lot of time at home. Since none of these women would defend the social or psychological realism of the soaps, I've always been fascinated by their appeal and its political implications. For that reason, I spent a week following two or three of them and found myself increasingly enraged and intrigued.

First the rage. Soap operas present the most blatant, heavy handed, and relentless propaganda for the nuclear family imaginable. They are geared to a captive audience of housewives and they intend to keep it that way. Stories and commercials alike present family life as the most meaningful and rewarding thing since organized religion. Within that context, women's work—cooking, cleaning, nursing, and worrying—is the mainstay of western civilization.

How do soap operas manage to project such a patently false picture of feminine experience and still keep women glued to their sets? Well, they make women's concerns seem terribly important in a world that usually treats them as anything but. Every crucial event, decision, and conflict takes place at home, usually in the kitchen. Criminal lawyers rush from their courtrooms and business magnates leave multi-million-dollar negotiations in the hands of lackeys to attend to the latest domestic crisis. The problems they rush home to are geared to the real concerns of women. Sexual relationships are the dramatic staple, with characters rotating partners endlessly. And the reason is clear: since emotional fulfillment and family responsibility are the highest values of private, domestic life, the greatest crises naturally occur when they are threatened.

Illness is the next most popular crisis. There wasn't a single program of the nine I watched in which a major character wasn't critically ill, and at least one other character wasn't a doctor or nurse. Illness is followed by crimes against individuals and natural catastrophes. Soaps present crisis and tragedy as strictly personal or accidental matters, the causes and solutions of which never involve social or economic factors.

In soap world, the range of characters is limited. All the men are doctors and lawyers, with an occasional police chief or millionaire thrown in for plot variety. And the women are wives and mothers. This is as true for the women doctors as for the housewives. And why not? The hospitals of daytime TV are really just convenient settings to play out human dramas with the largest number of characters plausibly available to participate. No social or even professional issues ever come up. Sickle cell anemia, for example, would be as out of place in a soap opera conversation as socialized medicine.

Taken as whole then, the world of soap operas projects a clear political message that is as simplistic as it is reactionary. First, there are no class differences. There are, of course, poor people and criminals, but they are defined not by their economic or social status but by their moral condition. They are either "good" or "bad." In fact, all behavior is seen as morally motivated. The girl from the wrong side of the tracks who schemes, lies, and cheats to get a man is simply an evil person. On one show, for example, at least four different characters, within two or three days, wondered whether the older man seeing this "evil" younger woman knew "what kind of *person* Rachel is?" Everyone lives in a spotless, elegant home, has a beautifully middle-class lifestyle, and is always, even when vacuuming, groomed and dressed to the nines.

But it's not what's left out that makes soap operas popular: it's what's put in. The main ingredient is love, love, love, and a very appealing king of love at that. Soap operas are the fairy tales of capitalism. Soap operas, unlike real life, fulfill women's need to be loved and appreciated. Every doctor, lawyer, and merchant chief thinks and acts solely for the benefit of the woman he loves. It is typical in a soap opera for a lawyer to look soulfully at a client and say, "I'm going to devote all my time to your case because I care about you so much."

Needless to say, this a far cry from the reality of sexual relations under capitalism, and an even farther cry from most other popular art. In movies like *The Godfather* and *Death Wish*, for example, women are brutalized, lied to, ignored, and worse. Supposedly exemplary, public real life isn't much better. No self-respecting soap opera politician would make the crass remark Rockefeller made about his wife' mastectomy: "Well, guys, you're not gonna believe this!" If Watergate had been a soap opera, women would never have been kidnapped, drugged, or mysteriously killed in plane crashes by wrong-doers who go unpunished. In fact, the entire drama would have been played out in the chambers of the wives and daughters.

As long as women's feelings, actions, and social contributions are not in their own names, not of their own choosing, and not acknowledged or rewarded, they will turn to soap operas, where women really have what we were all promised when we first heard "Cinderella."

It is the task of socialists and feminists to understand the justified needs that soap operas fulfill, and point out why they can never be attained in a society based on competition, greed, and sexual, racial, and class conflict.

The Politics of Soap Operas

A close look at the classic soap conventions and some recent profound changes in their treatment of women will explain a lot about how the media often manage to incorporate and co-opt positive social values into institutions that are unswervingly reactionary at heart.

On soaps, issues not easily discussed are often dramatized in useful, compassionate ways. A while back, a vain character in "Days of Our Lives" lost a breast to cancer. She and her fans went through the ordeal and learned of the many medical treatments as well as how to cope with the emotional trauma.

Recently, this educational aspect has gone further than usual, as many soaps—responding to the general sexual ferment created by feminism—have taken up taboo subjects. Rape, incest, wife battering, and changing sex roles have all turned up in recent scripts. On "Guiding Light," a young woman named Beth—long abused and ultimately raped by her stepfather—learned to feel rage, fight back, and seek help from a rape crisis center. She convinced her abused mother to accompany her, and the counselor presented sound advice and information from a feminist perspective.

The most interesting aspect of the episode concerned Beth's boyfriend Philip, who went through the typical male responses of disgust and sworn vengeance against the villain, before returning to comfort and support the victim and apologize for his male insensitivity. (ABC's *Something About Amelia* aired at the same time and treated the same issues far less adequately, yet ironically received much publicity and praise.)

Another criticism of typical male attitudes appeared in a recent episode of "Search for Tomorrow." A young journalist was raped by a co-worker who was angered by her professional skill and sexual rejection of him. She pressed charges, and then stood up to crass questioning by the police. Asked if she was ever married, she replied with a firm, "No." Asked next, "Were you a virgin at the time?" she replied, again, with a dignified, "No" and a withering, silencing stare.

Such episodes, and there are many of them, keep women watching and cheering. A young unemployed black man on "All My Children," for example, recently told off his macho friends who teased him for babysitting his son: "Raising a kid is the most important thing you can do, man," he insisted.

At this point some of the contradictions of the genre set in. Is it true, for example, that "raising a kid is the most important thing you can do?" And even if it is, where do all these feminist men come from?

Such males exist only in this very special, media-distorted part of "America." Soap actions rarely go beyond the town limits. Characters may visit "Chicago" or even a foreign country, but location footage is rarely shown.

In fact, soaps take place almost wholly indoors and in very few settings, for the most part. Kitchens, bedrooms, and living rooms are ever present. So are a few restaurants and clubs, a hospital, police station, and perhaps a corporate office. The only business transacted, even in public places, is personal. The curing of a disease, the scheming of a villain, or the kindness of a boss are the only things done "at work." The reason for this oddly limited vision is that the prime values and concerns of most women—long confined to the private sphere and now tracked into stereotypically female jobs—have been formed by personal, domestic responsibilities. And it is the great trick of soaps to create an entire universe dominated by these values—indeed to pretend that all of capitalism is run by them.

In a world of perfect doctors, lawyers, and merchant chiefs, a world in which good people rose to power and ran things fairly and humanely, feminist demands would be met quite automatically.

But capitalism isn't fair or humane. It is run by the values of the public sphere of commerce and global conquest. And most popular culture is quite blatant in glamorizing and promoting these brutal values. Is it any wonder, then, that so many prefer these daytime fantasies of a gentler world?

Solace in Soapland

So what do you do when things get really bad? When your checkbook won't balance, your relationship is on the rocks, your job may be phased out, your kids are threatening to run away, or worse, to never move out, and the headlines are giving you nightmares and indigestion? Most of our traditional escapes from such moments have been discredited. Drugs, alcohol, chocolate, shopping, sex—you name it, it's forbidden these days at risk of jail, death, or, at best, a Twelve-Step Program.

Never mind. There is hope—daytime soap operas, where the air is pure, the money flows into your bank account automatically, and most people have a profound capacity for intimacy, compassion, and emotional growth—or are quick studies.

Soap operas are among the most popular and lucrative of all popular culture forms. Women of all ages, and an increasing number of men and children, for that matter, watch them religiously, staying loyal to a favorite show for years and passing on their particular rituals to later generations like family cookie recipes. The growing number of fan magazines like *Soap Opera Digest*, the increasing number of prime-time award shows for the genre, and the growing fad of college students—male and female alike—watching favorite shows together are clear signs of that. But, while you're likely to overhear private discussions of favorite soaps in office cafeterias, school corridors, and dentists' waiting rooms, most soap fans, in less "safe" environments, are likely to deny their guilty pleasure and even to join in the mockery and denigration that is the standard "official" attitude toward soaps.

Never mind, soap lovers, it's time to come out of the closet. Repeat after me: "it is not a sign of dementia, stupidity, or intellectual laziness to like soap operas." In fact, there are very good reasons for preferring the company of soap characters to one's usual daily routine, especially for women. As fantasies go, the ones presented by soaps are extremely seductive. They offer a lot of things that most of us need and desire but don't get much of in reality. The men on soaps, for one thing, are infinitely supportive and available, living for the women in their lives and never forgetting to buy flowers, gifts, and plan surprise parties for their loves. The women on soaps, even single working women, have beautifully furnished homes, professionally coiffed hair, and the most stylish, expensive wardrobes you've ever drooled over in *Vogue*. Good friends and functional families are pretty much a given for anyone who wants them. Which, in Soapland, is everyone, even the villains, who always have at least one or two understanding supporters who believe in their ability to reform.

And—contrary to popular opinion—soaps are more intelligent and progressive in their treatment of personal and social issues than most of what passes for "serious" fiction, film, and prime time television. Amidst the current furor over date rape, for example, it is interesting to note that this topic has almost never been treated (as a problem as opposed to an accepted style of courting) in movies or on prime time. But in the last several years, at least two soaps have treated the issue from a decidedly feminist perspective, at great length and in some psychological and social detail. In both cases, the victim was a lover of the rapist, a woman whose past (as is inevitable on soaps, the most sexually graphic shows on the air) was certainly checkered. In both cases the jury, realistically, acquitted the man. And, in both cases, he saw the light (in one case after witnessing a gang rape and realizing, at last, the horror of his deed), confessed, and set about working with other sexual violators in treatment programs!

As long as relationships make the world go round and money and power are trivial afterthoughts, feminism can, conceivably, triumph. And if that's absurd, so be it. Realism offers cold comfort these days.

I could go on almost endlessly with similar examples of feminist story lines and influences. Media scholar George Gerbner has documented that the single greatest source of medical information in America is soap operas, which religiously present information and advice about things like breast cancer, venereal disease, drug and alcohol abuse, and other medical problems. A few years ago, when the AIDS crisis broke, one soap actually had professionals from treatment programs appear as characters on the show and run a town meeting to inform people and correct misinformation.

Soaps are also particularly good at helping people deal with tough issues in their daily lives that arise from changing mores, often brought about by the demands and successes of the Women's Movement. What a half-hour sitcom will, at best, cautiously mention and moralize about superficially, a soap will often treat for months on end, involving perhaps 30 different characters in endless discussions and raising many different points of view, representing the many angles that tough issues engender.

When black and white characters fall in love, for example, it is likely that everyone in town will discuss and argue about it and that popular characters will start off as downright bigots and gradually, through persuasion by friends as well as the dramatic examples set by the loving couple themselves, come to change their views. And because audiences so identify with and respect their favorite characters on these shows—after all, they've "known" them for years and visit them daily—the characters who represent unpopular but progressive ideas gradually gain audience sympathy and support, as first one and then another of the town Fathers and Mothers and Elected Officials come to their senses.

The most remarkable example of this process happened several years ago, on "All My Children," when a regular character, a young woman with many scars from the heterosexual relationship wars (a given on soaps), got a crush on the woman who was treating her daughter for emotional problems. The therapist, an "out and proud" lesbian, was a model of dignity and integrity and, gradually, as everyone watched and talked, and talked and watched, the parents of the young woman went from horror to acceptance. After all, on soaps, it's love that matters and "good" characters eventually recognize healthy love when they see it.

Of course, nothing came of this relationship. We aren't in feminist heaven, after all. But this was no small thing, nonetheless. And I bet you are hearing about it here for the first time. That's because, as I said, people don't usually take soaps seriously enough to write about them or talk about them in highbrow discussions of "the horrors of mass culture."

But this doesn't mean these shows don't affect public opinion. They certainly do. I have no doubt at all that the initial reaction of outrage on the part of so many women at the accusations of sexual harassment against Clarence Thomas—and the way in which this reaction took the Senate Judiciary Committee by surprise—had a lot to do with the fact that women were emotionally primed to take this issue very seriously. Unlike the aging white men in Congress, who follow *The New York Times* and "The MacNeil-Lehrer News Hour" but wouldn't deign to watch "Days of Our Lives," they had been participating, vicariously, in all sorts of dramatic presentations over the years in which feminist assumptions and values are increasingly taken for granted as "common sense." Soap fans know a male chauvinist pig when they see one.

There are a couple of reasons why soaps treat women's issues more seriously than more "highbrow" art forms. Most obviously, soaps cater to a largely female audience targeted by the sponsors—the guys who pay the bills—as the major consumers of household products like cake mix, aspirin, and yes, soap. And women—as the guys who do the marketing research for sponsors and networks are paid to know—have, in the decades since feminism hit the cultural scene, come to think about things very differently from their pre-1960s foremothers. Issues like rape, domestic violence, sexual harassment, incest—the list goes on—are taken very seriously by female audiences these days, because of feminism, and sponsors know and respect that.

Of course, these issues also show up on prime time and in movies and novels, but not as emphatically—trust me. And that's because, for better or worse, soaps are a female ghetto that those in power (read men) don't take seriously or worry about too much. You won't hear Ted Koppel leading lofty discussions of the date rape incidents on "Santa Barbara" or "All My Children" (both of which took place years ago). But women all over America discussed these cases passionately.

But it's not just as audiences that women with feminist ideas influence soaps. Another effect of feminism has been to push women increasingly into professional work previously done by men. Television, a medium with less status than film or print journalism, and less rigid "old boy network" exclusiveness, has proven more fertile ground for women in creative fields. (The number of women film directors and hard news correspondents, for example, can be counted easily.) Television has been easier for women to get into than other media. But even in the looser television world, prime time is infinitely more male-dominated than daytime, for obvious reasons. The best place for ambitious, creative women to begin as writers, directors, and actresses, then, is daytime TV—especially soaps and talk shows. And so, we have an interesting situation: a daytime ghetto peopled and watched by women while the big guys—they still don't get it—tear their hair out over the significance of Murphy Brown's pregnancy. (Women on soaps have been bearing and raising children alone forever.)

Okay, you're thinking, if soaps are so hot, how come when I check them out they seem so incredibly stupid? You've asked the right question. The answer is, because they are. And here's where the question of realism comes in. As a culture, we have come to equate quality with "true-to-lifeness." We buy our kids books with titles like *Uncle Jim Gets AIDS*, which explain, simply and antiseptically, how such tragedies occur, and we steer them away from "upsetting" fantasies like *Hansel and Gretel* in which two kids, abandoned by their horrible parents, successfully battle a wicked witch and stick her in an oven.

And we proudly assert that shows such as "L.A. Law" and "Thirtysomething" are "the only TV I watch" because—like *Uncle Jim Gets AIDS*—they are simplistic but "realistic." Daytime soaps, like

Hansel and Gretel, are incredibly unrealistic. They are also—in both cases—melodramatic, violent, intense, extreme in their portrayals of both good and evil, danger and pleasure. And that is their great appeal and their great virtue. (Who ever accused Shakespeare of being unrealistic, Wagner of being melodramatic or emotionally extreme?)

I raise the issue of children's drama because the analogy to women's drama is important. The appeal of *Hansel and Gretel* is that it allows children to fantasize being so powerful that they can survive abusive, negligent parents, and, if things get too scary, even kill them. Soaps have the same appeal. They create fantasy worlds in which women are all powerful, in which men and male institutions, like banks, corporations, the FBI and CIA, are shadowy structures in the background of life, while the really important people and institutions are women and women's arenas—houses (especially kitchens and bedrooms), boutiques, restaurants, health clubs. Of course everyone works on soaps, but workplaces, like everything else, are totally dominated by traditionally female values, values that women, in sexist societies, are socialized to maintain but that—except in the fantasy worlds of soaps—are in fact given little real importance or power.

It is this total lack of social realism that allows soaps to present the most progressive feminist storylines on television while at once—and here's where they are totally contradictory and wacky—presenting a vision of political and economic life that is downright feudal in its reactionary nature. You can't have everything. The trade-off for presenting a kind of women's utopia in which traditional female values run the show is that all larger issues—inequality, poverty, foreign policy, and militarism, whatever—are ignored or sugar-coated to fit the most asinine Reaganesque "City on a Hill" scenario the Great Communicator ever dreamed up. But then, "realistically" it couldn't be any other way, could it? Only by ignoring the realities of the marketplace and global conflicts—the male concerns that really run the show—could we possibly envision a world in which traditional feminine values—caring, sharing, communication, intimacy, neighborliness, and so on—could be seen as socially determinate.

And so we have a female fairy world where dreams come true and everyone lives in castles, or at least visits regularly. Everyone on soaps lives in a small town that is pretty much run by two corporate patriarchs who employ everyone in the town and whose extended families of relatives and loyal employees intermarry and reproduce endlessly. That's why you have all those long explanatory sentences about who's been married and divorced and in bed with whom. If you miss a week or two the musical beds are likely to have been rescrambled any number of times, leaving assorted offspring in danger of unwittingly committing incest or betraying family loyalties at every turn.

People on soap operas are not concerned with race or class difference. Such things just don't matter in Emotion Land. Like the Smurfs and Care Bears, soap characters judge people strictly on moral grounds: are they Good or Bad? Moreover, when a Bad character becomes popular (this often happens), she or he is likely to undergo a rapid character transformation. Suddenly, a lying, scheming would-be murderer becomes a caring, self-sacrificing pillar of virtue. At which point, he or she is given a job as vice president of one of the town multinationals and soon runs for mayor. It happens a lot.

Doctors, lawyers, and cops are the only other people in these towns. Oh, except for the people who run the local meeting places—restaurants and clubs, boutiques, hair salons, and, recently, health clubs. People on soap operas eat out a lot. They also shop and visit a lot. And they are notorious for using any old excuse to throw a masked ball or gala dinner dance at which everyone gets to wear elaborate gowns and coiffures and someone ends up dead in the swimming pool while everyone else was sneaking off to the bushes to commit adultery or plan and scheme someone else's downfall.

Weddings and holidays are equally popular and elaborate. No one who watches soap operas need fear the holiday season. Christmas, Thanksgiving, even Valentine's Day will be filled with warmth, companionship, and a suitable moral message from one of the Good Fathers even for those who are home alone. That's one of the big appeals of the genre. It does not desert you when times get tough. You or anyone in the cast, for that matter. People who go through crises and tragedies—which are the narrative mainstays of soaps—do not suffer alone. They are visited, cajoled out of their misery, befriended by former enemies, and ulti- mately—even when their misfortune is of their own doing—reintegrated into the community, reformed, and, in short order, remarried or at least in love.

This sense of community and warmth prevailing, even in the worst of times, is obviously one of the major draws of daytime soaps. We live in an age when more and more of us simply have no sense of community, no family gatherings that are not themselves causes of trauma, and no support systems during times of need, and in which—worse yet—our troubles are multiplying. In and out of the home, on the streets, in the political arena, at work, things are scary. Pine Valley, on the other hand, is never scary in that generalized, free-floating way. Evil is contained in the persons of specific evil people and it is invariably thwarted either through the banishment of the bad guy or his or her (at least temporary) reformation.

In this insane world, anything, obviously, is possible, as long as it concerns personal, emotional life. And since feminist issues for the most part do concern emotional and sexual matters, it is easy to see that they can be incorporated into the soap world and negotiated in ways that promote happiness and justice. As long as we stay in the world of economic and political fantasy, gender justice can, conceivably, exist. If love, rather than money and missiles, made the world go round, after all, women would be in pretty good shape.

And so it goes in the strange world of American media and politics. Life is a trade-off and what's touted as "good for you"—like socially realistic prime time drama and "pro-social" kiddie fare—is generally pretty thin stuff, stuff so marginally progressive, so cautious and grudging in its lip service to the real needs and desires of children and other weaker folk, like women, that it is insulting. (For every "positive" message about women's rights I've seen on "L.A. Law," I've suffered through a dozen smirky little sexual "jokes" and inanities, offered as "liberated" but really meant to assuage the prurient tastes of male audiences and producers. Remember the transvestite lawyer? The secret sexual device that made the less-than-classically attractive Stuart an instant lady killer?)

But if you're willing to swallow your college-girl (or -boy) highbrow values and go where MacNeil and Lehrer have never tread, if you're willing to suspend your disbelief and jump into the swamp of outrageously unrealistic and corny daytime drama, your "inner child" will thank you and so will the other kids in the house. After all, it was Nancy Drew and Wonder Woman, not June Cleaver, that inspired us to dream of a better world for women, back in the 1940s and 1950s. And I'm willing to bet you Clarence Thomas's porn collection that little girls today are collecting more dangerous attitudes from the amazingly tough and powerful women on "Guiding Light" than Steven Bochco and Norman Lear have dreamed up in their entire collective lifetimes.

Oprah, Phil, and Sally

"On Oprah today: Women who sleep with their sisters' husbands!"

"Donahue talks to women married to bisexuals!"

"Today—Sally Jessy Raphael talks with black women who have bleached their hair blond!"

These are only three of my personal favorites of a recent television season. Everyone's seen these promos and laughed at them. "What next?" we wonder to each other with raised eyebrows. And yet, these daytime talk shows are enormously popular and—more often than we like to admit—hard to stop watching once you start.

The personal is ever more political, and inquiring minds not only want to know, they need to know. Or at least they need to talk about and listen to these things. And so the coming of daytime talk shows, a financial gold mine for the media and sensationalized, trivialized "political" television for confused and frightened people everywhere.

The political roots of this form are apparent. In structure and in subject matter, they take their cues from an important political institution of the 1960s: the women's consciousness-raising movement. In those small consciousness-raising groups, through which hundreds of thousands of women passed during a highly charged four- or five-year period starting in about 1968, women invented a democratic, emotionally safe way of uncovering things we never spoke of before.

Of course, the purpose of these consciousness-raising groups was political empowerment. The idea that the personal was political meant developing strategies for social change. We hoped that when previously isolated and privatized women recognized the common sources of our unhappiness in the larger political world, together we could organize to change things.

The words "political" and "organize" are not, of course, uttered on daytime TV. The primary goal of television talk shows is to sell curious audiences products, not make revolution. Thus the circus-like atmosphere and the need for bizarre and giggle-inducing topics and participants.

Still, feminism (and other social and cultural movements) did influence the form, and thus the results are more interesting and contradictory. Donahue, Oprah, and pals have reproduced, in a plasticized format, groups of people who share deeply personal and significant matters with others in the same boat.

In line with the democratic thrust of 1960s feminism, the structure of these shows approaches the nonhierarchical. The host is still the star, of course. But in terms of authority, she or he is far from central. The physical set enforces this fact. Audiences and participants sit in the round, and—this is the only TV format in which this happens—speak out, sometimes without being called on. They yell at each other and at the host, disagree with experts, and come to no authoritative conclusions. There is something exhilarating about watching people who are usually invisible—because of class, race, gender, and status—having their say and, often, being wholly disrespectful to their "betters."

The discussion of black women with blond hair, for example, ignited a shouting match between those who thought blond-haired black women wanted to "be white," and those who insisted they should be judged no differently from white women who dye their hair or tan their bodies. The audience, selected from the black community, took issue with everything that was said. Participants and audience members attacked the "expert," a black writer committed to "Black is Beautiful."

This is as close to open discourse on serious issues as television gets. But it is only possible because the issues discussed are not taken seriously by those in power. And that is why the sensationalism of these shows is double-edged. If they were more respectable in their style and choice of issues, they'd be reined in more. By seeming frivolous and trashy, they manage to carry on often serious discussions without being cut off the air or cleaned up.

This may seem contradictory, but it's not. The truth is that the fringy, emotional matters raised by Oprah, Donahue, Sally, and others are almost always related in some way to deep cultural and structural problems in our society. Most of us, obviously, wouldn't go on these shows and spill our guts and open ourselves to others' judgments. But the people on these shows are an emotional vanguard, blowing the lid off the idea that America is anything like the place Ronald Reagan pretended to live in.

A typical recent program, for instance, featured a predictably weird ratings lure as its topic: Families Who Date Prisoners. It featured a family of sisters, and some other women, who sought out relationships with convicts. The chance for humor at guests' expense was not spared; Procter & Gamble doesn't care if people watch just to feel superior, as long as they watch. But in the course of the program, important political points came out.

Two issues were of particular interest. The "expert," a psychologist, pushed the proto-feminist line that these women had low self-esteem—they were "women who love too much." Some admitted to it. Others, however, refused to accept that analysis, at least in their own cases. They stressed the prejudice against prisoners in society and went on to discuss the injustices of the criminal-justice system and to insist that their men were good people who had either made a mistake or were treated unfairly by the courts.

Our discomfort, on watching what seems to be gross exhibitionism, is understandable. As children we are taught not to air our dirty laundry in public. We learn to be hypocritical and evasive, to keep our tragedies and sorrows secret, to feign shock when a public official is exposed for his or hers. It is not easy for most of us to reveal difficulties to neighbors. The result of this decorum is isolation, which keeps us frightened and alone, unwilling to seek out help or share problems.

And so we sit at home, from Omaha to Orlando, and watch Oprah in order to get some sense of what it all means and how we might begin to handle it, whatever it is. These talk shows are safe. They let it all hang out. They don't judge anyone. They don't get shocked by anything. They admit they don't know what's right or wrong for anyone else. They are, for many people, a great relief.

Let me give one final example of how these shows operate as forums for opposing views. A recent segment of "Donahue" concerned women and eating disorders. It was a gem. Apparently, Phil had not yet understood that women suffer and die from eating disorders. Nor had he grasped that eating disorders are a feminist issue, the result of sexist stereotypes imposed upon women who want to succeed at work or love.

Donahue's approach was to make light of the topic. His guests were actresses from Henry Jaglom's film *Eating*, which concerns women, food, and body image, and he teased them about their own bouts with food compulsions. After all, they were all beautiful and thin. How bad could it be?

First the call-in audience, then the studio audience, and finally the actresses themselves rebelled. Women called in to describe tearfully how they had been suicidal because of their weight. Others rebuked the host's frivolous attitude. Still others offered information about feminist counseling services and support groups. And finally, one by one, the celebrities rose to tell their stories of bulimia, anorexia, self-loathing, many with tears streaming down their faces.

Donahue was chastened and, I think, a bit scared.

Ted Koppel would never have allowed such a thing to happen. He would have several doctors, sociologists, or whatever, almost all of them white and male, answer *his* questions about what medical and academic professionals know about eating disorders. There would be no audience participation and very little dialogue among guests. Certainly none would yell or cry or show any other "excessive" emotional involvement in the matter. If they did, Koppel, the smoothest of network journalists, would take control and redirect the show. Only when a subject is deemed nationally important by the media gatekeepers will it ever get on "Nightline," anyway. Daytime is less cautious.

I have been stressing the positive side of these shows primarily because of their differences from their highbrow, prime-time counterparts, which are far more reactionary. Given the grand scheme of things as they are, these arenas of ideological interaction and open-endedness are a good thing.

But, ultimately, these shows are a dead end, and they're meant to be. They lead nowhere but to the drug store for more Excedrin. What's most infuriating about them is not that they are sleazy or in bad taste. It is that they co-opt and constrain real political change. They are all talk and no action. Unless someone yells something from the floor (as a feminist did during the eating discussion), there's no hint of the world of political action, or of politics at all.

This makes perfect sense. Mass media, in a contradictory social environment, take on progressive ideas once they gain strength and contain them in the large, immobilizing structure of the political status quo.

We are allowed to voice our woes. We are allowed to argue, cry, shout, whatever. We are even allowed to hear about approved services and institutions that might help with this or that specific bruise or wound. But we are not allowed to rock the political or economic boat of television by suggesting that things could be different. That would rightly upset the sponsors and network heads. Who would buy their Excedrin if the headaches of American life went away?

Romance Novels and Female Fantasy

Have you ever wondered what's inside those seductive-looking paperback romances that seem to be multiplying like fruitflies in supermarkets, newsstands, and drugstores across the country?

In the scant three years that U.S. publishers—green-eyed over the multinational empire built by the tiny Canadian Harlequin publishing house—have been printing them, pulp romances have become the hottest item in the trade. In 1988, they accounted for a full 45 percent of all paperback sales. *Publishers Weekly* estimates that 22 million women read them regularly.

In all, there are close to 200 new romance titles printed monthly in the United States. Most mass-market paperback houses have several marginally different lines, and the major "brands" are marketed through mail-order subscriptions, which bring four to six new titles to your door each month.

Janet Daily, the secretarial school graduate who has written over 75 romances, is among the four best-selling authors of all time. In dollars and cents, that makes her one of the top-earning women in the nation. In fact, the apparent sky's-the-limit appetites of U.S. romance readers have created a seller's market for untrained neophytes.

Even the public schools are selling them. The major educational materials distributors—Scholastic and Xerox—push four different series of pulp romances for "the 12- to 15-year-old girl" in school libraries and classrooms everywhere.

Once the kids are hooked on this sugary "homework," it's a short walk to the supermarket where they can pig out on a variety of similarly schlocky confections at about $1.50 a read. So, while schools are increasingly being pressured to cut such "offensive" authors as Kurt Vonnegut and Mark Twain, school board and local business leaders are filling the slack with the less "controversial," easier-to-sell junk.

And it is easy to sell. Where a typical quality adolescent title will get a first printing of 7,500, the teen romances go as high as 200,000. Simon and Schuster laid out $1.4 million for its first-year First Love advertising budget, and hasn't regretted a penny.

Having established the financial and cultural impact of this trend, the question of what's inside may seem more intriguing. The prose, as one might guess, runs from turgid to unreadable: the intellectual and emotional content, from corny to farcical. The plots religiously follow the one- or two-paragraph guidelines sent on "tip sheets" to would-be authors. And while very popular new forms—teen romances and explicitly sexual romances—diverge from the classic romances in many ways, they manage to convey the same basic message.

First comes the classic European Harlequin Romance, the model from which all U.S. varieties diverge: it features a young—no more than 18-year-old—virgin/heroine, who falls for a worldly, forbidding, mysterious older man with a name like Devil Haggard or Damien Savage (really) and a character to match. The girl—pure and devoted to Love—manages to transform him from cruel, sardonic, and morbid to a melting lump of love-sick putty, while still remaining a virgin.

When U.S. publishers picked up the form, they simply switched the heroine to a contemporary U.S. virgin and took it from there. The hero was still older, often European, and vaguely cruel and mysterious.

The essence of this genre is the "otherness" of the opposite sex in sexist society. The essential inscrutability and insensitivity of the typical male, in a society where power inequalities and the sexual division of labor make communication, respect, and sharing all but impossible, is portrayed as almost mystically romantic and sexually attractive. The logic-defying fantasy makes an unbearable situation seem thrilling. The heroine breaks through the "mystery" of the male to discover a wholly unlikely "inner" man whom she alone can bring out. Such is the fantasy of female "power" in a male world. And such is the fantasy that keeps women believing in a magical "transformation" in their own male partners.

The need for new markets, and the realities of contemporary female life, led to the development of the most recent and potentially significant forms of romance—the teen and the explicitly sexual. Twentieth-century high school girls do not succumb to cruel, mysterious strangers and live happily ever after in Gothic castles. And adult women, who have lived through the economic and cultural changes of the last decades, find such fantasies even harder to swallow. Women now have "careers," lovers, and consciousnesses raised by *Ms.* magazine. The new romances incorporate all these things. Both varieties cleverly manage to maintain the essence of the classic form despite seemingly drastic changes.

The teen romances are nothing if not mundane. To quote the various, almost identical, "tip sheets," they feature a 16-year-old heroine who is "an ordinary small town or suburban middle-class school girl, with a family to match." Divorce and working women have crept into the scene recently, but, in various ways, these subjects have been made to fit the general "moral" strictures. The love interest must be "no more than two years older." The plot must dramatize "the first meaningful romantic interlude in a young girl's life." And there must be "no explicit sex, only feelings of attraction and kissing."

All of this is treated in terms of a misleadingly enlightened rhetoric. "Being oneself," following one's "inner instincts," and turning away from snobbery or pure materialism are big in these books. The hitch is that snobbery and materialism are merely matters of degree, since clothes, looks, and popularity are all-important. The even bigger hitch is that "finding oneself" and following one's "inner instincts" is somehow always determined in terms of boys' approval.

In this way, the teen romances, through careful sleight-of-hand, reproduce the "Men and Love are All" theme, while denying it in their rhetoric. It's easy to be against snobbery in a middle-class suburb where there is no poverty. And for all the talk about "good values" and "independent thinking," looks and popularity remain the only real rivals to "Him" in the heroines' life priorities.

The new, sexually explicit romances are even cleverer at confusing "social" ideas and values. They all—Dell Ecstasy, Silhouette Desire, and Second Chance at Love are typical—feature "women of 26 to 45" who are "sexually experienced" and "have important meaningful work." Typically, the heroine and hero clash over that work. A civil engineer fights her boss about procedures. In the end, the man comes around. The engineer agrees to marry the boss when he agrees to let her travel and pursue her career.

The "issues," then, as in teen romances, are smoke screens covering the "Love is All" theme. Even sex—graphic, and at times even erotic—is removed from social reality. There is no pillow talk, no sense of sex as an integral part of a whole relationship. It's pure pleasure and perfection—in a word, fantasy.

In both the teen and sex romances, the males are, on the surface, very different from those in classic romance. They are gentle, supportive, and more Robert Redford than Heathcliff. But they are not less preposterous for that. They are sill wealthy, handsome, and glamorous. And they still fall for the "little me" heroine and change everything in their lives and habits when they do. They are adoring and giving, 24 hours a day.

The Love idea is not the most interesting aspect of romances, because it's so obvious. What helps explain its pull is the fantastic social (or asocial) context in which it occurs. These books create a universe of luxury, sensuality, pleasure, and fulfillment that is wholly self-involved and private. And love is only the main ingredient. The heroines spend as much time on clothes, restaurants, travel, and furnishings as on men.

What's lost in aristocratic elegance and luxury is made up for in capitalist, consumerist elegance and luxury. Substitute brand names for titles, soap opera doctors for Heathcliff, and you've got it.

One could say of romances what Marx once said of religion: for women, they simultaneously symbolize "real suffering and the protest against that suffering." They acknowledge and address the very real emptiness of women's lives and create a fantasy world that seems to fill that emptiness with spiritual and emotional fulfillment. But like religion and its dream of heaven, they deny and obscure the economic and political factors that have created the emptiness and put forth, instead of political solutions, a never-never land of fantastic happiness.

Tupperware and Women

My first experience with Tupperware and "Tupperware parties" came when I and my family moved to a new neighborhood where we hoped to do community organizing. Although we were in some ways an unusual family—a female college teacher and a male cab driver, both of whom were known to be politically active in feminist and union organizing—we, and our two school-age children, were welcomed to the neighborhood. Since the women in the neighborhood interacted socially and helped each other with child care, my children and I became involved in a certain amount of neighborhood activity.

It was only natural that I would be invited to a Tupperware party held at my next-door neighbor's house, and only natural that I would attend. Indeed, I soon found that Tupperware and Tupperware parties were a regular part of the community life of the neighborhood women, serving various functions and fulfilling various needs, the least of which was the use of plastic food containers.

Tupperware parties were a women's institution in many working-class urban and suburban communities. Many women loved to go to them. And in many cases, when extra income was needed, women, especially working-class housewives, chose to sell Tupperware over other available job options. There were many reasons for this, starting with the pleasure of attending the parties, and ranging through various economic and cultural aspects of Tupperware as a corporation and a social institution.

Entering a Tupperware party, one immediately felt a sense of comfortable anticipation. About 15 to 20 women would be chatting pleasantly in a relaxed manner. Most already knew each other from the neighborhood and other parties. Some had at least seen each other around. Parties were never held more than a few blocks from any guest's home. A hostess, to insure a successful party, may have invited one or two friends or relatives from further away, but this was not common. Parties were intentionally organized around neighborhood networks for several reasons. First, it was easy for women to get to a neighbor's house. Second, women saw the socializing with neighbors and getting to know new people as a major advantage of attending. And finally, the ethnic, geographic, and class similarities of the women made the atmosphere familiar. During the pre-party socializing people discussed local issues, such as school problems and food prices, and shared light gossip, political and personal.

Most of the women were working-class housewives who didn't get much chance to go out. They spanned three generations—from young mothers in their late teens to grandmothers who had attended Tupperware parties for 30 years. Clothing ranged from synthetic knit pant suits and tightly curled hair, to jeans and long, loose hair. (The dealer, on the other hand, was always dressed in a business-like fashion. Older guests had been known to complain about sloppily dressed dealers.) Most guests, if they worked outside the family at all, usually did work in their homes typing, doing laundry, or running play groups for working mothers.

The official party began with some games, chosen or invented by the dealer, which served to break the ice and help women open up to each other. Much had been made of how silly and insulting these Tupperware party games were. The participants themselves clearly enjoyed them. When I asked questions about the negative image of Tupperware parties, people were straightforward, taking pride in the ability to be silly and have fun, in contrast to the "snobs," "phonies," and "stuffed shirts" who they imagined made these remarks.

After the games, the dealer, who had already met with the hostess to plan the physical layout and arrange the display table, began the demonstration. Since most guests were regular party-goers, emphasis was placed on new items and original uses for standard items. The dealer herself was invariably poised, articulate, pleasant, and often witty. She had a major advantage: she believed in what she was selling. Tupperware plastic containers, while priced slightly higher than other conventional brands, are in fact superior. They keep food fresh for long periods of time, are dishwasher safe and guaranteed for life. So rare was product failure that the dissatisfied customer received two items in replacement.

Since the products did last, the market was satiable and selling depended on factors other than need. On the average, a woman may have attended two parties a year and purchased two to four items. I saw kitchen cabinets and refrigerators literally filled with Tupperware containers holding items that often were merely transferred from store packages to containers. Greater freshness was one factor ("Rich people don't buy Tupperware," one woman told me. "They think nothing of throwing out two pork chops. But when your husband's laid off and your furnace breaks you need to save every penny you can."); the other was that Tupperware was a way of life. Many women simply enjoyed the parties and therefore continued to buy. Indeed, Tupperware relied almost entirely on word of mouth and neighborhood networking for its sales. Almost no advertising was done. Moreover, almost all the work was done by dealers and consumers themselves. At the product demonstrations, old-timers chirped in with personal testimonials to help the dealer out. "My kids love to play with the stacking canisters. It teaches them spatial relationships." "My husband makes block ice in the square keeper." "I never buy packaged snacks anymore. We make loads of popcorn and it keeps all week in the giant canister."

There was virtually no paper work or distribution done by the company. After the games and demonstration, order blanks were handed out. While the hostess set up the refreshments, the dealer took her seat at a card table, set up in advance, and collected order blanks and money. Customers not only filled out their own order blanks and paid in advance, but they also went to the dealer's home to pick up their merchandise, after the dealer had picked it up from the distributor.

The hostess' part in the party was to invite her friends and relatives, provide refreshments—as much as four or five homemade cakes and jello molds—and help coordinate activities. For this, she received a gift from the dealer, who also provided the game prizes.

A successful party could bring in $150 to $200, of which the dealer kept 25 percent. The dealer also hoped to recruit new hostesses. I spoke to women who organized as many as nine parties in a single week. At other times, of course, they chose not to work at all.

It was also the dealer's responsibility to recruit new dealers to the "Tupperware family." A dealer who recruited five new dealers from her area became a group manager and was entitled to more money and fringe benefits, including a station wagon and gas.

Social factors, prizes, and personal self-esteem were obvious and important motivating factors for the dealers. Indeed, I rarely saw any group of women quite so confident and self-assured. Dealers were terrific organizers. They believed in their products and they liked their work and their customers. Since the lines between consumer and seller were blurred, recruiting went on as a part of the selling. Honest and mutual respect were built into the structure.

The importance of good feeling, self-respect, and mutual enjoyment was apparent when the official parties ended and socializing began. Many participants and dealers stayed, as late as 2 a.m. at times, laughing, gossiping, and sharing experiences.

This was one of the few social, non-family activities these women engaged in in which they didn't hesitate to stay out late. Their husbands knew where they were and approved. They were in the neighborhood, away from men, and engaging in activities thoroughly integrated into their roles as wives and mothers. Indeed, this attitude on the part of their families was another major reason why some women chose Tupperware over other ways of earning extra income. On the surface at least, Tupperware was no threat to the traditional marriage. A dealer made her own schedule, worked as little or as much as she chose, and always stayed safely within the feminine stereotype.

And yet, in subtle ways, a woman's life was changed when she became a dealer. She gained confidence in her abilities and earning power. She began to make demands on her husband and children to do more around the house. And she began to relate to other women as co-workers. This was why it was so easy to recruit dealers out of parties. Whatever the popular image of the "Tupperware lady," the reality, to those involved, was totally different.

In Pittsburgh, steel workers' wives were common in Tupperware circles. I met many wives of salesmen and insurance agents, too. For practical reasons, related to the product as well as the structure of the work, women with strong, traditional family ties predominated. Pittsburgh has a heavily Catholic population, largely of Slavic background, and this was the predominant base of the Tupperware dealers. Virtually no blacks or Jews were visible at any event I attended. Besides Slavic Catholics, however, there were women of other ethnic backgrounds.

Formal as well as informal remarks at dealers' meetings stressed certain conservative themes. Sacrificing for one's children, protecting them from the decadence and moral anarchy of modern society, and participating in church affairs were commonly expressed themes. Discussions of soap operas provided social cohesion but did not develop further. However, there was a gut-level kind of class consciousness present in their conversations that, if translated into political terms, sounded more liberal.

If anything, working for Tupperware reinforced a mixed and contradictory consciousness. Dealers were proud of their simplicity and the fact that they worked hard. Presentations at sales meetings often made much of the fact that Tupperware dealers were busy, active women with family responsibilities at home and outside. This was in strong contrast to "those bored housewives you hear so much about, with nothing to do but watch TV." There was also plenty of griping about their husbands' shifts, wages, and working conditions. I met only one dealer who was married to a professional—an architect. She was one of the few who seemed self-conscious about being a "Tupperware lady," having chosen to escape from the competitive, snobbish social world of her husband's associates and their wives. Overall, while the implicit message of Tupperware rhetoric was conservative, dealers themselves did not see their work as politically defined.

This was in marked contrast to other direct selling companies like Amway, which pushed a strong rightwing, free enterprise line. Amway was unlike Tupperware in almost every way except the direct-selling method. It was centered on the entire family and oriented toward the male patriarchal figure as the decision-maker. Amway's products themselves were not limited to household goods but were meant, again, to appeal to male consumers.

In Tupperware (until you got to the executive level), women did all the work. The consumers were women, and, most importantly, the product itself was a tool of women's work as homemakers. This is a subtle but important point. Women who used and sold Tupperware took pride in their skills as homemakers and enjoyed sharing those skills and "talking shop" at Tupperware parties. While this reinforced sexual stereotypes and sexual divisions of labor, it, nonetheless, viewed women's work as important, serious, and skilled. "Tupperware is Love" was the name of one of the many Tupperware "anthems." It implied, in this corny way, the double significance of women's work in the home: the practical labor as well as the emotional responsibility of nurturance and love.

Tupperware also had no heroines. Its line was quite different: that every woman is already a heroine—busy, competent, important. These qualities were not illustrated with Tupperware products; they were illustrated by the women themselves, who did, in fact, run homes, organize parties, and earn their own income.

Given this sense of pride in housework and the fit between doing housework and selling Tupperware, it was easy to see why women moved easily from going to parties to becoming dealers, and did not feel threatened by the move. Still, when women became dealers, they changed. They entered the world of business, where they were treated with some degree of respect.

Area sales meetings, or assemblies, took place one morning a week in each district. They were strictly voluntary, and yet, an average of 200 to 300 women found sitters for their children and drove many miles to attend these meetings. Like other professional meetings, these assemblies were places to share and brush up on organizing techniques, honor those who had done well in sales or innovative party ideas, and learn more about new products. Women often went to assemblies in car pools, sometimes stopping to shop on the way home.

As a woman rose in the Tupperware hierarchy, from dealer to manager to distributor (the highest level a woman could reach in Tupperware), she spent more and more time at her job. Typically, the distributor was a woman whose children were older and whose husband was willing to share involvement in the business and its social aspects. It was not uncommon for husbands to give up their own jobs and join their wives in building the distributorship, thus forming "Total Tupper" families. Such couples may, at one time, have worked at such jobs as manicurists or bus drivers. But now they were members of the petit bourgeoisie, owning and managing their own warehouse and overseeing an entire district of managers and dealers. The income of such couples was hard to establish. Like all Tupperware workers, they were paid partly in gifts. Distributors drove silver Mark IV Continentals. They often even owned two company-furnished homes as well as a boat, airplane, furs, and swimming pools.

Thus, for all its pro-traditional family rhetoric, the activity of selling Tupperware had made structural changes in dealers' lives and consciousness. First, they no longer functioned simply as wives and mothers, seeing to the needs of others. Quite to the contrary, the children and husbands of Tupperware dealers were increasingly drawn into the Tupperware world, which became an increasingly important aspect of family life. Dealers were seen by themselves and their families as competent and productive. Demands on their time were accepted, and new work was taken on by the family to help her out. Thus, while the cultural and emotional aspects of family life were preserved, the sexual division of labor, and the power relationships it implied, were seriously and sometimes permanently altered.

"Total Tupper" families spent three days a year at the annual Jubilee, a Tupperware convention held at the national headquarters in Florida, a luxurious estate designed by Phillip Johnson. The Jubilee was a combination inspirational revival, training sessions, and vacation. Conservative entertainers like Pat Boone and Glen

Campbell performed before huge displays of American flags formed by red, white, and blue plastic bowls.

These events clearly moved very far from the world of individual Tupperware parties. The point at which men came on the scene was the point at which the corporate structure itself came into focus. To most Tupperware women, this level was a mystery. That was the company's intention.

According to the official company *History of Tupperware,* "Tupperware products were first introduced to the public in 1945 by Mr. Earl Tupper, one of the pioneers in the conversion of polyethylene in the housewares field and founder of Tupper Corporation."

Nineteen forty-five was an important year for at least two reasons. First, it marked the beginning of the wide-scale use of plastics in American manufacturing, a scientific breakthrough with profound effects on American marketing and consumption patterns. The special technique developed by Mr. Tupper did in fact produce a product superior to other plastics.

Originally, Tupperware was distributed conventionally through retail stores and franchises. However, the special nature of Tupperware products, and its slightly higher price, created a problem. According to the company, "in 1946, Mr. Tupper had a choice of either becoming just another housewares manufacturer [sacrificing] quality for price" or finding another way to demonstrate and distribute his product.

He developed the idea of the home party plan using women's existing networks, which proved, for cultural and economic reasons, to work quite well. In 1951, a sales organization called Tupperware Home Parties was created to administer sales. In 1958, Dart Industries (formerly Rexall) purchased the Tupperware Corporation as well as Tupperware Home Parties.

Today Dart Industries is a multinational corporation with five lines of business, of which the direct selling division is by far the most successful. There are Tupperware plants in 14 countries besides the United States. There are Tupperware distributors, managers, and dealers in 30 countries, serving a potential market of one billion.

The secret to Tupperware's success was more complex than the "build a better mousetrap" story. It related to another important event of 1945: the end of World War II and the return of American women from war-related jobs to full-time housework, thereby creating the enormous, if shifting, reserve labor force of women whose primary responsibilities were at home. And it was this group from which Tupperware recruited its workforce. To quote Dart Industries, "direct selling is contra-cyclical to declines in the economy in that more people are interested in part-time selling during such periods."

From the company's point of view, one is tempted to agree with the former Tupperware research chemist with whom I spoke, that "Tupperware is an evil company" that "exploits women." After all, women did all the work and received little of the profits. Moreover, as Betty Friedan has pointed out, "Tupperware dealers are like migrant workers"; that is, they receive no fringe benefits since they are not employed by the company.

Yet the two most important aspects of the Tupperware approach had to do with its attitude toward housewives themselves. First, Tupperware dealers were told again and again how competent and important they were. Blue ribbons, stars, prizes, and hugs were given out freely. As one woman told me, "no one ever notices what I cook for dinner, but at the assemblies I feel really important." Second, Tupperware spoke to the very real problems of full-time housewives: loneliness and isolation. At both parties and assemblies there was a sense of communal sharing of work skills. There was a strong sense too, that women knew better than scientists what housework and child care were about. Tupperware was not a technical innovation; its use was based on common-sense knowledge of food and storage.

No special training or education was required to sell Tupperware. No rigid eight-hour day away from home was needed. Women assumed new responsibilities in safe, nearby environments where schedules were flexible. Not even a new work wardrobe was required. Tupperware was, psychologically and economically, an escape from the family and its all-consuming claims on women. It was a career which, like any other career, became a major part of a woman's life and changed her self concept and her attitudes and behavior.

When we put the Tupperware party into a broader political context, it looked a lot less rosy, of course. First, women earned only 25 cents on a dollar of sales, and much of their income was in merchandise rather than cash. They were thus both exploited and manipulated. Also, the make-work nature of the Tupperware life-style—essentially transferring foods from packages or plates to plastic containers—was hardly meaningful work.

Next, dealers were totally cut off from the business and scientific end of things and had no say whatsoever in policy. The line of ascent was from dealer to manager to distributor. That was as high as a woman could go in the company, and she had to be married and have an involved family to do that. No woman sat on the board of directors. And when a "Total Tupper" family did rise to executive status, the husband, rather than the wife, got the position. "What we are trying to do is decide what is in the best interest of good marital relations," said one Tupperware spokesman.

The success of Dart Industries' many enterprises, including Tupperware, Vanda Beauty Products, and West Bend Housewares, was linked to the growing concern, pushed by the Right, for home and family life, and to its goal of spreading the Tupperware idea and "the American way" around the world. Thus, one of the common themes in the Tupperware anthems was to "Spread our love to every nation, that's our goal in Tupperware!" Both to "give a helping hand to others" and to "watch our Tupperware family grow and prosper."

It is interesting that Mr. Tupper himself, along with many members of the publicly hidden "inner circle," are Mormons. Mormons share a commitment to the patriarchal family structure and a belief in community self-sufficiency based on mutual support and self-started institutions. Thus, the contradictory elements of reactionary thinking about the family and a collective, self-help-oriented sense of process were merged in ventures like Tupperware.

It was this contradiction that informed the equally contradictory, but institutionally harmonious, existence of the two separate levels of Tupperware—the male and female. For while many of the immediate personal and social rewards for women were, I believe, progressive, the overall purpose of the company was to make money by keeping the most traditionally defined nuclear family intact and maintaining women's subordinate position. Indeed, in one sense, Tupperware acted to preserve the reactionary nature of the family structure by the very fact that it provided a way for women to earn just enough money, and develop just enough self-esteem and autonomy, to keep them happy and thus dependent at home.

But that is also the nature of capitalism. Tupperware was a part of working-class women's culture in many places. It provided a network for socializing and sharing. It created the kind of atmosphere of intimacy and closeness that the Women's Movement had always understood to be politically important to women. Also, because it was based in neighborhoods and the work centered in the homes, it created an accessible and important new space for housewives to begin moving out of the family structure and develop new support relationships and activities. It was one of the few ways such women could significantly alter the nature of their family roles.

In a larger sense, women at Tupperware parties often expressed a desire to feel more a part of a community and to know their neighbors. Most Americans suffer from this sense of atomization and social isolation. These women wished to break through this, partly to form helping relationships, and partly to overcome loneliness. As Leftists, we are not exempt from these feelings. Participating in neighborhood networks makes sense politically and personally. The time I spent participating in and thinking about Tupperware was valuable to me. I learned about and experienced a level of women's culture about which I feel good and even hopeful. There were no easy conclusions to be drawn from that experience, but there was much to be considered.

Hooked on a Feeling

Pick an addiction, any addiction. You don't have one? You're hopelessly out of it. According to the current wisdom—or at least the "experts" who write self-help books, lecture, and run workshops for the "addicted generation"—addiction is nearly a universal malady. A recent *Mademoiselle* article on "Addiction Chic" states that "there are an estimated 12 to 15 million people—up from 5 to 8 million in 1976—currently involved in about 500,000 organizations" for people suffering from a mind-boggling array of psychological disorders now characterized as "addictions."

From the well-known Alcoholics Anonymous to the newer groups, Debtors Anonymous, Impotence Anonymous, Overeaters Anonymous, Sex Addicts Anonymous, Gamblers Anonymous, Depressives Anonymous, and Love Addicts Anonymous (sometimes called WWLTM, after Robin Norwood's enormously successful and influential 1985 book, *Women Who Love Too Much*), these groups are multiplying wildly. Robin Norwood herself, in her recently published second book, *Letters From Women Who Love Too Much*, says "there are over one hundred varieties of Anonymous Programs that exist today." Moreover, she states that, as a psychotherapist, she has "never encountered a troubled individual who didn't qualify" for one of these groups.

I became intrigued by this trend because it has touched many people I know and because of its implications for feminism. The most popular of the groups are the ones about love or relationship addictions, almost all of which implicitly or openly are addressed mainly to women. Go to any B. Dalton or Barnes and Noble and you will be astonished at the number of books with titles like *How to Break Your Addiction to a Person* and *Overcoming Romantic Sexual Addictions*. After all the gains women have made in work and public life, why are so many still in sexual relationships that necessitate buying these books and attending these groups?

One way to get a take on the phenomenon is to look at the blockbusters, the ones that stay for months on *The New York Times* bestseller list. Robin Norwood and Melody Beattie are clearly the queens of codependents (the current term for people who stay with abusive, unreliable partners). Norwood's 1985 book and her new follow-up are bestsellers, and have helped create the nationalized network of WWLTM groups. Melody Beattie's 1987 *Codependent No More* stayed in the top five of the *Times's* How-To List for three years, and her recent follow-up, *Beyond Co-dependency*, is currently number one.

These four books have much in common. Before examining their disturbing implications, it's only fair to point out what is healthy and useful about them. For one thing, they lay out, in plain English and with extensive examples, what is clearly a serious problem for many women and some men. In fact, few women reading these books—whatever their current situation—will fail to feel a shock of recognition at reading Norwood's and Beattie's analyses of heterosexual relationships.

Whether or not Beattie and Norwood realize it, they often present a watered down version of feminist theories of the dynamics of the traditional family and the pervasive media-generated images of "love," both of which influence the socialization of boys and girls and provide unhealthy models of male/female relationships. Norwood, for example, after narrating the tragic case history of "Lisa," comments that "her condition wasn't helped any by the fact that both suffering for love and being addicted to a relationship are romanticized by our culture [and that] very few [media] models exist of people relating as peers in healthy, mature, honest, nonmanipulative, and nonexploitative ways."

Beattie's examples typically describe the results of traditional family conditioning, in which women caretake and rescue while men, infantilized by their all-powerful but ultimately rejecting mother-image, retain a great deal of neediness and hostility toward their partners. This elicits, in the woman brought up to care for others and not herself, a deep anxiety and sense of guilt. "Marlyss," for example, is a compulsive caretaker. She "resents how her family and their needs (emotional, physical, and sexual) control her life" but, she says, "I feel guilty when I don't do what's asked of me...live up to my standards for a wife and mother."

Most Leftists, male and female, will find this pretty obvious. In an urban world, where dinner party conversation addresses the newest theories about sexual and social life, and people talk about their shrinks the way other Americans talk about their grandchildren, this is not exactly headline news. But many others (and a lot of us who—no matter what we "know"—are still in relationships that fit the "codependency" model) find something useful and healing in these books. They do some of what the consciousness-raising movement did 20 years ago: they let us share our deepest, perhaps most shameful pain with people in the same boat, and they provide examples of how others have extricated themselves from similar situations.

Unlike the early Women's Movement, however, these books do not show how the personal becomes political. Instead, they present addiction as a disease from which one never fully recovers, which only the most vigilant and permanent adherence to the Twelve-Step Program.

The first seven of the 12 steps reek of the kind of religion typified by televangelism. Members must first "admit they are powerless over" the addiction, whatever it is. Then they must accept that only "a Power greater than [themselves]" can cure them and then make "a decision to turn [their] wills and lives over to the care of God." Beattie and Norwood, both recovering addicts of more than one variety, give heavy personal testimony about the crucial role of surrendering to this very traditional, patriarchal God in their recoveries. Neither is aware of, or interested in, social or political factors that may contribute to their "diseases."

Their new books—which stress recovery and new beginnings rather than getting out of a bad situation, as their first books did— are far more pushy about accepting one's powerlessness and surrendering one's life to God. Beattie, for example, tells us that she overcame her problems by "trying gratitude." She got down on her knees and "thanked God for each thing I hated about my situation. I forced it, I faked it, I pretended," she says, and "after three or four months, things started to change."

What's wrong with this picture? From a political point of view, just about everything. Passivity and the surrender of personal agency subverts any faith in the power of political action. Then there's the question of race and class. It's ironic, to say the least, that at a time when drug addiction—of the ordinary street-drug variety—is wreaking havoc in poor communities, these books discuss addiction as a primarily middle-class problem. Eating disorders, gambling and overspending, relationship dependency—these are not, surely, the most serious addictions of people living in poverty and/or suffering the effects of systemic racism. They are, however, the obsessions that affect the people who buy self-help books.

Barbara Ehrenreich, in *Fear of Falling,* comments on the national hysteria over drugs. She says that drugs "symbolize the larger and thoroughly legal consumer culture, with its addictive appeal and harsh consequences for those who cannot keep up..." She is right, but consumerism is not the only aspect of modern life that encourages addictive needs. Whether we are heroin addicts or credit card addicts—and the differences are to some extent class-related—we all got that way in the process of growing up in a world based on impossible goals and values. It is not just consumerism that induces addictive needs. It is also the fact that we are all, whatever our milieu, taught to be competitive, acquisitive, power-hungry, and controlling. But while boys strive to control nature and the public realm, for girls, alas, relationships are still the main arena for playing out power games. Thus the epidemic "addiction" to dysfunctional, unreliable men.

In my perusal of the "love addiction" shelves, I was grateful to find at least two books that seemed to address the larger social context of addictive behavior. The first, written in 1987 by Anne Wilson Schaef, promised more than it delivered. *When Society Becomes an Addict* is an explicitly feminist analysis that is at once insightful, superficial, and theoretically murky. Schaef, to her credit, understands that the institutions of society perpetuate addictive behaviors. "The Addictive System operates out of a scarcity model," she says at one point, "a model based on the assumption that there is not enough of anything to go around and that we had better get as much as we can while we can," a perfect description of the 1980s mentality. Unfortunately, her gender-based explanation for this is so simplistic, and her suggested solutions are really silly. Schaef sees this society as made up of three Systems: the White Male System (which she equates with the Addictive System); the Reactive Female System, which is the traditional way women have been taught to respond to the White Male system, with total compliance and a willingness to be dominated and abused; and the Emerging Female System, the sole hope for the future of the world. This system is based on theories that depict women, who are socialized to be emotionally caring and sensitive, as inherently superior leaders.

But in real life, women in power—Margaret Thatcher was the obvious example—don't necessarily have wonderful compassionate qualities. Since Schaef believes they do, she proposes a pie-in-the-sky mass therapy movement as a way to change the generation's power structure. Individual men—George Bush and Donald Trump, for example—should, she suggests, deal with their neurotic need for power by voluntarily "feminizing" themselves. Apparently they will be brought to such radical self-transformation by reading Schaef's book.

The most interesting (and ultimately depressing) book I read was Stanton Peele's *Love and Addiction*. Written in 1975, it also makes connections between addictive relationships and the larger social context. Reading it was like waking up in an earlier era—it is filled with the utopian thinking about social change characteristic of the late 1960s and early 1970s. It is also extremely savvy about class and race. It is the only book I read, for example, that analyzes the differences between working-class styles of negotiating relationships and those of the middle class.

What's most impressive about this book is its political conclusions. "The real cure for addiction," says Peele, a social psychologist, "lies in a social change which reorients our major institutions and the types of experience we have within them...[for] we cannot begin to cure it in the absence of a more universal access to our society's resources, and to its political power."

Now that 1960s nostalgia has depoliticized what the 1960s vision was about, this book seems both unsettling and instructive.

Returning to Norwood and Beattie, I was even more disturbed by their approach to the very real pain that drives so many people to destructive behavior patterns. They have helped promote "addiction" as an explanation for personal and social problems and Twelve-Step Programs as the appropriate response. Their success challenges us to take their ideas seriously. Should we, as Beattie recommends, learn to "practice gratitude" for the unbearable circumstances of our lives? Or should we set about changing institutions and power relations? I think we know the answer.

Needed: A Radical Recovery

During the 1992 presidential campaign, *Time* magazine ran a piece on Al Gore's frequent use of "recovery talk"—the now widely spoken language of the Twelve Step/Addiction/Self-Help movement—in his campaign appearances. *The New York Times*, a few weeks earlier, ran a similar piece about Bill Clinton's frequent references to his experience with family "dysfunction," drug and alcohol abuse, and therapy.

To which Bush aide Torie Clarke responded—invoking the days when a candidate could easily be defeated by the mere disclosure that he had sought treatment for emotional problems (Thomas Eagleton) or by allowing the camera to see a single tear-filled eye (Edmund Muskie)—that "real men don't lie on couches."

But, as the Republicans found out, the times they are a-changin'. "Codependency," wounded "inner children," "adult children" of various kinds of "dysfunctional" parents are the cultural, and increasingly, the *real* currency of today's marketplace of ideas and things.

If any of this makes sense to you, if you recognize the language and gestalt it refers to, you know that this recovery stuff represents a major cultural phenomenon in American life. Nor is it obviously, as too many critics blithely assume, a politically "conservative" (as opposed to "liberal" or "progressive") movement. Not with such Left-feminists as Gloria Steinem writing bestsellers on the need for "healing" one's "inner child" and developing the "self-esteem" destroyed by "dysfunctional" family dynamics.

No, traditional political terminology is not so easily applied to this brave New Age world of recovery. Like all totalizing discourses, "recovery thought" reflects a worldview that explains and addresses everything in its own terms. Any troublesome behavior pattern, from shopping "too much" to worrying "too much," can be made to fit the loose definition of "addiction." Any objection or doubt can be answered with the all-purpose dismissal that one must be "in denial."

Do you worry that such self-absorption takes people away from political matters? You are using political activity "addictively" as a way of avoiding "your problem." I've been told so many times, "You can't change the world until you heal yourself," that I don't raise the issue anymore. Do you insist that your own moderate, but regular, use of alcohol is a pleasure rather than a problem? You are, so far, "controlling" your addiction, but it will soon "progress" and "become unmanageable." Just wait.

It is this totalizing, politically reductive aspect of the movement that critics—most notably Wendy Kaminer in *I'm Dysfunctional, You're Dysfunctional* and David Rieff in "Victims, All? Recovery, Codependency, and the Art of Blaming Somebody Else," in the October 1991 *Harper's*—most oppose.

Movement people call everyone a "victim" of "dysfunctional,""abusive" family systems: John Bradshaw and friends use a widely quoted figure of 96 percent as their official statistic on dysfunctional families, and most agree with Robin Norwood that virtually everyone in therapy "could use" a Twelve-Step Program. Their critics argue, however, that to do so is to trivialize the very idea of "victimization" and "oppression."

"A quick way of seeing just how specific the recovery idea is to prosperous Americans," says Rieff, "is to think how preposterous it would seem...to a man whose daughter had just been killed by a terrorist bomb, to someone who was hungry, to someone, anyone, in Croatia, the Soviet Union, or South Africa." And Kaminer agrees. "The Recovery Movement's cult of victimization mocks the notion of social justice by denying that there are degrees of injustice," she says. "It equalizes all levels of abuse...The personal subsumes the political."

While I agree with much of this argument, I am deeply offended by its tone. Kaminer and Rieff, progressives both, actually ape the smugness and cold-bloodedness of such rightwing Republicans as William F. Buckley, Jr. and Pat Buchanan when they dismiss the suffering of everyday people in this vicious world as so much whining and whimpering and suggest that they simply pull themselves up by their Bruno Magli bootstraps and get on with the dirty business of being grownups in a tough world.

"Imagine everyone grappling with their problems and forging their identities, using their own intuitions and powers of analysis," says the tough-minded, I-did-it-my-way Kaminer. That, agrees Rieff, would be facing the "splendor and misery of being an adult."

But this kind of Emersonian self-reliance misses the political point. It assumes that the pain for which so many seek help in the Recovery Movement is wholly "personal," which it certainly is not. That people drink, take drugs, shop, and spend themselves into oblivion or the poor house; that they starve themselves into fashionability; that they endlessly and compulsively seek sexual conquest and novelty—these are not merely "personal" matters. They have everything to do with capitalism and its effects on daily life and social relations.

The fact is that much of the thinking found in recovery books makes perfect sense, as far as it goes. Bradshaw's analysis of dysfunctional family dynamics actually says a lot of things feminists and Leftists have been saying for 20 years. The family isn't working. Patriarchal power relations breed abuses of power, both emotional and physical. They encourage women to feel they can't function without men and to bond with (typically patriarchal) men who won't communicate with them and who use the cultural capital they were born with to dominate, manipulate, and exploit those who are less powerful.

The workplace is just as bad. Now that men have gotten into

the recovery thing—via Robert Bly and pals—there are almost as many books that use New Left and feminist ideas to decry the emotional toll taken by life in corporate and bureaucratic settings as in the family. Ann Wilson Schaef has built her own empire of books, conferences, consulting gigs, and recovery retreats and hotels to go along with her many bestselling treatises on the "addictive" nature of American society as a whole. Using feminist and New Left ideas, she explains how the stresses of work and politics grow from institutional "male-style" power "addictions" that can only be ended by putting "success" and "work" addicts into their own recovery groups.

Most of the self-help stuff about addiction, unhealthy sexual and child-parent relationships, and self-destructive, compulsive habits uses this king of Left-feminist model. Much of it reads like a 1972 issue of *Ms.* or *Liberation* magazine.

Except for the political conclusions. There aren't any.

Instead, we are given a complete ideological system of explaining human suffering which replaces political and economic forces with biologically determined genetic causes. It offers prayer, group conformity, and the giving up of one's personal and political agency as an ultimate "cure" for everything.

Since, according to this model, the "disease" of addiction is not only inborn but incurable, there is no help for it but to put oneself—permanently—in the hands of the movement and religiously attend meetings and work one's programs. Once in the movement, one always discovers more addictive tendencies: how could it be otherwise? These are the feelings and behaviors of people trying to live up to the *common* demands of advanced capitalism and to avoid the *common*, socially caused kinds of stress, misery, and loneliness that this system breeds. Lest one be accused of a lingering case of "denial," however, one must forget about trying to change institutions and power relations until one is "healed."

The recovery rhetoric works because it manages to shift attention away from social reality and redefine *actual* political, social, and personal ills and miseries in ways that contain and control impulses toward realistic social solutions. In fact, the rhetoric of addiction and recovery has become a subtle form of social control in a world in which more and more of us are at the end of our ropes, our wits, and our emotional resources. Just as the managed-media Gulf War thwarted Vietnam-style protest by redefining reality in terms of images that masked the actual situation, the Recovery Movement thwarts protest against domestic madness by redefining *that* reality in ways that keep us from seeing the real situation.

In fact, the discourse of addiction and recovery, now circulated so effectively and ubiquitously through the mass media, can be seen as a subtler version of the War on Drugs aimed at inner-city, mostly male African Americans. Hard drugs like crack and heroin, it is argued, lead to street crime and violence, and so we must put users in jail. This is a form of social control widely accepted as necessary, even though theorists of the Left and Right agree, more and more, that it is erroneous, costly, and ineffective. The real causes of crime and violence are, after all, the same as the real causes of drug use—poverty and despair. The law-and-order solutions, then, are public relations smoke screens for a society that has never had any intention of ending drug abuse, only of "controlling" and demonizing it, making it a scapegoat for systemic social crises.

This PR strategy of keeping us confused and agitated over the mysteriously intractable "drug problem" can be seen—if you look carefully—in the media's approach to the "softer," middle-class "addicts" so in vogue these days. This time the socially dangerous "abusers" being "controlled" are not violent, dark-skinned young criminals, but white, middle-class men, women, and teenagers whose inability to function has become socially problematic.

These people don't rob banks, of course, but they do get out of control personally. And that leads to problems in the professional workforce, in family stability (which women are depended upon to maintain), and in the socialization of middle-class youth into productive work habits.

The real "solution" would be to go back to the original Left-feminist analyses of these problems and take another look at the ideas about changing institutions and power relations that they laid out. But that has never been consumer culture's way of doing things.

Better to sell Excedrin than find a cure for headaches, after all. So television keeps things up close and personal, within the family unit, where it seems as though we cause and can therefore solve our own problems, with the help, at most, of (free) self-help groups, private therapy, and mass-market paperbacks. It offers us Nytol, Calgon bubble baths, an occasional trip to Disney Land, and now the Recovery Movement.

On "Oprah" there have been many examples of how this works, but I'll use just one. A group of people who, as children, were subjected to emotionally painful teasing and ridicule because of the way they dressed were the guests. In the audience were some of the very people who had persecuted them. During the opening segments—when the problematic experiences were re-called—the emotional distress felt by these "adult children" was extreme. After the passage of decades, after their lives had gone in different, adult directions, they still could not recall these incidents without tearing up and stifling sobs.

Oprah's method of handling the situation, typically, was to force a therapeutic confrontation between abusers and victims, in which the persecutors came to acknowledge the effects of their behavior, accept responsibility, and ask forgiveness. This technique, quite moving and effective as far as it goes, was also used recently in Oprah's exemplary prime-time special about sexually abusive fathers and their daughters/victims. It is no small thing to get a grown man to cry on television, acknowledge his sexual abuse of power, and beg his victim not to blame herself even if she can never forgive him.

Nonetheless, here, as in the segment on childhood teasing, the real political issues are not only avoided; they are ideologically reformulated to fit a nonpolitical worldview. The children who had been tormented were working-class and poor. Among the hurtful labels used against them—which still pained them to the point of tears—was "white trash." But when the "expert" came on to give closure to the matter, she ignored the entire class basis upon which children shame each other in this materialist, consumer culture for failing to own the right "things." Instead, she advised the victims to find a group (Bad Dressers Anonymous? People Who Cry Too Much?) and "heal your inner child." Given time, I'm sure she would have offered the same advice to the middle-class tormenters who were, by now—judging by their fashionable and expensive clothing—surely in the grip of their own inner-child problems with addictive shopping, workaholism, or credit-card debt.

TV movies about such issues do much the same thing. The

codependency/sexaholism movie, for example, was actually—in the first half—a good portrayal of a destructive marriage between a successful woman and her insecure, competitive, subtly hostile husband. In the 1970s, when movies like *An Unmarried Woman* and *Alice Doesn't Live Here Anymore* were popular, a woman in this kind of marriage would have gone to a consciousness-raising group, or at least gotten support from friends in leaving the marriage. Today, she is sent to a group where she gets support in "recovering" from a problem that is defined as "hers," not his—not sexism's.

Or take the case of the prize-winning *Shattered Spirits*, in which Martin Sheen played an alcoholic who abused his children and wife emotionally and jeopardized them economically, until he finally "hit bottom" and agreed to family therapy. There they learned that they were all "sick" members of a "dysfunctional family system." No mention of the economic and power relations that kept the woman and children captive and emotionally complicit in this "sick" system. No mention of the economic and power relations of the demeaning Willy Loman-esque job the man had.

The usefulness of this kind of "help" in keeping people functioning, just barely, in intolerable, unjust circumstances is obvious. These experts' and therapists' ideas aren't wrong. They do address one level of socially induced suffering and failure. Nor, I am eager to explain, do I underestimate the value and efficacy of therapy, support, and self-help groups in helping us negotiate the treacherous terrain of daily life. These kinds of things are often lifesavers and godsends for people in distress.

I am concerned, however, politically and theoretically, with the broader social implications of their theories, taken out of their proper therapeutic context and used, as the media now use them, as panaceas for socially induced troubles.

To suggest, as the media do, that nothing more is needed to keep us happy and at peace is—implicitly—to ensure that nothing changes in the broader structure that causes this suffering and injustice. These groups and experts and dramas turn things upside down and insist that our problems are internal and the solutions personal. As the critics say, they do dissolve the political into the personal, but that's only because they deny the political nature of personal problems, as do Kaminer and Rieff themselves.

Instead of simply attacking the Recovery Movement and alienating millions who have experienced it as a lifesaver, we need to reclaim its ideas as our own and reformulate them in our own politically oriented terms. The social movements of the 1960s did not "fail," as Gloria Steinem suggests, because we were too emotionally damaged to be politically effective. It was never "us" that was the problem. It was the "damaged," "dysfunctional" society itself, and it still is.

In fact, we were much too politically effective for comfort. So much so that our ideas and analyses have had to be incorporated and redirected into "self-help" directions in order to contain their very dangerous—still very dangerous—implications. Nor are the many problems addressed by the Recovery Movement just the whimperings of a bunch of rich, spoiled babies. As Bradshaw and others rightly suggest, they are experienced by the vast majority of Americans these days. The pain and anxiety are real enough. It's the "Higher Power" Savior solutions that are phony.

American Nightmare

Long ago, in another galaxy, I was a very young faculty wife. My husband was an up-and-coming star at a prestigious school, being groomed for big things. The idea of a deanship had come up. I remember feeling an unexpected terror at the thought. I had just started graduate school and sensed, vaguely, that the two jobs would not easily meld. Luckily, I trusted my instincts and moved as far as possible from the duties and obligations that go with traditional marriage to a successful man. I didn't know the half of it.

Kitty Dukakis's new autobiography hit the bookstands, newsstands, and airwaves like so much garbage hitting the fan. The media were quick to exploit the nastier elements—the drug and alcohol abuse, the repeated hospitalizations, the final, horrifying ingestions of a variety of potentially fatal substances including hair spray and rubbing alcohol—for all they were worth. There was no reason not to expect a fast sequel, in which our always perfectly coiffed and groomed anti-heroine would inevitably take yet another step to rock bottom—this time, hopefully, with the help of even more bizarre concoctions.

From all this publicity I assumed, when I decided to review this book, that I'd be dealing with the trendy subject of women and addiction. But much to my surprise, the media ambulance-chasers had led me down a blind alley. The facts I've just told you pretty much cover the addiction aspect of the book. Of course, there are the various hospital stays, none apparently of much use, and the obligatory quotes throughout of basic Twelve-Step-ism. The book begins, not surprisingly, "My name is Kitty Dukakis and I'm a drug addict and an alcoholic." By the last page she's added "manic depressive" to the humiliating public declarations.

Nonetheless, in reading this sad and horrifying tale, I found that something entirely different was its major theme. In fact, anyone with an ounce of perspective or integrity, it seems to me, would notice immediately that in terms of sheer pages, the topic of addiction and mental illness is a minor, if continuously mentioned and acknowledged, theme. What is equally apparent and significant is that there isn't a page here that isn't essentially about Michael (to whom the book is "especially" and lovingly dedicated) and her marriage to a public figure. One needn't be a deconstructionist, then, to realize that it is this, rather than addiction, that Dukakis has made her central concern.

Sure, the issue of addiction gets intertwined with her marriage and public life. But it, like the author herself, is never allowed to emerge with any sense of reality or clarity. Over and over again, Kitty insists that her ambitious, high-powered mate, the man who ran for president while his wife was disintegrating before his eyes, and plans perhaps to try it again—with her support, she insists, of course—is flawless. It is Kitty herself, she repeats till you want to cry, who is the problem, the damaged cog in an otherwise perfect political and familial machine. "In spite of Michael's attempts to reach me," she says, typically, after one drinking episode too ugly for the family to ignore, "I couldn't give anything back...Anyway, it wasn't really Michael's issue."

In fact, the book was undertaken, after the election and the first public declaration of substance abuse, as a journal of the campaign by the would-be first lady. Yet there was no real reason to give Dukakis a book contract or publish such a book. Even with a ghost writer, it is badly written, chaotically organized, and filled with trivia and boring and/or cloying anecdotes about such already media-battered figures as Jesse Jackson (he didn't eat the dinner she served him) and Lee Hart (Gary didn't notice she was gone for an afternoon, while Michael rushed attentively to Kitty's side). What her publisher and the press really wanted (and what the perfect hubby allowed her to subject herself to) was a nasty tell-all about yet another Washington—or Hollywood-style—addict.

Thus the book's schizophrenia, disorder, and frustrating superficiality. There are really two Kittys here. One is the cheerful, attractive, political trouper who emerges, in some ways, as a truly awesome figure. She is never late, unprepared, or even tipsy during the grueling course of the doomed campaign. In what seems like a mad effort to find something to say without ever letting her guard down, she pulls every dull incident or sunny scene from her campaign journal and her married life. There she is, committing a minor political gaffe in Alaska where she spouts environmentalism, unaware that the Democratic gubernatorial candidate has a different position. There she is again, being embraced by Danny Kaye, a friend of her musician father. And here we see her winning over her father-in-law, who is opposed to Michael's marriage to a Jewish divorcé with a young son.

Occasionally we see a hint of emotional strain (although never in a political situation). Her description of her behavior at her daughter's eighth-grade graduation is a rare but vivid one. There she sat, fidgeting, making nasty cracks, "talking loudly and snapping," while her family sat nervously dreading what, apparently, were fairly common outbursts of unstable behavior. But this incident (at least in the book) stands in isolation amidst the Norman Rockwell details of a blissful American Dream of a life, and goes pretty much without comment. The dominant image is of a woman who has a perfect man and a happy, successful family and is a tireless organizer of numerous projects to help the disadvantaged and beautify the state of Massachusetts. So when she throws in a rare tidbit of emotional distress, it's as if she has been reminded by her collaborator that there has to be a clue every now and then to indicate some sort of character flaw or inappropriate behavior, or else the ending will make no sense.

Unfortunately this minor effort doesn't work. In fact, it's the kind of thing that produces the jarring, almost absurd quality of the book as a whole. One is left wondering: Just what is going on with this woman? Who is she and why does she need so desperately to maintain this weird facade? She never even admits to an escalation of drinking or the mildest of squabbles with the Great Man. All is perfect here.

One must wonder. Here is a woman who, at one point, having left three treatment centers only to reach greater and greater depths of despair and self-destructiveness each time, enters a psychiatric hospital. She no sooner unpacks, learns the rules and the route to the gym for "a strong physical workout" followed by "a hearty breakfast" each dawn, than she is insisting on being released for Christmas. Here comes the sensitive teary-eyed spouse to collect her. And then, having managed to survive one dinner, she retreats to her room in a desperate search for anything "to kill the pain." What pain? Who can guess? Not Michael; he plies her with anxiety-provoking compliments, praising her "to the skies at a time when I felt like two cents." Good move, Mike. That's what I call communication.

She does offer one quick answer early on—the one the media unquestioningly embraced, by the way—when she tells of discovering that her mother's birth mother was an unwed woman who gave her child to a wealthy Jewish family and went to work as her nurse. The title, *Now You Know,* was her mother's only comment upon revealing this secret to Kitty. Okay, that's certainly traumatic. But how in the world can that be responsible for everything that followed? Why so strong and happy for so long only to fall, in her mid-1950s, into what seems to be a continuing, worsening breakdown?

There is no answer here. Nor, tragically, is there supposed to be. This book, like everything else in Dukakis's life, is obviously meant primarily to embellish her husband's image and support his career. In fact, the suspicion arises more and more frequently, as one reads on, that this itself may well be the major factor in her escalating crises. Why else—if not to keep up appearances compulsively—the urgent need to be at home for the holidays? She wasn't needed and she clearly required rest, privacy, treatment, and an absence of stress.

Why did Michael and her doctors permit so obviously dangerous a home visit so soon after her arrival in the hospital? It's worse than ridiculous; it's infuriating.

When I began this book, I probably hadn't thought in years of that moment, long ago, when the possibility of becoming a dean's wife filled me with terror. Half-way through, though, I recalled it vividly and with full knowledge of what scared me so. I saw in Kitty Dukakis's life story a feminist nightmare of loneliness, subservience, and a near-fatal need to be the Good Girl, the Perfect Helpmate, the classic fairy-tale version of every American girl's Cinderella story. Being a dean's wife, of course—especially today but even then—does not in any way bear comparison with being the First Lady of the Land. Kitty Dukakis lived in a crystal palace through which everyone she knew, and most she didn't know, ogled her endlessly. Her husband, apparently so caught up in his own thoughts that he was oblivious to her emotional condition, kept praising her performance in her second-bill role in his drama. Her doctors kept prescribing medication and signing release orders. The presses rolled on.

That's about all you'll learn from *Now You Know*. It's a strange and depressing book about a woman who seems to be perfect in the process of killing herself. I said earlier that the dominant theme here wasn't women and addiction. Maybe I was wrong.

Contested

Feminisms

The Future of Motherhood

The brave new world of reproductive technology—contraceptive techniques, labor and childbirth "management," fetal monitoring, artificial insemination, and surrogacy—more than any other social or scientific phenomenon, forces feminists to confront central issues that have plagued us for 20 years. What is motherhood? What is a family? What is the relationship between sexuality and reproduction? What is the relationship of women to the scientific establishment and the capitalist economic order? And perhaps most difficult of all, what does it mean—really mean—to be a woman?

In the late 1960s and early 1970s, heady days for feminists and Leftists, radical approaches to these matters were the order of the day. Questioning established thinking about motherhood and femininity was a radical and exhilarating act. For a generation raised on "Leave It to Beaver" and Freudian biological determinism, the realization that biology need not be destiny was liberating.

Things have changed since then, for reasons that are in some ways understandable and in others—to me at least—mysterious. In the heat and passion of feminist debate about reproductive technology one hears the rumblings of an at times alarmingly conservative view of the personal and political future of women, and of the relationship among women, men, children, and the larger community.

Before getting down to the nuts and bolts of the technical and political issues facing us today, it seems important to retrace the history of radical and Leftist-feminist thinking on these matters. It is in the imaginative literature that these feminist movements spawned—the novels we read and discuss with passion—that the convergence of the feelings and ideas that fuel our politics is often most clearly revealed. This seems particularly true in matters of motherhood.

In the groundbreaking 1970 political study, *The Dialectics of Sex*, Shulamith Firestone, a radical feminist in those innocent days when Left and radical feminists shared some crucial political visions, presented a theoretical and programmatic response to those who argued that women are biologically determined to be mothers: "the freeing of women from the tyranny of their reproductive biology…and the diffusion of the childbearing and childrearing role to the society as a whole" through the development of the very reproductive technologies that now seem, to many, anything but liberating.

Some of Firestone's ideas were given imaginative life in Left feminist Marge Piercy's 1976 futuristic novel *Woman on the Edge of Time*. In it Piercy describes in fascinating detail a future world in which all resources—technological and natural—are used to further democratic, life-affirming values such as pleasure, beauty, and individual development and expression in the context of full personal choice. Part of this vision, the most radical part, includes a fully delineated program for childbirth and parenting wholly separate from biological imperative and from the nuclear family. Each child, artificially produced in special reproductive nurseries, has three biological parents, none of whom are lovers. Men are as capable of nursing as women, and the choice to be or not be a parent is as accepted as the choice to be celibate or nonmonogamous.

Such feminist political utopias, whether fictional or theoretical, seem a quirky, aberrant glitch in today's gloomier approach to sexual and family matters. As early as 1979, British feminist Zoe Fairbairn's *Benefits* presented a dystopian futuristic response to Piercy's idyllic vision. Fairbairns's future is one in which genetic engineering, controlled by a misogynist government, is the greatest weapon against feminism and the ultimate force for the enslavement of women. Socially and racially "fit" women are given rewards for returning to the traditional wife/mother role, while poor, black, and otherwise "unfit" women are deprived of their reproductive rights and forced to fill demeaning roles. Margaret Atwood's more recent *Handmaid's Tale* envisions a similarly bleak and terrifying future for women at the hands of an all-powerful reactionary government.

Sue Miller's 1985 book *The Good Mother*, about a single mother who loses custody of her daughter when her ex-husband charges her and her unconventional lover with "sexual irregularities," brings home—depressingly—how little progress women have actually made in our quest for sexual and political freedom. Divorced, impoverished, but happy for the first time in a fulfilling relationship with a man who loves her and her child, Anna Dunlap capitulates immediately to the obvious power of the male-dominated state once her lifestyle is challenged. Losing her beloved Molly, she embarks, like some latter-day Hester Prynne, on an apparent future of penance and personal misery. She breaks with her lover and moves to another city in order to have the few hours a week granted to her with her child.

Anna's plight is heartbreaking and tragic. The sensitive reader cannot judge her too harshly; after all, mother love is real, as is male power and sexual guilt. What's troubling about this novel is the way it poses its heroine's problems. While the first half of the book presents Anna's new and hopeful life from a perspective of optimism and spiritual growth, the second half—devoted to the custody case—switches perspectives in a way that is literally brilliant but politically disturbing. The male power structure—represented by almost every man in the book—speaks, and Anna crumbles in total defeat. Sexual fulfillment and motherhood are seen—once more—as mutually exclusive, not because of Anna's own nature but because of the immovable force of patriarchal ideology. And when forced to choose, it is motherhood—even the disfigured form in which it is offered her—that she chooses. In the end, this child is Anna's reason for being. She imagines no future life, no future children. More distressing, from my own perspective as a mother, she chooses to present herself to her growing daughter as a fallen woman, a loser, a victim. The real needs of a child must surely include the need to see one's mother as a model, a woman whose life is meaningful and dignified.

This novel embodied the state of much feminist (or post-feminist) thought in the 1980s. In its sense of women's powerlessness against masculinist institutions, and in its reversion to an image of motherhood as the sole arena of female power, it mirrors the dominant feminist responses to the issues raised by the new reproductive technologies. Male power, in the realism of science, law, economics, and politics, is seen as absolute. Challenging that power is implicitly brushed aside by feminists in favor of a feverish focus on individual control of one's body and its offspring. Outside the context of a broader social vision, this narrow, single-minded focus too often leads not only to contradictory, even dangerous, political positions and alliances but to unconscious reversion to an essentialist view of femininity as defined by the ability to bear children.

With rare exceptions, feminist responses to the reproductive sciences have been grounded in totalizing visions of male power and female victimization. Andrea Dworkin, in a 1980s version of radical feminism as dour as Firestone's was hopeful, sets the tone in *Right-Wing Women*. "Motherhood is becoming a new branch of female prostitution with the help of scientists who want access to the womb for experimentation and for power," she states in a chapter called "The Coming Gynocide."

Gena Corea, another radical feminist who works with members of FINNRET, the Feminist International Network on the New Reproductive Technologies, paints a similarly harrowing and far more technically detailed picture in *The Mother Machine*. In chapters with titles such as "Cloning: The Patriarchal Urge to Recreate" and "Reproductive Control: The War against the Womb," she depicts a social and scientific world in which these techniques are used solely to exploit and oppress us. Jan Zimmerman's *Once upon a Future* is a similar but broader study of the science and technology, including the reproductive technologies, wholly controlled by men who exploit and destroy women. *Test Tube*

Women, an anthology of scholarly and personal essays, includes a few articles defending the use of reproductive technologies in individual cases. But like the others, it is primarily a critique of reproductive science as wholly oppressive. *Made to Order: The Myth of Reproductive and Genetic Progress* echoes this refrain.

I do not for a moment question the vital political truths these books present. Certainly women are being exploited by the scientific/medical profession. Certainly there are fascistic overtones to the current technologically based regimes that rate some women fit for motherhood on the basis of class, race, and marital status, while channeling others into "surrogacy" for their more fortunate sisters and depriving them of the right to reproduce and mother for themselves. A feminist would have to be a fool not to understand the class, race, and sex biases of capitalism. She or he would have to be worse than a fool not to see the importance of a feminist response to the situation. But what is the correct response? "Discourses of totalizing morality," says Rayna Rapp, astutely, in a review of some of these books, "persuade at a high price. When we accept them, we give up precious ground so recently won: on that ground science as well as nurturance, culture, not just nature, could be women's turf."

It is that precious ground that I am concerned to reclaim, because once we give it up, we easily fall into thought and behavior that feeds into the worst rightwing agendas. As German writers Juliette Zipper and Selma Sevenhuisjen remind us, "the opponents of surrogacy in the Social Democratic Party in West Germany" fell into a program that "the right would applaud: the ties between marriage, love, sexuality and reproduction may not be loosened; surrogacy must be prohibited and reproductive technology may not be applied outside of marriage."

The Socialist-Feminist Response

While the books above primarily express radical-feminist thinking, socialist and other Left-feminists have more often than not concurred. The case of Baby M—in which the birth mother, Mary Beth Whitehead, reneged after being inseminated by William Stern and legally committed to giving him the child—brought the issues raised by reproductive technologies into the mainstream media dramatically. In the process, it also forced feminists of all stripes to take positions. Many of these were particularly revealing of the widespread postfeminist sense of political pessimism about social change.

For example, 125 prominent feminists signed a statement supporting Whitehead's claim to her birth child. For the Left-feminists who took this position, the primary issue was class. If Whitehead, a working-class housewife, was seen as less fit than the Sterns, who were both educated, wealthy professionals, then theoretically, millions of women could be deemed unfit and lose their children on the basis of their class standing.

On this level the argument is irrefutable. Poor women, black women, lesbians, and sexually unconventional women do in fact lose children all the time to those rare fathers who choose to sue for custody. But the Baby M case raised deeper issues for feminists. It demonstrated how socialist analysis of class and race bias can lead to a retreat from an equally crucial Leftist-feminist tenet: that motherhood is socially, not biologically, constructed. Sympathy for Whitehead, the class underdog, led socialist feminists to not so logically agree with Whitehead's own political argument: that the child "belonged" to her as the birth mother. As a result, a number of feminists—liberal, radical, and socialist—were suddenly arguing as vehemently for the rights of the biological mother and the sanctity of the biological bond between mother and child as they had once argued for the right not to mother and the need for fathers to share equally in child rearing.

The May 1988 issue of *Ms.* magazine, devoted entirely to the matter of reproductive technologies, was telling. After presenting an overview of "the dilemmas posed by the new reproductive technologies," the bulk of the issue, the really hot articles, were almost uniformly "pronatal." Phyllis Chesler, in an excerpt from her book on the Baby M case, asks—as though no sane person could disagree—"How can we deny that women have a profound and everlasting bond with the children they've birthed; that this bond begins in utero?" A few pages later the mother of physician/novelist Perri Klass describes helping her liberated daughter deliver her first born as "a transcendent moment" shared with her daughter and son-in-law (white professionals with the time and money to "choose" the most intimate, natural setting for the occasion, one that was also safe, comfortable, and efficient). And Barbara Ehrenreich worries—as have so many feminists recently—than legitimizing "surrogacy," which defines the birth mother as something less than a "real" mother, "flagrantly trivializes the process of childbirth," reducing it to "womb rental."

What all these pieces have in common—and they are simply a representative sampling of feminist opinion on the matter—is an implicit and largely emotional sense that in a post-Reagan world where so much has been taken from us and so much that we dreamed of 20 years ago has not materialized, we must at all costs hang on to the two things we can still hope to own and control, our bodies and our biological offspring. And yet, these articles are fraught with political blind spots and contradictions. Motherhood, after all, is not experienced by all women as an unmixed blessing. Nor do all women have the material advantages of many white feminists, which allow childbirth and parenting to be experienced in such romantic terms.

Motherhood Demystified

The truth is that most women today live lives characterized by emotional and material deprivation, compromise, and a healthy dose of spiritual and/or physical suffering. Among my own friends the issue of motherhood is often painful and usually at least difficult. Among those fortunate enough to have financial security and supportive mates—and, often, to have been lucky enough to conceive later in life than biology prefers—there are still the problems of child care, curtailment of social and political activity, and coping with a dangerous social environment. But more distressing are the problems of single women: those whose personal and economic positions prohibit them from having longed-for children; those who struggle to raise children alone, on inadequate incomes and with no help from ex-partners; and those who use reproductive technologies to become single mothers by choice at enormous economic and emotional sacrifice.

Among my own children's friends and acquaintances I see even greater misery and trouble looming. Teen pregnancy, especially among poor, black women, is widely known to be epidemic. What may be less well known is that many of these young women are among the brightest in their classes. Yet their futures—their potential for self-fulfillment, much less material security—are cut short because they believe, as do the writers in *Ms.* and Anna in *The Good Mother*, that biological mother love is at any cost the greatest, most meaningful fulfillment for a woman.

Finally, there are the women, whom I do not know personally, who do in fact choose to "rent their wombs" to men because, in fact, this is the best option they see for surviving in this cruel, sexist society. What of their right to control their bodies? What of the realities of their situations? I am not suggesting that prostitution or surrogacy, as now practiced, are good things. I am suggesting that any Leftist-feminist discussion of these matters must take into account the realities of capitalism for most women and the choices that exist.

From a broader, less personal perspective, the issues surrounding motherhood and reproduction appear even more politically difficult and confusing. Women's needs, desires, and situations do differ, after all. To assume that the fight for the "maternal rights" of the biological mother and against technical or commercial intrusion into this "natural" realm is the obviously correct feminist position is more than theoretically regressive. It is simplistic in its failure to confront political reality in its entirety. Looking more closely at the specific reproductive techniques available, we see a maze of political contradiction more mind-boggling than any survey of one's personal circle of friends could reveal.

The categories of reproductive technologies are varied, but each is fraught with its own apparently irreconcilable contradictions. Birth control itself is the most common and accepted of these techniques, yet its promise of sexual freedom to women has always been compromised by the social and economic context in which it was developed and distributed. Health risks, unequal access by poor and Third World women, and sterilization abuse of women who want to have more children than society wants them to commonly occur. Moreover, the possibility of fertility control is balanced by a strong ideological belief—widely held in the medical professions and society at large—that "motherhood is the natural, desired, and ultimate goal of all 'normal' women." Those who "deny their maternal instincts are selfish, peculiar, and otherwise disturbed." This thinking influences political decisions to invest more in fertility research than in contraception. Still, who would do away with contraception because it is badly used by those in power?

The management of labor and childbirth and the monitoring of fetal development by the scientific community are also fraught with contradiction. Financially secure women have access to the best care and are in a position to make choices about continuing a pregnancy when the fetus is less than "perfect." On the one hand, such techniques can be a boon to the individual woman fortunate enough to have access to them. On the other, control of the birthing process, once in the hands of female midwives, is now taken from us. Moreover, the fascistic implications of a set of techniques and policies that allow for the production of "perfect" babies and the possibility of aborting the less than perfect are obvious. But again, what pregnant woman would wish away these methods?

In the realm of conceptive technologies—artificial insemination, in vitro fertilization, and surrogacy—the political contradictions are most extreme. Poor women, single women who are not economically privileged, Third World women, lesbians, and others do not have equal access to this technology. Surrogacy today is certainly an economically exploitative practice. Yet for individual lesbian, single, or infertile women, this technology can be a godsend.

In even so sketchy a survey, two things become obvious. First, single-issue fights for "maternal rights" or an end to the commercialization of sex and childbirth are inadequate, often wrongheaded and at cross-purposes with other feminist values. And second, the real issues we need to be addressing are the big ones that we started with: What is a mother? What is a family? What is the responsibility of the community to women and children? And how does technology fit into this picture? These questions demand a return to visionary thinking and to a view of technology that sees it—despite what we know of the male power structure—as potentially progressive, liberatory, and positive in its promise of a better world, a better human family.

To begin rethinking our relationship to technology, we might reread Piercy's *Woman on the Edge of the Time* from the less idealistic perspective of current realities. While reading this, we might want to remind ourselves how we have trapped ourselves, as Zipper and Sevenhuisjen suggest, "in an opposition between [views that stress total] oppression or liberation." Technology inherently serves neither; "it is not technology itself that complicates theory and strategy" but "the *terms* in which technology and its social consequences are spoken about." Free in her imagination, Marge Piercy envisioned a world—albeit a fantastic one—in which people do control technology and make it work for them. We may be far from the power to do so, but that is all the more reason to remind ourselves, in these hard times, of what we are ultimately fighting for, what kind of world we want our grandchildren and great-grandchildren to inhabit.

A Feminist Future

This brings me to the first matter, the questions about motherhood, family, and community as Leftist-feminists would like them to exist. As feminists, we began by challenging patriarchal notions of family and sexuality. In place of paternal ownership and control of women and children, we demanded individual freedom, shared child care, and social responsibility for the human family. In place of blood ties and inherited property as the basis of the distribution of wealth, we demanded social ownership, control, and sharing of our common resources. In place of hierarchical structures, we demanded democratic institutions in which each of us had some power and importance. In place of a single norm for "proper womanhood," we demanded choice and a recognition of the vast differences not only in women's natures and desires but in the material and emotional situations of women of different backgrounds and lifestyles. And in place of the good girl/bad girl dichotomy, we demanded the right to be fully integrated persons, capable of experiencing sexual freedom and intellectual fulfillment without losing our right to be—or not be—mothers.

As grandiose and unrealistic as all this may now seem, the fact is that we were right to make these demands. While some of us are shoring up our little havens in this heartless world and counting our blessings, most of us are in worse shape than we imagined 20 years ago. The feminization of poverty, rising divorce rates, sexual and physical abuse of women and children, illiteracy and alienation among youth, loneliness and isolation among the old and not-so-old—these are the realities of life today. We don't have the choice of returning to the family structure of the 1950s except in isolated cases. In fact, to be politically realistic is to face the fact that terms such as "family" and "mother" have lost their traditional meanings for most of us, and no amount of romanticizing the mysteries of pregnancy will change that. In the face of these truths, the need for imaginative, even visionary speculation seems obvious, if difficult to manage.

Difficult, but not impossible. If Marge Piercy seems bizarre and fantastic to today's young women, there is another literary tradition, that of black women novelists, which is easier for young readers to relate to and in its own way often visionary in its view of family, motherhood, and community. *The Color Purple* is Alice Walker's marvelous example. In it, we see the most oppressed woman imaginable grow into a heroine of mythic proportions in the context of a radically progressive, supportive community. The novel, as fantastic in its way as *Woman on the Edge of Time*, pictures a community of black women that creates the kind of family and lives out the kind of sexual and emotional relationships that earlier feminists envisioned. In a world in which white and male power can at any moment separate families, destroy people, and leave children motherless, Walker shows what family—certainly for blacks and increasingly for all of us—must become if love and community are to survive.

In *The Color Purple*, children are raised by friends and relatives when parents disappear. Sexual relationships end abruptly, if not because of forced separation then because of the enormous strain under which relationships exist in a world of pain, trouble, and powerlessness. Sexual jealousy is overcome in the interest of sisterhood and community survival. Most marvelously, sex roles and heterosexual norms are turned on their heads. Love between any two people is a blessing, albeit one that will almost inevitably be short-lived. Even men—those emotional laggards—are allowed to grow and change under the influence of these magical, majestic women.

The vision is very close to what 1960s feminists believed in. It's not surprising, however, that it is now black women who are the feminist visionaries of family and sexual matters, given the breakdown of the black community under the stress of capitalism. The role of women in preserving it—in lovingly raising whatever children need care, in constructing a new definition of family much more realistic than the one white society has tried to impose upon it—stands as a model to white socialist feminists. It is a model that is accepting of difference, the fragility of the biological "maternal bond," and the need for radical alternatives in these nasty times.

To be sure, *The Color Purple* is economically and technologically anachronistic in its portrayal of a small family-based craft industry as the material basis for the extended family's survival. Which brings us back to the matter at hand—reproductive technologies. Rather than hanging on to our little bit of biological power to reproduce, we might consider the issues raised by reproductive technologies in the context of creating a truly loving, democratic, nonsexist, nonrepressive environment in which technologies are widely and inexpensively available and used in the interest of women and children themselves. It is only in that context that the contradictions raised by these technologies, as they affect different kinds of women, can be resolved. The idea of social responsibility for "family policy" is discussed ad nauseam, and to little effect, these days. A socialist-feminist agenda that transcends immediate special interests to raise large questions of what a decent society would like, and how it would distribute its economic and technical resources, is not unrealistic. It is the only realistic approach to the increasing impoverishment and deprivation of our lives and our political imaginations.

I am particularly concerned with the return of the visionary in political discourse because I have a grown daughter of my own and teach young women of her age every day. These daughters of the Second Wave are remarkable and irritating. They have a vast sense of their own personal potential, their own right to "have it all": meaningful love, important work, children, pleasure, and joy. But their sense of how to achieve these things is as narrow and socially constrained as their self-confidence and energy are vast. They understand Anna in *The Good Mother* perfectly. They accept the limits and contradictions of her choices as given, and in their own lives they plan to avoid her tragedy by being smarter, more careful about their life choices. Implicitly, they have opted for less than sexual freedom, less than real freedom of any kind, less than what we, their biological and spiritual mothers, hoped to be able to offer them—although they cannot possibly know that that is what they are doing.

They can't know because they can't understand *Woman on the Edge of Time* any more than they could understand Shulamith Firestone, should I be foolhardy enough to assign it. Yet they will be inheriting the world we leave them and the values for which we fought. Most alarmingly, they will be inheriting a world in which technology is an ever greater part of their lives, while their control over that technology is virtually nonexistent. Surely they need to know that their biological and spiritual mothers thought, wrote, and even tried to do something about that state of affairs and that it is therefore possible, necessary, even imperative that they do the same.

The Second Time Around?

My college-age daughter was calling for comfort. "My generation is really out of it," she moaned. It was July 5 and she had just returned from a holiday camping trip with her closest friends. She, it seems, was "*the only one*, can you believe it?" who was distraught over the Supreme Court abortion ruling in *Webster v. Missouri.* The others seemed not to feel it had much to do with them.

Usually I manage to cheer her up by reminding her she is just a bit ahead of her friends because she grew up with the Women's Movement and that the others "would find out" in time. This time, however, I wasn't much comfort. Yes, it's true that most of my friends were up in arms over the ominous threat to the constitutional right we had fought hard to win, we thought, for ever. But lately I hadn't been feeling all that sanguine about feminism for other reasons. My generation, I had come to feel vaguely, had won important battles but, perhaps, had lost some crucial war. I wondered if, like our daughters and students, we might not be veering dangerously near the edge of "it" ourselves.

In this gloomy mood, I was heartened to receive *Women Together, Women Alone: The Legacy of the Consciousness-Raising Movement* in the mail, a perfect read for a rainy "post-feminist" night. Written by a journalist and filled with the kind of first-person narratives, laced with gossipy chunks of personal detail, typical of *Ms.* or *The New York Times Magazine* (where an earlier, much shorter version first appeared), it told a juicy story.

The author, Anita Shreve, spent four years crossing the country, interviewing over 100 women who had been in CR groups between 1970 and 1973, when what she calls the consciousness-raising movement numbered between 80,000 and 100,000 members. Using a composite, fictional group of seven women as her core, she begins with an imagined Greenwich Village reunion meeting in which each tells what happened to her over the years and what her life is like now.

The rest of the book is divided into sections according to topic—"Sex and the Secret of Life," "Motherhood: A Bitter Debate," "Women Exploiting Women," and so on. Each begins with a return to one core member's story and is followed by a chapter which gives a quick history and analysis of the significance of the theme and its current status. Here Shreve includes a few references to key works, mostly by radical and liberal "stars" like Betty Friedan and Robin Morgan, and many quotes from her far-ranging interviews.

Like a lot of the women in the book, I "discovered feminism" when I was already a wife and mother of two, and—like a surprising number of them—I felt that "it saved my life." Unlike the majority, however, my involvement was always inherently political. I went from the anti-war movement to the New Left, where I helped found a "women's caucus." We didn't call it CR, but it was. Since most of us were involved with men in the same organization, we never doubted for a minute that "the personal was political" in the broadest sense, that changing social institutions was a part of changing our daily lives. We developed theories to prove it and called ourselves socialist feminists. It was the most exhilarating and hope-filled time of my life.

I lay this out, in the spirit of CR, because it helps explain my somewhat schizophrenic response to this book. On first reading I found it irritating. It is all too glib and superficial, for one thing. For another, it's written in, if not a political vacuum, at least a very limited political universe. It's overwhelmingly about personal life as an end in itself. While Shreve's core group includes Daphne, a black professional woman fighting for joint custody of a son she had given up, and J.J., a Marxist-Leninist turned lesbian separatist struggling to keep body and mind together, its assumptions are overwhelmingly white and middle-class. Larger issues are occasionally raised by these two women, but the texture of this (unlikely) group renders the political comments merely symbolic—background music meant to suggest "the times." At one point during the initial reunion, J.J. gives a somewhat impassioned speech:

> If you ask me how things are for women...I'm gonna tell you right now, from where I see them, they're in pretty bad shape...I see a lot of single parents; I see a lot of women who can't make it economically; I see a lot of women with no child care...

As for Shreve's own analysis, it's equally lacking in political depth and texture. There is no way to conduct interviews with veterans of late 1960s and early 1970s feminism without running up against larger political matters, and Shreve dutifully gives a certain amount of this. But it is personal life—men, children, work—that delimits "feminism" as she and her informants seem to define it.

In the chapter called "Female in America," for example, Shreve gives a brief overview of female life before feminism. "I was brought up Catholic by a mother who believed in fairy tale endings," says "Margaret S., the vice-president of a wine firm in Manhattan," in a quote typical of the many that pepper this chapter. From them Shreve weaves together her summary of what CR meant historically. "The overhauling of this traditional adult female role was among the more successful ventures of the CR process," is one of her conclusions.

Later chapters point out areas where women felt CR did not go far enough. The tyranny of the media image of beauty—you can't be too young or thin—persists. Competition and exploitation of women by women still mar personal and work relationships. Motherhood—handled so differently from our mothers' generation—is nonetheless as fraught with conflict and confusion as ever.

"Between 1972 and 1982, the rate of first births for women in their thirties rose 50 percent; the rate of first births for women in their late thirties rose 83 percent," says Shreve in a rare bit of documentation. "By the time they had children these women were firmly ensconced in the workforce." The women speak eloquently about the work/family juggling act, the inequality of domestic responsibilities in marriage, and their guilt, exhaustion, and isolation.

While all of these things are true enough, they are pretty obvious to anyone who reads, watches TV, leaves the house, or breathes. Shreve tells us no new facts and provides no new insights. While most of her informants recall CR with great nostalgia, at least half no longer consider themselves feminists in any sense, and the rest rarely think it means doing anything beyond "being the best that you can be." "We took what we learned and invested it in our personal lives," says one. "I guess that's what we meant by 'the personal is political.'" That is certainly what my daughter's friends would say if they could even make sense of the mysterious phrase.

My first response to this book was, "So we haven't created feminist utopia; what else is new?" I was even more irritated by Shreve's overblown conclusion: a step-by-step blueprint for re-forming the CR movement. Actually, I suspect this "how-to" ending was the idea of some editor who knows the formula to self-help books and who saw this book—perhaps rightly—as a candidate for that now bulging section of the chain bookstores. After all, we have a common "problem": women are still hurting. Since problems today never have "no name" or no solution, publishers insist on a few quick rules and catch-phrases—suitable for five-minute TV talk show gigs—to which viewers can latch on.

As for the grand scheme of revitalizing the CR movement, there were a million reasons why that seemed silly. For one thing, movements grow out of history, out of a shared, intensely felt sense of frustration centered on specific agents of social repression. The Civil Rights and anti-war movements had put issues of equality and public acts of protest on the national agenda. We were younger then, and less invested in where we were since we hadn't created or chosen our lots. And what would be the point of solving the problems of Beverly Hills corporate lawyers when women were losing basic rights and starving in alleys everywhere?

My cynicism seemed to dissipate in the next 24 hours, however. Why, I wondered, had a glib, superficial book so moved me? Why, even as I scribbled marginal notes of annoyance, did I often have tears in my eyes? The reason was my profound sense of empathy for so much the women in the book were saying. They—we—were still suffering. Careers, children, sexual and personal independence were not giving us everything we had imagined.

No matter what the weaknesses of the book, Shreve had managed to draw out of 100 women the kind of painfully honest truths I had been muttering to myself and a few "safe" friends for a while now. The women I know best are mostly pretty successful. We have all managed to get a lot of what we changed our lives to get. We certainly wouldn't go back. But there are areas of pain and regret in the lives of every close friend I have. Those who have permanent relationships—heterosexual or lesbian—are envied a bit by those who are single, while they, in turn, having made hard compromises, envy the others for other reasons. So it is with mothers and childless women, working mothers and those who stay at home.

With more delicate matters—personal appearance, for example—things get even more hairy. As we age, and times change, more of us resume behavior we gave up in the 1960s. Some of us wear make-up and "feminine" clothes, others color our hair and do other things to head off the aging process and the loss of youthful good looks. Those who consider these decisions reactionary are horrified and condemning.

Tensions around political issues are also strong. Some of us are politically active, others absorbed in personal and career issues. Some of us have "made it," other never will. We tend to censor ourselves a bit around those whose choices differ from ours.

Reading Shreve's tales of what one woman calls "the Glory Days," it was hard not to feel sad. We all had a common vision then. Women friends came first. Natural looks and cheap, rough-and-ready lifestyles united us culturally. We read *The Golden Notebook* and *Woman on the Edge of Time.* We could talk about anything. We had the whole world ahead of us. Today, as Shreve points out (although without due recognition of the enormous importance of women friends in most of our lives today), we have no such community, not even the ones women traditionally have had.

No quilting bees, no mothers meeting in parks to gripe and share information, no kaffee klatsches—nothing but "networking," and very male, often cutthroat groupings of professionals on the make.

While my political doubts remained, I couldn't help but think wistfully about some of what Shreve was suggesting. The pleasure and gratification of meeting with a stable, safe group of women in similar circumstances to "speak bitterness" and be heard and understood—it would be nice, wouldn't it? What if at least this much could be revived? Would we give the time and emotional investment? The Women's Movement, after all, did grow out of a historic sense that women collectively were suffering and that society was at fault. Well, we are still suffering and society is still at fault.

I let myself fantasize. Even if women began meeting for personal reasons, might they not regain a sense of social consciousness and even, occasionally, decide to become active? After all, we began with the assumption that action came from making connections between daily life and social issues, rather than abstract resolves to "do good works." And the activist Women's Movement—as now constituted—isn't drawing as many regular participants, even in a time of crisis, as it once did. This may well be changing now, but mightn't our ranks swell even more if, as in the old days, women's groups legitimated and fostered personal sharing?

I don't know the answers to any of these questions and am far from convinced that a book like this is the proper tool for testing them, in any event. I do know that Shreve's apolitical, isolated women are far more open about these things than I usually am and that this book, whatever its problems, movingly captures a lot of painful realities about our lives.

Pleasure and Danger

When I began writing about the sexuality/pornography debate raging within the feminist movement, strange things happened. Strangers commended me for my "courage." Friends asked why I had gotten mixed up in this "divergence from real politics." These reactions—more than the expressions of disagreement and outrage that I anticipated and heard—forced me to search for the reasons this subject arouses such interest, passion, and fear.

My efforts at understanding were greatly aided by the release of *Pleasure and Danger*, the edited compilation of the papers presented at the (in)famous Scholar and Feminist Conference: Toward a Politics of Sexuality, held at Barnard University in 1982, where the "sex wars" began. Because it finally let us read the papers that caused the commotion, this book was a political landmark.

The conference sought "to address women's sexual pleasure,

choice and autonomy, acknowledging that sexuality is simultaneously a domain of restriction, repression and danger." The conference organizers were concerned that the anti-pornography movement, with its exclusive focus on the "danger" aspect, had prematurely stopped debate and set a program for feminist action in an area only partly and somewhat erroneously understood. How right they were.

The week before the conference, members of Women Against Pornography, Women Against Violence Against Women, and New York Radical Feminists enlisted prominent feminists to denounce the conference and its participants as "anti-feminist" in sexual theory and practice. This group of women picketed the conference, wearing T-shirts marked "Toward a feminist sexuality" and "Against sadomasochism," and handed out leaflets attacking the sexual practices of individual panelists. Barnard's administrators were so intimidated by the antagonism that they confiscated 1,500 copies of the conference proceedings.

These events introduced a different kind of danger to feminists—the danger of the use of sexual and political repression as a response to sexual danger.

What the conference hoped to do "was not to weaken the critique of danger" but to "expand the analysis of pleasure." With the publication of these papers, we saw that it indeed had done that. Though the protesters charged that the conference only aired "anti-feminist" sexual opinions, practices, and fantasies "such as pornography, butch/femme and sadomasochism," in fact the issue of danger was explored in many of the papers in *Pleasure and Danger*.

Far from avoiding the question of sexual danger, the conference sought to place it in a broader, more politically useful context. As conference coordinator and *Pleasure and Danger* editor Carole Vance explains in the book's introduction, the discussion reflected "changes in material conditions, and social organization wrought by capitalist transformation and the women's movement itself, most notably in the weakening of the traditional bargain women were forced to make with men." That bargain, whereby women agreed to "be good" by reserving sex for marriage and procreation in exchange for protection against male sexual aggression, has unraveled.

With that as a backdrop, the conference asked the question: How has sex changed? Does sexual danger stem from male nature or from the way society is organized? Are women sexually gentler beings who must restrain men? Or is female sexuality muted and repressed under capitalism? What are the connections between sex and gender, between sexuality and reproduction, between fantasy and action?

Sexual desire is "for each of us unique, necessary and absolutely terrifying," as Dorothy Allison's article in the book says. *Pleasure and Danger* explores the roots of that fear and ways diverse women have struggled to free themselves from it. Articles examine the sexual myths and realities of black women, Latina women, teenagers, children, and others. These articles help us to see our way clear of ahistorical, white middle-class stereotypes, and to understand the often subtle consequences of sexual mythology that we live by.

The papers dealing with daily experience are startling. Psychologist Muriel Dimen's piece, "Politically Correct: Politically Incorrect," for example, examines moral judgments we have imposed on sexual practices, and sheds light on the experiences and feelings those judgments have helped keep hidden from consciousness. For instance, she describes graphically what she sees while examining male crotches. Horrors! But what a liberating experience, really, to discuss things women have done but have rarely admitted or analyzed together.

Lesbian authors Joan Nestle and Amber Hollibaugh, who also wrote two of the best articles in Monthly Review's "Powers of Desire," gave talks at the Barnard conference that serve as models of how to look openly and seriously at what we think, like, feel, and do in bed.

Nestle, a self-identified "femme who came out in the 1960s," argued that butch/femme role-playing is legitimate for lesbians in the context of a heterosexual culture. She argued that while butch/femme may seem to the straight world—and even to some of the lesbian world—a capitulation to patriarchal sexual norms, role-playing is in fact an act of resistance involving ingenuity in the creation of a personal style. It is, she wrote, a way of reflecting the "colonizer's image back at him" in a way that is quite obviously a rejection of the sexual power system it has traditionally represented. "Resistance lies in the change of context."

Hollibaugh's closing remarks carried Nestle's implications even further. After sharing aspects of her own varied sexual history, Hollibaugh suggested that the desire at times to "resist," to "surrender," to "fight," and to "scream"—in short to act out the fantasies society tries to repress—may be healthy and pleasurable. She insisted that feminists must follow her example to discuss openly the infinite variety of our desires, "recognizing how class, race, and sexual preference will influence the discussion," she said. Women must be able to take sexual risks, Hollibaugh concluded, without fear of political excommunication, if we are ever to understand the nature and scope of our own sexual powers and capacities for pleasure.

Filmmaker Bette Gordon's illustrated description of her movie *Variety* is absolutely provocative. It tells of a woman who works at a porn theater and fantasizes about and even acts on the feelings the films arouse in her. How outrageous to suggest to women that male-created pornography might stimulate us! What's liberating about this piece is its insistence that it's okay to admit having sexual feelings about porn; that feelings are okay, while actions are often not.

In this distinction lies the crux of what's fallacious about the anti-pornography movement's politics. By insisting—against common sense—that pictures, and the feelings they arouse, lead directly to action, these feminists deny us not only the complexity of our political and social experience. They also deny us our dreams, our sensations, our rational and healthy free will.

It is understandable that some feminists, outraged at revelations of widespread rape, incest, and other sexual violence, sought to quickly stamp out its seeming "root cause." It is also understandable that they found legal strictures on porn attractive.

What is less understandable is the way these activists used McCarthyist tactics to try to stop other feminists from challenging anti-porn theories on sex. That they behaved so irrationally and repressively speaks to the depth of the belief that sex is a dangerous, even fatal, subject for women. Even the hint that women might be someday free to have unfettered pleasure and the ability to create and be thrilled by erotic images conjures up for them the fear that women might instead reproduce existing power relations. Thus, the thought that women might, even in today's perilous world, find limited ways of dreaming and experiencing pleasure is unthinkable to them.

As an alternative to that kind of tunnel vision, *Pleasure and Danger* made me often exclaim, "What a relief!" Feminism has helped to free me, and so many others, from irrational, paralyzing ideas and behaviors. Surely we can trust it a little further, bringing up our deepest, most sensitive, and scary feelings. If feminists can't trust each other to discuss sex, who can we trust? And where can we feel safe? Surely not the U.S. legal system. To do that is to cede our sexuality to the New Right, to admit that we have allowed them literally to scare us to political and sexual death.

Backlash,
The Beauty Myth,
and Responses

Susan Faludi and Naomi Wolf—both in their twenties or early thirties—certainly don't suffer from my sense of middle-aged muddle about things. They are absolutely certain that things couldn't be worse for women, that all we have struggled for is in danger of going down the drain as we speak, that there is a monster loose upon the land, which looks, acts, and talks very much like a full-blown conspiracy of powerful woman-haters whose boots are already in our faces.

It's encouraging and exciting to find such signs of renewed passion and urgency on the part of the twentysomethings in these days of waning feminist activism, of so many young women who have reaped the bounties of the Second Wave retreating nervously from the very term "feminist." And it's hard to disagree with the main thrusts of Faludi's *Backlash: The Undeclared War Against American Women* and Wolf's *The Beauty Myth*. Who hasn't felt a sense of panic at the threats against our fragile gains, of rage at the cruelty of the ascendant rightwing misogynists, of sorrow at the suffering that so many of us still endure daily? And yet, while my first response to both books was exhilarating, as I read on, in both cases, I became gradually more irritated and even bored.

Susan Faludi's book is the more ambitious and less interesting of the two. Faludi is the Pulitzer Prize-winning journalist who blew the lid off the sloppy statistics of the infamous Harvard-Yale study—the one that attempted, with the help of a mainstream media blitz, to scare women to death with its dire predictions about our chances of "catching a man" as age and education level increase. She parlayed that coup into a full-length study/exposé of similar terror tactics on the part of individuals and institutions—in league with the main culprit, the media—across the culture. From film and fashion, to Washington politics and think-tank ideology, to national policies on work and reproductive rights, Faludi finds an almost uninflected landscape of hostility and intentional injury toward women on the part of those in power, as a response to the threat of feminist gains.

Her "theory" is based upon what she learned from investigating the marriage scare studies: that the media are eager to print almost anything anti-feminist without much checking for authenticity, while almost equally unwilling to print material that challenges or disproves such stories. In other words—and who could doubt it?—the media are inherently sexist.

It's not that she's wrong, exactly. In fact, women new to feminist thinking may well find much of the book informative. It covers so many areas of life and it ferrets out—often anecdotally—so many horror stories and shocking numbers. My own less than amazed response, however, was largely due to the fact that I was aware of virtually everything in the book. Much of it, in fact, is very old news indeed. The misogyny of *Fatal Attraction*; the new pro-family vogue; the woman-hating of George Gilder and Allan Bloom; the radical Right anti-abortion movement; the Robert Bly

"New Man" cult—these and similar bits of bad news make up her quite long list of quite short, superficial chapters.

That these various items are fairly old news is of course no reason to deny their importance. Books are long in the making, and they are supposed to synthesize and analyze large amounts of material in ways that give us the kind of perspective and insight that daily or weekly journalism can't provide. But Faludi doesn't really do that, and therein lies the problem of this book. It's ill-thought-out, badly argued, and way too often simply erroneous or uninformed. She indulges in nasty personal slurs of the Kitty Kelley variety. She lumps large amounts of material together under generalizations that don't work. She misrepresents things to make her points. She oversimplifies and distorts complex theoretical positions.

The book starts out well enough. Two introductory case histories of media misogyny—the first retelling of her exposé of the Harvard-Yale study—arouse the proper indignation. She goes on to chart the pattern of backlash following periods of women's gains. This is her strongest chapter, because, unlike the rest of the book, it places the backlash phenomenon in the historical context of dialectical interplay with progress. The tendency to polemicize and make exaggerated, out-of-context claims is diminished.

She makes some nice points, too, about the inconsistencies of so much media hype. On the question of marriage, for example, she notes that on the one hand we are supposed to be returning to an age of traditionalism. More and more women, according to the media, are having traditional weddings and marriages and there is, we all know, a new "baby boomlet." And yet the media harangue us equally often about the horrors of the new single woman, lonely and unable to find a man, who blew it all for a shot at the glass ceiling and has lived to regret it.

Of course, the reason this section works better than others is that it acknowledges that the media are less monolithic than Faludi's organizing theory presumes. In this case, of course, both trends are anti-woman. In others, where being similarly even-handed would force Faludi to admit that the media sometimes don't conform to her assumptions, she chooses not to see contradictions. Her world is as black and white as that of her rightwing adversaries, and it gets that way, unfortunately, by similar methods.

To take the example of pop culture: Faludi would have us believe that virtually all 1980s movies and TV series (except "Murphy Brown") were misogynist. But she mentions only films like *Fatal Attraction* and *Overboard* and includes in her list some films that are open to far more complex and contradictory readings. *The War of the Roses*, for example, can easily be seen as anti-marriage rather than anti-woman. Of course we can disagree about movies, but that's just the point. She gives so little attention and time to her readings—her sections average less than 10 pages each—that they don't hold up against questions from anyone, friend or foe.

And when it comes to actual subtleties in media politics, she is hopeless. She complains, for example, that the AIDS storylines in so many soap operas all portray women as the victims, and calls this sexism. In fact, while the soaps have been particularly commendable in their quick response to the AIDS crisis, their homophobic fear of presenting gay male characters was responsible for their uniform portrayals of AIDS victims as white, middle-class women. The focus on women, then, is anti-gay, not anti-women.

Faludi's often slapdash, irresponsible judgments are most dangerous in her section on individual thinkers. In a typically injudicious move, she assigns the serious, if controversial, feminist Carol Gilligan, with whom she disagrees, to the same anti-feminist camp as the viciously sexist and racist philosopher Michael Levin. Putting Gilligan on the "enemies list" is unfair to her ideas—and to the complexities of current feminist debate. Feminists certainly disagree (more than Faludi seems to realize), but distinctions between colleagues and enemies can't be thrown out in the interest of proving a totalizing thesis.

The Beauty Myth is more interesting and useful. Rather than taking on the entire universe of discourse, Wolf sticks to a narrower focus and a more manageable thesis. She argues, convincingly, that in the wake of women's gains in the public sphere, the male power structure has upped the ante on the one area in which feminists have had least success: the struggle against socially enforced standards of physical appearance. Women—or at least white, middle-class women—have indeed entered the worlds of business, power, and thought in unprecedented numbers, but we suffer enormously, both psychologically and socially, for our failures to be ever more thin, youthful, and commercially "beautiful."

Wolf calls the new discriminatory criteria the Professional Beauty Qualification (PBQ), and she needed only to begin listing its manifestations to arouse a shock of recognition in me. There is no question that women today are expected, by the media, by employers, and by themselves to achieve levels of physical "perfection" unheard-of before. Wolf is good with statistics, and when she tells us that models used to be 8 percent thinner than the average woman but today are a substantial 23 percent thinner, she is simply naming a trend that, once pointed out, seems obvious. The same is true of her statistics on eating disorders, cosmetic surgery, and money and hours spent on diet products and programs and exercise equipment and activity.

This is one of those books that, at least in its early sections, changed my perception of myself and the world, if only temporarily. Suddenly every magazine, every friend, every shopping trip looked a bit different, a bit ominous even. Wolf is both more perceptive and more clever than Faludi. She points up, nicely, that articles in women's magazines today (contrary to Faludi's wholesale dismissal) are, in fact, filled with feminist assumptions and perspectives, but that for that very reason they are forced to balance their feminist messages with advertising and beauty articles that instill more and more anxiety about appearance, in order to sell the products of the advertisers on whom magazines depend.

So far, this makes a lot of sense. Wolf's account of the beauty industries themselves works on a very obvious level of economic analysis. After all, we're dealing with big business, both selling commodities and keeping women out of top positions. Unfortunately, Wolf doesn't leave well enough alone. In the last two-thirds of the book she goes so far afield theoretically and rhetorically that her book begins to sound like a jeremiad about the end of the world. Like Faludi, she omits all opposing analyses and statistics in her map of an unbearably oppressive social and psychological environment.

The worst section is the one on pornography. Oh, how I wish she'd let that one go. She ignores the voluminous amount of important theoretical debate around this issue and takes an uncritical, unexamined Andrea Dworkin/Women Against Pornography line. Assumptions about causal relationships between sexual imagery and violence are presented as gospel; and issues of female sexual freedom and repression, as well as the complexities of, and disagreements about, media reception and use—both so thoroughly a part of any informed feminist discussion of this matter by now—are simply ignored. Nowhere in the book does she seem aware of the complexities of class, race, and sexual preference that have so preoccupied feminists in recent years—although attention to these would significantly undermine her homogenizing account. It is as though feminist debate had stopped in 1975.

The porn chapter is followed by others as rhetorically hyperbolic and theoretically simplistic. Wolf's analysis of what she sees as women's religious relationship to the worship of physical perfection is clever but ultimately unconvincing. She finds any number of parallels in ritual and attitudes between beauty regimens and Christian religious practices: women feel the same guilt about eating as they used to feel about sex; they "confess" to their diet group as they once confessed to priests; and so on. But Wolf so exaggerates the extent and significance of this kind of thing that her melodramatic descriptions begin to resemble *The Story of O.* It is as though women were sealed up in some claustrophobic counter-universe where the concern with beauty was the only operating variable.

This tendency to overstate horrors continues in the chapter on cosmetic surgery. The descriptions are predictably nauseating and distressing, but ultimately become a bit absurd, as gothic prose raises the stakes ever higher. It is indeed appalling that "at least 67 women are dead so far" as a result of elective cosmetic surgery. But Wolf makes it sound as if all women have already entered the world of *The Handmaid's Tale.* Surely we are oppressed by beauty standards, but walking down the street in a dress and heels is not akin to traversing hot coals barefoot. And yet Wolf makes it sound like it is. "Enough pain makes people numb," she writes, in a lengthy passage of which these are only brief excepts:

> Look at a done-up woman walking down a street...wearing a costume, part flamenco dancer, part Carmen...She painted her face for an hour...Her legs in black silk are numb from the windchill. The deep parting of her dress is open to a blast of wind. Her achilles tendons...are throbbing.

As I read page upon page of such purple prose, I began to feel I was in a time warp. The impulse to sound the call to the crusades is admirable. The backlash, to be sure, is real and frightening. But the fact is, these are far more confusing and contradictory times than Faludi and Wolf seem to admit. Some of us like to wear sexy pumps and dresses on occasion. Others of us wear only pants, jackets, and flat shoes and do fine. This really isn't the 1950s, and all is really not lost.

In fact, what most troubled me in these books was that they seemed so out of touch with the mass of women—especially young women—in their dogmatic puritanism, as to turn off readers to what's really valuable in them. There are reasons, both theoretical and pragmatic, for feminists to back off a bit from this kind of ultra-correct rigidity. Because these are hard times, economically, politically, and emotionally, and the feminist revolution dreamed of in the 1960s is still on the horizon, women have good reasons for making certain kinds of compromises in their personal and professional lives. The media are not entirely wrong about some of the "trends" they report, and to say they always are, as Faludi does, is to risk credibility and possibly scare a new generation of women who are hurting and confused away from feminism.

The same is true of our relation to fashion, cosmetics, and even pornography. Most women get pleasure from adorning themselves. They do not, in fact, feel pain or numbness when dressed fashionably. They feel a whole lot of different things, I suspect, which they are not willing to give up for an abstract revolution. Many use pornography in ways they feel fine about and which, in any event, many feminist theorists interpret very differently from Wolf and Faludi.

More and more, such "yes, but's" jumped into my head as I read these books. In a truly weird and surprising way, by the time I finished reading, I felt better about women's situation than I had in a long time. True, I thought most about more privileged women, like my own daughter, who is of Wolf's and Faludi's generation and whose professional and personal life—not to mention her mental health—are so far superior to mine at her age that she could be a walking ad for the results of the Second Wave. If we are so much more aware and so much more outraged over what's left to be done, it's at least partly because our expectations have risen from zero to infinity.

How was it possible for these two women to write books so oblivious to the ferment in feminist theory, so locked into an ideologically dated world? At least one possible reason strikes me as particularly relevant to academic feminists. In the years since the Second Wave began, a troubling gap has developed between academic and public discourse. So much of the important work on sexuality, fashion, and popular culture, for example, which should have informed and enriched the analyses of these two young writers, appears in esoteric academic journals and in language accessible only to initiates of theory-talk. Among the many contradictions of the current age, one of the most depressing perhaps is that women have gained power within the academy even as our involvement in the larger public battle diminishes.

Backlash will probably be widely read and discussed. *The Beauty Myth* has already made an explosion in the media; Naomi Wolf has been on more than a handful of talk shows that I've seen, and her book has had plenty of publicity. She is perceived as speaking for feminism and, in the vacuum left by the rest of us, she has a right to that title. I think we need to think about that some. Second-Wave feminism began in the 1960s with a public agenda and a political project—to transform the world. That project is still our primary responsibility—or should be. Faludi and Wolf, to their credit, have taken on that challenge, at a time when few of us seem to be thinking in those terms. But they are going to need a lot of help in order to get it right.

Letters to the Editor

This piece originally appeared in *The Women's Review of Books*. Readers responded with the following letters.

"Dear Editor,

"I regret that as a result of a bad review an important book may be overlooked by some of your readers. Especially now, in the wake of the Clarence Thomas hearings on TV, Susan Faludi's *Backlash: The Undeclared War Against American Women* takes on relevance as a valid, forceful, and thoughtfully written analysis of the historical opposition to women's changing status. Faludi argues that for every advance in the Women's Movement, there has been an historical backlash. It is orchestrated by those who feel threatened with loss of status as the result of women's achievements. The backlash is supported by the media which plays to the sensationalism of bad news at the expense of accuracy and truth.

"Faludi's book is broadly encompassing in scope and indictment; it is a masterpiece of investigative reporting on topics ranging from New Right think tanks to TV soaps, from the fashion industry to Operation Rescue, from Ronald Reagan to Randall Terry—all of which may not be so far apart. It is richly supported by a scholarly apparatus that alone is worth the price of the book. It is written in a witty, intelligent and accessible style. It respects women.

"Not so, Elayne Rapping's review. Rapping's major complaint is that young women—the 'twentysomethings'—don't properly appreciate the sacrifices and achievements of the fiftysomethings like herself. The review is inaccurate (beginning with Faludi's age which is in the thirtysomethings); unsubstantiated by evidence of having read the index, much less the content ('short, superficial chapters,' Rapping complains, referring to 14 chapters in 542 pages); and patronizing ('Women new to feminist thinking may well find much of the book informative....I was aware of virtually everything in the book.').

"In contrast, Teresa L. Elbert's review in the same issue of Camille Paglia's *Sexual Personae* is a stunning example of a review that is informative about the book's content as well as intelligently and persuasively critical. It is the best evaluation of Paglia that I have read, and there have ben many."

Edith Gelles, Stanford, CA

"To the Editor:

"Elayne Rapping's review of books by Susan Faludi and Naomi Wolf was undeniably well written and thoughtful, but it was also offensive. Toward the end of her analysis of Wolf's book she concludes: 'Some of us like to wear sexy pumps and dresses on occasion. Others of us wear only pants, jackets, and flat shoes and do fine. This really isn't the 1950s, and all is not lost.'

"These seemingly innocent remarks unveil Rapping's sexist bias. She has disguised it, dressed it up in judicious language and created an ostensibly fair-minded analysis. But her remarkably traditional and patriarchal view of what is sexy and what isn't (pumps and dresses are sexy, 'only' pants and flat shoes are simply 'fine,' perhaps not inferior, but certainly not sexy), ultimately made a greater impression on me than her cautious academic prose and her reliance on theory and research.

"What is sexy, powerful, and necessary are not short skirts and high heels. What is sexy, powerful, and necessary (for the survival of feminism, and of women) is a generation of young women who are impatient and outraged, who intend to make damn sure that 'all is not lost.'

Sima Rabinowitz, Minneapolis, MN

"To the Editor:

"The recent disparaging review by Elayne Rapping of *Backlash: The Undeclared War Against American Women*, by Susan Faludi (Crown Publishers) is most regrettable.

"First of all, because *The Women's Review of Books* is taken as a reliable and credible source, many readers would be dissuaded from buying the book, pursuing the topic, and opening up this extremely important area of politics for urgent and passionate debate. This would be a great shame because those who do read this 'dazzling' documentation (as Barbara Ehrenreich so aptly labels it) will be much better informed about the processes that are at work to undermine feminist gains and to 'manipulate' women's minds.

"Secondly, some of the tactics used by the reviewer are unfortunate. We are not against a reviewer charging that a book is boring, or irritating, or anecdotal, although we do think they are political terms and need closer examination, as do their counterparts original, satisfying, and scientific. Our objections in this case are that such accusations seem to us to be without foundation, justification, or exemplification in relation to Susan Faludi's *Backlash*.

"Few are the feminists, particularly in the academic community, who have not been exposed to the distressing practice of having their work discredited by the suggestion that their research is 'anecdotal' (or subjective, emotional, irritating, or boring). And to see the reviewer refer to Susan Faludi's well-documented and supported thesis as a 'theory' (in quotes) is to add to our sense of unease.

"We would like the readers of *The Women's Review of*

Books to know that we consider *Backlash* one of the most daring, powerfully argued and politically oriented books that has appeared in the last few years. Susan Faludi, and Naomi Wolf (the author of the other book in the review), are ushering in Third Wave feminism and we, of the Second Wave generation of feminists, are delighted, proud, and relieved to see younger women restating the truths in their own terms. (We remember some of the First Wave feminists protesting that we had not invented the Women's Movement, but giving us their blessing to continue the quest. We too feel it is a privilege to be able to say to the younger women that we know something of what they are talking about—and that we will make any of our resources available to them in their work for women.)

"Susan Faludi has written a brilliant book. She has used the research skills of a superb journalist (and the prose of a professional—oh how we envy some of her phrases) to expose the role that the media has played in trying to convince women that feminism is not good for them. Again and again she shows how some of the greatest scare-issues of the decade have been nothing other than media distortions—'beat-ups' designed to drive women out of the work place, the economic stakes, the self-esteem and self-realization stakes, and back to serving men. 'Trend journalism' which ostensibly reports trends is unequivocally shown by Susan Faludi as journalism that promotes trends, many of which are anti-feminist and orchestrated by men who prefer women to be silent, subservient, and poor.

"We suggest that women in the thousands buy the book. Backlash can then become a different debate."

Chris Kramarae and Dale Spender, Urbana, IL
"To the Editor:

"I wish to strongly disagree with Elayne Rapping's review of Susan Faludi's *Backlash* in the front-page essay of your October issue. Rapping's broad generalizations about *Backlash* do not describe the book I just read.

"Rapping maintains that Faludi (and Naomi Wolf, author of *Beauty Myth*, the other book she is reviewing) 'are absolutely certain that things couldn't be worse for women.' *Backlash*, however, is not about women's actual lives, but about the *cultural* attack on feminism in the 1980s. In contrast to Rapping's claim, Faludi asserts that women never really succumbed to the backlash agenda.

"To Rapping much of *Backlash* is old news. She declares that Faludi, a Pulitzer Prize-winning journalist, does not 'analyze large amounts of material in ways that give us the kind of perspective and insight daily or weekly journalism can't provide.' She goes on to attack the book, saying it is 'ill-thought-out, badly argued, and way too often simply erroneous or uninformed.' But Rapping offers hardly any examples or arguments to back up such harsh dismissal. Let me offer an alternative evaluation with specific examples.

"The first part of *Backlash* does synthesize a huge body of popular and scientific writing to demonstrate persuasively that the mass media in the 1980s used selective statistics and social science studies to argue anti-feminist positions on five topics: the man shortage for professional women, the disastrous effects for women of no-fault divorce, the fertility problems of women in their thirties, the depression of single women, and the negative effects of day care on young children. Faludi argues forcefully that in all five cases other studies and more credible statistics prove that these now popular positions are false. She shows how the press coined the terms postfeminism, man shortage, biological clock and mommy track, and concludes that 'these articles weren't chronicling a retreat among women that was already taking place, they were compelling one to happen.' Faludi also demonstrates how the work of some avowed feminist social scientists (like Lenore Weitzman, Judith Wallerstein, and Carol Gilligan) left itself open for anti-feminist popularization.

"These topics were 'old news' to me precisely because they have been so much in the media, but Faludi's feminist critique was much more powerful than any I've seen or been able to articulate. Her first two chapters will be required reading in my introductory Women's Studies classes. I wish she had provided an equally cogent analysis of why the popular press and media has been so anti-feminist, and how we might begin to pressure them to change.

"The faults I find in *Backlash* are also different than Rapping's. Faludi doesn't adequately support her contention that many women resisted this media barrage. We need better analyses of both the interaction and independence of cultural constructs and women's real lives. I was also disappointed that Faludi didn't discuss the backlash against women of color. What about the attack on Alice Walker's *The Color Purple* by black male intellectuals? Anita Hill's dramatic testimony vindicates the focus on multiculturalism in the Women's Movement during the past ten years. It also supports Faludi's contention that backlashes aren't completely effective.

"Rapping's review was so negative that I doubt if your readers would consider looking at *Backlash*. In contrast, I believe that they will find much to enrich their thinking, teaching, and politics."

E. Kay Trimberger, Rohnert Park, CA
"Editors:

"I read with interest and admiration Naomi Wolf's book *The Beauty Myth* and Elayne Rapping's review, which partially disagreed with it. I was impressed by both writers' knowledge, intelligence, and honest conviction, hallmarks of a good debate whatever side we take. Let me branch off from their views and take one with a third, somewhat different emphasis.

"Wolf in her book tends to stress the 'they' component and, to be sure, 'they'—the media, the beauty industry, the patriarchal legal, political, and economic power structures—have played a powerful role in shaping a beauty myth which has become so stringent as to harm women. Rapping, while concurring with this, urges us nevertheless not to lose sight of women's desires: the majority of women want to dress up and conform to the code of a conventionally feminine appearance despite the burden of doing so. I would like to propose a view that connects these two positions and extends them toward a fuller sense of our lives as self-determining.

"After all, the 'they' argument, however valuable and necessary, takes us only so far because, while helping us understand our actions, it displaces the responsibility for them. The argument from desire, on the other hand, brings the issue back home, but not thoroughly enough, it seems to me. Desire per se, women's or anyone else's, is not sufficient explanation much less validation of a phenomenon. The two ideas need to be linked and then probed further: for women's desire has been programmed, and not only by 'they,' but also by 'us,' namely, individual women—from our mothers and sisters and colleagues to the hairdressers, manicurists, magazine editors, sales clerks, and countless others who influence us in the use of products and services, and who in turn have been able to make a living in one of the few fields that has not historically been closed to them. Virtually all of us as we go about our daily business continue to program our daughters, our students, our friends, if nothing else by the example of our acquiescence.

"I am not saying this hasn't been for purposes of survival within an unjust system, or that it isn't in any case part of a natural reaction of competitiveness within the real world. What I am saying is let's look at it straight on. Our trade-offs are strategies, sometimes brilliant, sometimes highly gratifying. They are still trade-offs. I think the time may be coming to look squarely at our continuing cooperation in the dissipation of our increasingly precious resources—time, thought, energy, money—even while acknowledging the complexity of its sources. We deserve sympathy and understanding: we have been victims. But we also deserve a little laughter: we have been buffoons, often willing ones. I need only to point to fashions like platform shoes and beehive hairdos to bring a smile to a lot of faces. Maybe we should see more of that smile as regards current trends. Maybe we should hear more laughter, at ourselves and at the Rube Goldberg machine of beauty we have had a hand in creating. Because I think that once we begin to laugh—truly laugh—the sound will drown out those whispers in our ears that seduce us not so much by telling us that we should be perfect as by implying that it is possible."

Marlene Miller, Laguna Beach, CA

I replied:

"In light of the thrust of the responses to my review of *Backlash* and *The Beauty Myth*, I was moved to consider the politics of book reviewing. Only Rabinowitz and Miller actually address the theoretical issues raised in my review. Both disagree with me about the politics of personal appearance and clothing style, about what is actually 'sexy' and to what extent actual female desires can be expressed in terms of traditional 'patriarchal' cultural conventions. Fair enough. I'd love to debate this issue further. That's why I wrote the review. Unfortunately, however, it seems more important to devote myself to the issues raised in the other letters, issues I anticipated and which I find troubling.

"Gelles, Trimberger, Spender, and Kramarae are all concerned that my review may keep women from reading these books. They believe this would be a very unfortunate circumstance because they believe that the books, especially Faludi's, are saying things that are politically important. Here we move from theory to political strategy, to considerations of what is politically advantageous for women, in the larger public sphere. In fact, I believe I am being accused of political incorrectness. I accept the challenge.

"Gelles begins with a provocative statement, in the form of an unquestioned, almost throwaway-style line, 'Especially now,' she says, 'in the wake of the Clarence Thomas hearings on TV, Susan Faludi's *Backlash*...takes on relevance...' While I wrote my review long before the events of October, my own response to the hearings was exactly the opposite. I found them exciting and encouraging, evidence of something I (as a person who has written and taught about media representation, especially of women, for 20 years) have long believed: that in fact women's consciousness of and anger at traditional cultural assumptions about gender/power relations are far grater than anyone—especially the male power structure—had understood. The proof of that growing anger—of the increasing refusal of women to quietly acquiesce to things like harassment, date rape, domestic violence—has been clearly reflected in the mass media, in particular in the popular culture forms viewed (and in fact increasingly produced) by women. Anyone who follows soap operas, made-for-TV movies (I have just completed a book on this topic), or daytime talk shows (these are the richest examples, but there are many; the film *Thelma and Louise*, written by a young woman, is the most obvious) will be aware that the media, in its woman-oriented programming viewed by many more women than regularly read books, has long portrayed and discussed issues of sexual violence and coercion in terms set by feminists.

"The point is that the media are not a monolithic presence, nor are they oblivious to feminist ideas. On the contrary, since the 1970s, women—as consumers, viewers, and, increasingly, media professionals—have had an enormous impact on media representation of women and women's issues. And that impact was evident in the spontaneous, unpredicted outrage of so many over an issue that was not taken seriously by the Senate Judiciary Committee when they first heard about it because they didn't know it would matter so much. Like most of us who read this journal, they were not keeping track of popular culture, especially women's culture.

"I feel justified in developing this one point (as opposed to doing something space forbids, now and in my review: refuting each and every error in Faludi's media analysis and pointing out each and every example of things she missed or ignored) because it gets to the heart of why the book made me angry and why I am troubled by these letters. Surely, we all know, every scientist or student of Thomas Kuhn knows, that once hypotheses are developed, they influence the search for evidence, that we are likely, if we try hard enough, to find the evidence we need to support our thesis. The media are easy targets for thesis proving, especially about sexism. No one is disputing that those who control the media are sexist. Nor am I denying that there is a backlash. That would be insane. What I am arguing, and I am sorry my readers didn't find it interesting enough to consider, is that politically, the situation of women is contradictory and confusing, that the Women's Movement—and I take pride in this—has in fact made an enormous difference, especially in media (remember any segment of 'Father Knows Best' or 'I Love Lucy' and then compare any sitcom today), and that, therefore, the game has changed since the 1960s and women, feminists, now have—at least—more chips and more points than we started with.

"This is a political point. It speaks to the main issue here: what is in fact 'good for women' in books and book reviews. My critics seem to worry that women won't read these books because of me. That's nonsense. Faludi has been hyped by everyone from *Newsweek* (selected last summer as the first on the list of fall must-reads), to *The Los Angeles Times* and *The New York Times*, *Mother Jones*, you name it. Both Wolf and Faludi have been all over the media, hyped as major writers/thinkers. There's no question their books will be read, taught, reprinted, discussed, awarded. *The Women's Review*, however, is not the same as these publications. It is, at least I believed this when I wrote my review, a serious journal read by a select group of committed feminist activists and scholars, a place to debate and disagree about feminist theory and strategy, a place where it was safe to raise issues that were theoretically divisive. (It's not like I'm the only theorist who finds mass media more hopeful, especially from a feminist perspective, than the monolithic manipulation theorists of the Left and Right believe.)

"I would not mind being disagreed with; I did mind being accused, in tone and implication, of betraying feminism. There is no unitary version of feminism; nor is feminist dogma established and unchanging. Spender and Kramarae are 'delighted, proud, and relieved to see younger women restating the truths [of Second Wave feminism] in their own terms.' But what if our truths, then, are not so clear now? What if some of our good work has borne fruit? Is there some political value to continuing to rail about the uninflected sexism of the media instead of giving ourselves credit for and encouraging young women to build upon the chinks in the armor we've succeeded—at least somewhat—in making? I think not. In fact, politically, I think finding reason for optimism and hope, finding evidence of feminism's successes, is far more likely to fuel a 'Third Wave' than wallowing in tales of the monolithic media and women's powerlessness to change it.

"Finally, what about the media reception of these books? Why do the media push to celebrate books that attack them? Here too I think we need to consider. The media love to be told they're all powerful. They loved the anti-porn movement; they love the anti-violence-on-TV movement. But they also love theories that put attention on issues of representation rather than real social and economic causes of social ills. They do not like, and will not review or publicize, books which ferret out pockets of hope and activism (which exist all over campuses and communities). They do not want to give information or publicity about what women, especially young women and women of color, are doing to fight economic discrimination and problems like child care and reproductive rights on grassroots levels. But these things—and the media know it—are far more important than Christian Lacroix's fall collection."

Girls Just Wanna Have Fun

From the early days when feminists looked for "positive" and "negative" role models in the culture to more recent, theoretically sophisticated times, the stance of the feminist critic has remained consistent. She stands at an emotional distance from the object in question and, in one way or another, strips it of its power to seduce and enthrall. The strategy is to liberate us from what used to be called false consciousness.

There's a lot to be said for this position. No feminist in her right mind would deny that much of pop culture is not healthy for women and girls. It's demeaning, misogynist—you know the litany. Seen from another angle, though, it's not clear that this is the best way to approach the "problem" of sexist culture, either politically or theoretically. It's too extreme in its oppositional, either/or assumptions. Implicitly—and this is true of this kind of feminist criticism as well as much feminist alternative art and media—it takes an apocalyptic position about the horrors of mass art. Mass culture is here to stay; it is loved and enjoyed by most women and girls (whether it's seen as a guilty pleasure or not), and feminists have a responsibility, for that reason, to take it seriously and respectfully.

But there's another reason for being skeptical of the usual approach. It's based on an outdated view of the cultural scene. In fact, as every postmodernist knows, there is no more "inside" and "outside," no more clear boundary between high and low, mainstream and alternative culture. Artists today move easily in and out of these categories, and the old concept of co-optation is increasingly imprecise and useless. What does one make of Laurie Anderson, for example, doing interviews on MTV, of performance artists like Ann Magnuson doing Hollywood movies and then returning to New York's downtown scene?

All this is by way of introduction to two books that deserve attention because they take a totally different approach to women and mass culture. *The Female Gaze: Women as Viewers of Popular Culture*, edited by Lorraine Gamman and Margaret Marshment and *Gender Politics and MTV: Voicing the Difference*, by Lisa A. Lewis are both uneven but provocative and important contributions to the feminist critical debate. Nor are they alone. In recent years more and more works of feminist criticism have put forth the argument made in these volumes: that the realm of popular culture is not monolithic and evil but an arena of cultural/political struggle in which artists and audiences wrestle with the contradictions of commercial culture and sometimes even win. Implicit in this approach is another important idea: that women who like schlock can justify their enjoyment; that hidden beneath the glitz and idiocy there is often something valuable.

The Female Gaze is a collection of British essays on the pleasures of different kinds of trash. The essays are held together by a philosophy presented in the introduction. "We feel," say the editors, "that we cannot afford to dismiss the popular by always positioning ourselves outside it. Instead," they continue, "we are interested in how feminists can intervene in the mainstream to make our meanings part of 'commonsense.'" These are polemical and problematic words, and by and large the essays are too slight and theoretically weak to carry that burden. Nonetheless, as in the most interesting popular culture, there are moments of sheer brilliance here and enough of an argument to demand consideration.

The essayists take on the notion—popularized by feminist film theorists associated with the British journal *Screen*—of a "male gaze" in film and television, the assumption that the spectator is always male and the female the object, rather than the subject, of desire. They insist that popular culture, in Susanne Moore's words, is a site of "renegotiations" about the portrayal of both male and female bodies and that this process is the direct result of the influence of "radical political discourses." In other words, Moore argues, feminism has altered pop culture by altering the consciousness of both performers and fans. She uses as an example Debbie Harry's 1978 song "Picture This" (a favorite of mine for the very reasons Moore suggests), in which the female singer tells her lover, "I will give you my finest hour/The one I spent/Watching you shower." The rest of the piece analyzes similar examples, increasingly common these days, in which the male body is the desired object and the female the one who looks.

Other interesting pieces dissect Joan Collins's image and its meaning and the trashy but fascinating pulp novel *Lace*. In both cases the writers play with the contradictions of female representation and point out that the products themselves do the same. *Lace*, for example, shows women being exploited—even raped—by male characters. However, Avis Lewallen argues that "these women are not mere passive victims," because "even when abused and exploited, they fight back and their collective sisterhood provides them with an emotional and economic support network." Still, she admits that "the question is whether the context of this objectification alters the relationship female readers can have with it or whether it merely colludes with conventional, sexist ways of seeing women." Similar questions are raised in Andrea Stuart's defense of the Hollywood version of *The Color Purple*; in spite of its hedging on issues of class and lesbianism and its hokey Hollywood style, she argues, the movie not only represents a vision of black sisterhood that is rare in Hollywood but makes it available to poor black women who don't necessarily read novels.

Janet Lee's analysis of *Elle* magazine is more theoretically complex and satisfying. It begins with a personal statement: "I really enjoy *Elle* magazine...It is stylish, and that stylishness is appealing...[Its text] doesn't tell me what to do and it doesn't keep offering me advice." She ends by suggesting that we take seriously the appeal of such works because young women and working-class women like them. "There are clearly lessons to be learned from the marketplace about women's needs," she concludes, "which neither feminism nor post-feminism are adequately meeting."

Now we are getting to the heart of the matter: the lived experience of the woman viewer herself. Just what is the source of pleasure in this material and what can we learn from it? How do women use popular culture and what does it say about the failures of both avant-garde art and feminism itself to attract wide support, especially among the young, poor, and disfranchised?

Two articles address this matter by looking at the Madonna phenomenon. Jackie Stacey's "Desperately Seeking Difference" analyzes the Susan Seidelman film *Desperately Seeking Susan*, in which Madonna plays the Madonna-type character Susan to the counterpoint of Rosanna Arquette's repressed middle-class housewife Roberta. It is Roberta, not a male viewer, who is "the bearer of the look" in her obsessive interest in the Madonna/Susan character, a free spirit who does as she pleases and most definitely controls her own sexuality. Roberta herself—in a wacky series of plot twists—takes on that identity and uses it to change her destiny and escape from her oppressive life. Here we have a fascinating concept: a woman may look at another woman, even at the representation of that woman, and the look itself may be a catalyst for liberation.

Shelagh Young, in the final essay, picks up this theme, again using *Desperately Seeking Susan* and the image of Madonna to make her point. She quotes a critic who attributes to this film a kind of permission given women to "relax and admit that all along we'd loved Madonna." But, says Young, this idea that "we" were ever not relaxed about loving Madonna assumes that women, collectively, are represented by "semi-professional feminists." Young women have always loved her, Young points out, and so, interestingly enough, have blacks. Certainly gay men and lesbians have formed a significant part of her following as well. So, what's with us middle-class feminists, she asks. We might find out, she suggests, by "listening to the views of [our] wayward daughters who seem to be so actively resisting, rather than conforming to, any simple feminist model." Madonna, after all, is no bimbo, no pushover. She's a woman who represents herself as powerful, autonomous, and also very sexy—on her own terms. This kind of representation may not appeal to Second-Wave feminists fighting to escape the Marilyn Monroe/victim image. But their daughters have different agendas, different battles.

This brings us to Lisa Lewis's far more theoretically ambitious study of women rock musicians and their fans. Written in an academic jargon that is sometimes nearly unreadable, it nonetheless makes a strong case for the less-well-argued thesis of *The Female Gaze*: that popular culture is contested terrain and that women, as artists and as spectators and fans, can and have made astonishing inroads into a commercial, male-defined turf.

Her book, originally a doctoral dissertation that could have used extensive stylistic and thematic revision, sabotages its own goals in many ways. It's a paean to pop culture and its female fans, and her very upbeat thesis is that women rockers and fans have been able to use the contradictions, both ideological and commercial, of pop culture to do what the Gamman/Marshment anthology proposes: "intervene in the mainstream to make our meanings part of 'commonsense.'" Yet she addresses her academic colleagues rather than the women about whom she clearly cares and with whom she actually identifies. Teenage girls won't read this book; neither will women performers.

Nevertheless, the book is full of substantive theoretical gold. It's audacious, original, and—despite the assumed academic audience—very much engaged in its subject. In her introduction Lewis makes a point of stressing her own personal and emotional involvement in her subject. Attending concerts, watching videos, and reading popular media interviews with women rockers became a significant part of her life. "I...was affected by the musicians' address to women," she says, "and studying them was a way of using their texts in my everyday life." Clearly Lewis stands inside, participates in, and identifies with the female culture of fandom. One of her more compelling themes is that teen fans are not spaced-out groupies but rather an impressively articulate and autonomous "collective" of women who successfully battle—in their roles as consumers—for the cause of women-oriented cultural representation.

The book's strength derives from Lewis's comprehensive look at gender issues in commercial video—most obviously in MTV videos. She starts with the ingenious strategy developed by MTV executive Bob Pittman, whose market research told him that there was money to be made by focusing on 18- to 34-year-old white males. But video also provided a space for women musicians. Female performers and viewers became commercially important "properties" and "markets," and this gave both musicians and fans a new position of power to define what they did and demand what they wanted. Such are the sometimes fortuitous workings of capitalism.

The meat of the book is in the chapters that focus on the ideas and strategies of the musicians and fans themselves. The profiles of four performers—Madonna, Tina Turner, Pat Benatar, and Cyndi Lauper—are eye-openers. One after the other speaks loudly and intelligently about her battle to overturn the industry's male-defined ideology about gender relations, particularly in adolescent culture. Lewis cites such videos as Turner's "What's Love Got to Do With It?" and Benatar's "Love Is a Battlefield" as examples of female performers appropriating the male turf of the streets in narratives of female bonding and sexual antagonism. And of course there's the now-famous Lauper video "Girls Just Wanna Have Fun." In it a racially mixed group of working-class girlfriends literally take over the public space traditionally reserved for males and behave in delightfully outrageous ways that previously only boys could get away with. Lauper even changed the lyrics of the song—written and meant to be sung by a male—to make a consciously feminist statement.

But the most important and original sections of this book deal with fandom. I have never read an academic book that treated teen rock fans quite so respectfully and made so strong a case for the positive aspects of fandom. Lewis argues, plausibly, that groupies and intensely involved fans are not really dreaming of sexual relationships with their male idols. It is far more likely, as common sense and my own feminist assumptions would suggest, that female fans identify with them and want to be what their rock heroes seem to be in a world in which girls don't usually have such options. This is borne out dramatically in Lewis's discussion of how

MTV was forced to air tough women performers because female viewers, contrary to Pittman's original strategy, became as loyal to the network as their male counterparts and preferred to identify with women like Turner, Lauper, and Madonna.

So what can women realistically accomplish in mainstream media? Lewis thinks, and she's persuasive, that not just love but American pop culture itself is a battlefield in which some women—both fans and stars—have become aggressive, effective forces in the ongoing struggle over cultural hegemony. Lewis understands fully that most commercial and pop culture is far from liberating, and she never underestimates the power of commercial and political forces to sabotage progressive movements. Still, there's something exhilarating about her unfashionable cultural radicalism. She believes that we do have the power—limited but very real—to fight. And she also believes that artists and fans have more clout than is generally acknowledged by the classic discourses—the old Frankfurt School, the positive-role-model feminists, and now the postmodernist/post-structuralist crowd.

Lewis ends with a poignant appeal to Second-Wave feminists to listen to their daughters. She quotes two teens, wise beyond their years, to this effect. "The Women's Movement must now come to terms with the contradiction of needing young women to be part of it, and treating us as if we were smaller, inadequate, and immature versions of older women in it. Obviously," they go on, "our experiences are different from yours. But that doesn't make them less valid." Lewis concludes that the emergence of "girl culture" is important politically and that feminists must try to understand it.

The Female Gaze ends on a similar note. Both these volumes are tentative and flawed in various ways. But they are asking hard questions, challenging political and theoretical dogma, and provoking us to think about popular culture in a way that offers a more hopeful perspective on what's actually happening and where the contradictions can be made to work for us.

Feminism and Media in an Age of Reaction

Back in the 1960s, when we Second Wave feminists began revving up our motors for the war against sexism, one of our most obvious targets was the media. In those innocent days, before "gender representation" replaced "images of women," before media theory became an academic discipline, before women's studies became—in the nightmares of the Right—a threat to western civilization, we had a fairly simplistic, but powerful idea. We believed that if we could just replace the almost exclusively "negative role model" of women in movies, television, and advertising—the airheads, bitches, hausfraus, and sex kittens—with "positive" alternatives, we would go a long way toward destabilizing the ideological foundations of sexism.

Naive and starry-eyed as we were in those heady days, when songs about revolution made the Top Forty and no one had yet teased out the myriad ways in which the media might thwart and outsmart us, we were nevertheless onto something. The media obviously have enormous powers of persuasion. And, less obviously perhaps, they do, in significant ways, respond to public opinion and political pressure.

If we look closely at what's really on television—especially "women's" television—and analyze it historically, the whole backlash phenomenon may look a little less ominous.

There's no doubt that, in the legal and economic arenas, things look very bad indeed. Case by case, census figure by census figure, we are losing ground and hurting badly.

But that's just one side of things. The very term "backlash" implies that there is a battle going on, a pitched battle in which those on the Right are exerting enormous energy and resources in an effort to dislodge an enemy which they take very seriously indeed. And that enemy is feminism, which, in the last 20 years, has unquestionably and profoundly altered the way in which gender relations and values are understood and discussed in this country. And the proof of that is nowhere more dramatic than on television.

One reason it's so easy to trash television is that we have forgotten what things were like before the 1960s. More and more of us, of course, aren't even old enough to remember. And, because of feminism, our expectations and demands have grown from zero to infinity. But I'm old enough to be vividly aware of why the old men at the top are in such a panic about the power of feminism. And, after 20 years of monitoring, writing, and teaching about media, I believe they are right to be apoplectic. We are gaining on them.

Remember when Rhett carried Scarlet upstairs kicking and screaming? Remember her contented purr the next morning? That was rape, girls. In fact, it was only about 10 years ago that the hottest couple on daytime TV—Luke and Laura of "General Hospital"—acted out the same demented scenario with virtually no public outrage. In fact, even 10 years ago, it would have been inconceivable for two movies like *The Accused* and *Thelma and Louise* to be made and distributed in mainstream America. The political concept on which they were founded—acquaintance rape—simply was not understood back then. It is now, though—because of feminism.

And what is still mostly tokenism in film (where serious themes of any kind have become rarities) is everyday stuff on TV today, especially daytime. In fact, I cannot imagine a current daytime soap opera even considering a "Luke and Laura" storyline. A mere few years of consciousness-raising through national media by feminists, and television's representation of sexuality has been transformed. On at least two soap storylines I know of in the last two or three years—"Santa Barbara" and "All My Children"—date rape cases were presented from a decidedly feminist viewpoint. In both, the women had checkered pasts, the men were (realistically) acquitted, and then—amazingly—they saw the error of their ways and confessed. One even began volunteering at a rape crisis center. And this was long before the Thomas hearings or the Kennedy trial.

I could go on endlessly with such examples, from soaps, TV movies, and prime-time sitcoms and dramas. I could also remind everyone of June Cleaver endlessly tearing her lettuce into her Pyrex bowl, of Lucille Ball howling "Ooh, Ri-i-i-icky!" and collapsing in hysterics, of the Andersons steering "Princess" and "Kitten" away from football and chemistry and into pink organdy prom dresses, week after depressing week. We put an end to all of that too. Ask Roseanne.

No, we haven't made a feminist revolution. Lesbians are rare on TV; poor and minority women and older women are marginal. But we are in the game and we have more chips than we started with. And make no mistake about it, these changes are political victories for which feminists can claim credit. Procter & Gamble, who pays the bills for so much television programming, has marketing researchers telling it every day that women—who still buy most of the soap, cake mix, and cleaning supplies—have very different ideas about gender relations and sexism these days because of feminism. And money talks in corporate America.

There's another important factor in the political changes wrought by feminism in television programming that explains why so many critics have missed it. More and more women—as a result of feminism—are now in the professional workforce, especially in media. But, for obvious reasons, they are concentrated in less prestigious places—TV rather than film, daytime rather than prime time. Since we on the Left are often as guilty of unconscious sexism and class bias as anyone else in things cultural, we tend to focus almost exclusively on programs such as "Nightline" and "MacNeil-Lehrer" instead of the shows people really talk about, like "Oprah Winfrey" and "Sally Jesse Raphael"; on classy prime-time drama like "L.A. Law" and "thirtysomething" rather than the endlessly popular and ubiquitous daytime soaps. But for women writers, producers, and actors, it is TV, not film—and daytime, not prime time—that offers the most opportunity to develop skills and reputations. And of all media forms, it is daytime TV where risk taking is most likely to occur because, as everyone knows, it's a women's ghetto that policy-makers don't watch or care about. Since it's considered trash and not taken seriously, it's allowed to get away with a lot more than Ted Koppel or Steven Bochco—the guys that Standards and Practices and Walter Goodman keep track of.

But if the pundits and policy-makers are missing the boat, we should be paying attention. Once you get past your understandable distaste for the exhibitionism and sensationalism of daytime talk, you will hear things on Oprah and Sally that will, more than anything else in the media, prove how powerful feminism (and the other 1960s-spawned mass movements, to a lesser extent) has become in this country (even if it isn't necessarily called by that much maligned F-word.)

Where Ted Koppel will talk endlessly to other powerful white men about subjects deemed "serious" from angles deemed "legitimate," Oprah and Phil are likely to be chatting with regular people, many female, black, gay, and poor, about issues that often as not have been raised by progressives, especially feminists. Date rape, gay parenting, sexual harassment—these topics have long been familiar to daytime TV viewers. And, surprisingly enough, the folks who appear as guests and speak from the audience on talk shows are a lot more open-minded than George Bush would care to know.

When we consider all of this and then rethink the events of the last year—the Thomas hearings, the Kennedy trial, the *Thelma and Louise* scare—they take on different meaning. Of course the rich white men in the Senate wanted Anita Hill to seem crazy and shut up. Of course the legal system was rigged in favor of (more) rich white men like William Kennedy Smith. Of course the mainstream media were outraged to the point of talking censorship at the screams of support in movie theaters for a couple of working-class women who decided, on the spot, that they no longer saw the point in acquiescing to male desire, in sexual matters or anything else, and were willing to get nasty if pushed on the point. What did we expect? The power structure is not going to quietly accept the changing attitudes and values of women. They have too much at stake to give up the male sexual privilege upon which gender inequality ultimately rests.

We can choose to feel despair about the results of these trials and hearings, the attacks on these movies. But that would miss the point. The public outcry from women when Anita Hill first spoke, the endless discussions of date rape and sexual harassment that these two events engendered—all this was made possible by the work of feminists in the last 20 years in bringing these issues into consciousness in the first place, so they could be challenged and discussed. And it is television, more than we have so far realized, that has been the arena in which this fertile public discourse has been and continues to be carried on.

The lesson for activists is to start thinking more seriously about media strategy. We may have been selling ourselves short by misreading the political climate. Political change is slow and it takes a long time, especially for changes in attitude to show up in actual events. But if we are losing badly in the political arena right now, I'm convinced we're doing very well indeed in the hearts and minds department, especially where gender issues and cultural values are concerned.

About South End Press

South End Press is a nonprofit, collectively run book publisher with over 180 titles in print. Since our founding in 1977, we have tried to meet the needs of readers who are exploring, or are already committed to, the politics of radical social change.

Our goal is to publish books that encourage critical thinking and constructive action on the key political, cultural, social, economic, and ecological issues shaping life in the United States and in the world. In this way, we hope to give expression to a wide diversity of democratic social movements and to provide an alternative to the products of corporate publishing.

If you would like a free catalog of South End Press books or information about our membership program, which offers two free books and a 40 percent discount on all titles, please write us at South End Press, 116 Saint Botolph Street, Boston, MA 02115.

Other South End Press Titles of Interest

The Looking Glass World of Nonfiction TV,
by Elayne Rapping

Rockin' the Boat: Mass Music and Mass Movements,
edited by Reebee Garofalo

Beauty Secrets: Women and the Politics of Appearance,
by Wendy Chapkis

Sisters of the Yam: Black Women and Self-Recovery,
by bell hooks

Black Looks: Race and Representation,
by bell hooks

The Last Generation: Poetry and Prose,
by Cherrie Moraga